Colonel Blood
Soldier, Robber and
Trickster
A Novel

D. Lawrence-Young

A CIP catalogue record for this title is available from the British Library.

ISBN 978-1-912964-85-7 (Paperback)

www.cranthorpemillner.com

First Published (2021)

Cranthorpe Millner Publishers

Historical Novels by D. Lawrence Young

Fawkes and the Gunpowder Plot

Tolpuddle: A Novel of Heroism

Marlowe: Soul'd to the Devil

Will Shakespeare: Where was He?*

The Man Who Would be Shakespeare

Will the Real William Shakespeare Please Step Forward**

Of Guns and Mules

Of Guns, Revenge and Hope

Arrows Over Agincourt

Sail Away from Botany Bay

Anne of Cleves: Unbeloved

Catherine Howard: Henry's Fifth Failure

Six Million Accusers: Catching Adolf Eichmann

Mary Norton: Soldier Girl

Two Bullets in Sarajevo

King John: Two-Time Loser

Go Spy Out the Land

Entrenched

Emma Hamilton: Mistress of Land and Sea

My Jerusalem Book (Editor)

Villains of Yore***

Reissued as: Welcome to London, Mr. Shakespeare

**Reissued as: Who Really Wrote Shakespeare?*

***Also published by Cranthorpe Millner Publishers*

As: David L. Young

Of Plots and Passions

Communicating in English (Textbook)

The Jewish Emigrant from Britain: 1700-2000 (contrib. chapter)

Website: www.dly-books.weebly.com

Dedication

As ever to my wife, Beverley who, apart from helping me with her computer skills, has now learned from Colonel Blood's experience how to successfully raid the Tower of London in order to increase her jewellery collection.

Prologue

Blood. Thomas Blood or, rather, Colonel Thomas Blood. That's me, although some people doubt whether I'm a real colonel, but that's another story, which I will tell you about later.

I am sixty-two years old, it is almost the end of August, in the year 1680, and to my great regret, I am dying. My long, black, curly locks have turned grey; my skin is of a similar colour, and there are liver spots all over the backs of my hands and arms. A friendly physician told me recently that I am not long for this world and that if I wish to depart this life with a clear conscience, I should confess to everything I have done. Mind you, that's easy for *him* to say; he hasn't done much in his life. All *he* had to do as a physician was to understand anatomy, determine which herbs suited which diseases, and know how to saw off gangrenous limbs, preferably without causing too much pain.

But me, I've been very busy, and by busy I mean I have attacked castles, fought in a civil war on both sides, and rescued several friends from being hanged. I also once tried to kidnap a nasty aristocrat and was also imprisoned in the Tower of London. But my greatest achievement by far, the one which has made my name known in every household in the land, was the time I almost succeeded in stealing the Crown Jewels. But more about that later.

Still, you cannot knock the advice of a medical professional. And since I have a stiff drink of good old Irish whiskey in my hand, I'll tell you what has kept me so busy since 1618, the year I made my noisy entrance into this world that I am soon to depart.

Chapter 1
Early Days

"Tom! Tom! Put those pistols down, lad! What are you doing with them anyway?"

"But, father, I'm practising."

"Practising for what?"

"Practising to be a highwayman."

This is one of my earliest childhood memories. I was six years old when this happened in our home in Sarney, near Dublin. I know I was quite tall for my age, and my father told me that I was very tough. Whenever I was involved in a fight with other boys in the village, I would always win. My mother agreed that I was a strong lad, and would often ask me to help her carry heavy buckets of water, which I always did without much difficulty. She told me that she loved my thick, black, curly hair, and I knew from looking in the mirror that I had dark brown eyes and a rather square jaw.

But never mind me. Let me tell you about my family and ancestors. Although I consider myself Irish, my family, the Blood family, originally came from England. My grandfather, Edmund Blood, came from Makeney in Derbyshire and was a minor member of the Tudor gentry. He enjoyed an adventurous life in the army and in 1595 he became a cavalry captain. When he was aged only twenty-seven, he joined Queen Elizabeth's army to seek fame and fortune in the Emerald Isle.

On the ship to Ireland, my grandmother, Margaret, gave birth to a son. She was going to call him Edmund in honour of his father, but the Earl of Inchiquin, who was also on board, persuaded her to call the baby, Neptune. She wasn't too happy with that but, on the other hand, who tells an earl that you don't agree with him?

Another aristocrat they met whilst in Ireland was Robert Devereux, the Earl of Essex. He was a man you never argued with, either. According to my grandfather, the earl was hot-tempered, boastful, and constantly announcing to everyone that he had been specially appointed to be Her Majesty Queen Elizabeth's Chief Commander of the English Army. In truth, the Queen had simply dispatched him to Ireland to deal with the rebellious Irish Army led by Hugh O'Neill.

After spending some time chasing O'Neill all

over Ireland, my grandfather decided that being a soldier was not as exciting as he had imagined it would be. Unsurprisingly, he came to the conclusion that spending his life feeling cold, wet, and miserable, whilst risking his life for a Queen who lived hundreds of miles away in London, was not what he wanted to do. He thus resigned his commission and bought two hundred acres of land in County Clare, on the west coast of Ireland. At the same time he also bought two other large plots of land in the north of the country.

In addition to making money from his peasants' agricultural labours, he made a tidy fortune by blackmailing sea captains to pay him in exchange for a trouble-free voyage. He later became a Member of Parliament in the Irish House of Commons, and it was during this period of his life that his wife gave birth to two more sons, Edmund and Thomas. Edmund died three years before I was born, but Thomas, my father, became an ironmaster – a trader in iron – and later bought two estates, the first in County Meath, and the second in County Wicklow.

This, my friends, is where I came into the picture. I was born at Sarney, Dunboyne, in County Meath, twelve miles north-west of Dublin. I spent my first few years on my father's estates, enjoying each of them for different reasons. The wild ruggedness of the west coast was invigorating, and I spent much of my time walking along the high cliffs looking down at the huge waves rolling in from the Atlantic Ocean as they crashed against the rocks below. As the wind blew though my hair, I would listen to the gulls' squawking as they flew and drifted on the sea breezes, constantly searching for food and squabbling with one another for a place on the craggy cliffs.

In contrast, I also enjoyed going into Dublin with my father on business, and gazing at all the big houses and the ships on the Liffey. The places I liked best were the Customs House on the north bank of the river and the bustling Temple Bar on the south bank. The Customs House was an impressively long building that fronted the river, crowned with a green domed roof and sporting a central pillared entrance not unlike that of a Greek temple. Every time I accompanied my father there it was full of important looking men rushing around fashionably dressed in doublets with leg-of-mutton sleeves, wide collars or ruffs, and brightly coloured breeches and hose. My father always wore more sombre clothes, usually black, dark blue, or brown. When I asked him why, he replied that he wished to be taken as a serious businessman and not as a brightly coloured animal.

"Look, Thomas," he had said to me, pointing to a particularly brightly garbed man on the other side of the Customs House. "That man looks more like an exotic creature from the Indies than a trader in furs and skins. He may be carrying an expensive bag and have his secretary with him, but he himself has gone much too far with his gaudy clothes." With that, my father had turned away and set off to find the trader he had come to meet.

One day I asked my father why he took me with him so often, when he went into town for his business meetings. I remember saying to him, "You know, father, although I like looking at the ships on the river, sometimes, I get bored on these trips."

"When?"

"When I have to wait for you while you are talking to your friends and other people."

"That may be true, son, but your attendance is important. Whilst you may be bored, at the same time, you are learning about the world of business; about money and how to deal with people."

He was right and I nodded in response.

"You see, Thomas," he had continued. "Your grandfather came over to this country with very little money but with much ambition. He worked hard and so I was able to grow up in a comfortable state. I'm sure you wouldn't want to be like those beggars we saw at the entrance to this building, would you?"

I shook my head vigorously.

"Although the Good Book says that the poor should be blessed, I prefer it when it talks about the rich man being furnished with ability. And that is what you are: furnished with ability. You are no fool, and I want to see you do well in life."

It was because of his desire for me to make my way in the world that, soon after this conversation, I was sent 'o'er the water' to England, to attend a school in Lancashire. I don't remember much about my time there, except that it rained less there than it had done in

Ireland. And yes, I recall some of the pupils making fun of me because of my accent, at first anyway. After I had punched a few of my loudest classmates on the nose, and elsewhere, the mocking stopped and I was quickly accepted. It was a valuable learning experience for me really. I learned not to turn the other cheek and that if I wanted to achieve something, I should just go for it, and not worry too much about the consequences.

After I returned to Ireland, my father gave me more responsibility in helping him run his estates. On many occasions, I made decisions about managing the land and dealing with peasants without having to consult him, which only furthered my conviction in my own leadership abilities. It was a good time in my life. However, there were disturbing events occurring in England during this period, especially between King Charles and his Parliament. At first, I thought that all these 'petty squabbles' – as I called them – had nothing to do with me. I saw myself as an Irishman, and thought those problems 'o'er the water' concerned only the English. But my naive assumption was far from the truth, and in the end, a series of events led to me becoming drawn into the English Civil War.

Following the development of an atmosphere of increasing mistrust between King Charles and his Parliament, the King had raised his standard at Nottingham on the twenty-second of August 1642. At the time he had a small army of just over two thousand infantry and cavalrymen, but from that day forward the number of his troops grew extremely quickly. At around the same time, Parliament appointed Robert Devereux, the Earl of Essex, to be its own commander, and the rival Parliamentary Army also began to expand.

From the beginning of September 1642, both sides started moving their armies around England like they were playing a gigantic game of chess. Each side searching for its own strategic advantage, while trying to discover and penetrate the enemy's weakest points. The Royalist forces started moving south-west, towards Shrewsbury and the Severn Valley, while the Parliamentary opposition began concentrating its ever-growing army in the Cotswolds and Coventry. A major clash between these two armies seemed inevitable, and there were a number of minor skirmishes as each side tested out the other's forces, all the while learning the rules of war and how best to exploit their own resources. It was during one of these minor, local clashes, at Babylon Hill, a few miles east of Yeovil in Somerset, that I experienced by first taste of arms, blood, and chaos.

"At least none of this is our problem," I said to my good friend, Richard Cavendish, one evening, after we had heard that the King had declared war on the Parliamentary opposition.

We were sitting in the garden of his house near Preston in Lancashire, discussing the contents of a news sheet that a friend had brought from London.

"This war between the king and his Parliament is nothing to do with us," I continued. "He's down there, two hundred miles away in London, and we are all the way up here." I gestured to the hilly countryside surrounding us. "Look around you. Why should we get involved? Do you want to get killed for a king who has a Catholic wife, or for an earl whose father had his head chopped off for treason?"

"No, Tom, you're wrong," Richard replied. "We *have* to support the King. He may not be a strong leader, but this country has always worked on the premise that we, the people, support the monarchy. Just think what would happen if we had no king. We would end up as a *republic*. Can you see yourself living like that?"

After a moment of thought, I nodded my head. "I agree with you. We should definitely have a king but not necessarily *this* one. Think about it, if we could get rid of him, we could crown a stronger king. One who knows how to rule."

"Who?"

I shrugged. I had not given this much thought, and had failed to come up with an alternative on the spot. The King's two brothers, Robert and Henry, had both died at a young age, and of his four sisters, only one was still alive. "Can you see us having another queen?" I asked.

Richard shook his head, insisting that unless we had a king on the throne, even an uninspiring one like Charles, the country would descend into chaos. "Just as it did when the Lancastrians and the Yorkists couldn't agree on who should be King."

Soon after this conversation and still with some misgivings about what we were doing, we set off to join the Royalist forces. We caught up with them at a rough-and-ready army camp near Yeovil in Somerset. As soon as we arrived, we asked to see the commander, and were taken to the tent of Sir Ralph Hopton. He was sitting at his desk as we were ushered in, but he stood up to greet us. He was a large, impressive man, dressed in a dark blue jacket, breeches, and a white, wide-collared shirt. A diagonal red sash cut across his sombre garb. He was wearing a sword on his left side and a dagger with a jewelled hilt in his belt. I immediately noticed his sharp piercing eyes, his intelligent expression, and his well-trimmed, triangular beard. I guessed he was in his mid-forties.

"Gentlemen," he said, indicating that we should sit down in the chairs facing him. "What brings you here?"

"We wish to join you," I replied.

He carefully looked us up and down. "Can you ride? Do you have horses? Have you ever fired a musket?"

We both nodded.

"We're from the north, from Lancashire and Ireland respectively," Richard said. "We're country folk so we're used to horses and riding."

"And we both know how to use muskets," I added, "although we haven't used them much recently. We haven't had the need."

The Sir Ralph didn't say anything; he just

jotted down some notes in a large black ledger. Then, he looked up. "Have you brought any supplies with you? Blankets, warm clothes, food, and arms?"

We both nodded again. Sir Ralph stood up, walked to the entrance of his tent, and called for the guard to fetch a certain Captain Robertson. In the meantime, he gave us a few details about his forces, and told us where we were to be stationed.

"Don't be surprised if we meet the enemy soon. My spies tell me they are drawing near, a force of about four hundred men. That's about the same number that we have here."

By now, Captain Robertson had appeared, and soon Richard and I found ourselves sharing a tent with two soldiers from Bristol.

"Ah, so you haven't been involved in any fighting yet?" the short one, a man called Bill Radstock, asked.

"No, we've just arrived," I replied. "But we saw plenty of troops being mustered in the Cotswolds while we were on our way south."

"Ah, they must have been Essex's men, the Parliamentary lot," the second man, who introduced himself as Fletcher Howard, commented. "You can usually recognize them by the buff coats they wear."

"Do you know what our plans are?" I asked. "I assume we're not just going to be sitting around here all the time, doing nothing."

"You're right there," Bill replied. "We've been told to wait here near Yeovil to make sure the

Parliamentarians don't try anything."

"You mean prevent them from establishing themselves here?" Richard asked.

"Aye. About four hundred of them have retreated to this area. Tomorrow, we'll be setting out to keep an eye on them."

"That's right," Fletcher added. "Tomorrow we're off to Babylon Hill, just a few miles away. From there we'll be able to see what they're doing much more clearly. If I were you, I'd try to get some sleep. Tomorrow will probably be a very long day. And make sure your horses are ready, and also your swords, muskets, and pistols. You don't want to be caught out with a faulty weapon in your hands."

It was official. My career in the army had started.

Chapter 2
Civil War

We were woken early the following morning, and after a hurried breakfast and inspection by an officious captain called Frobisher, we set off for Babylon Hill. We spent most of the day there, just hanging around doing nothing and in the evening we received orders to retire for the night to Sherborne. This was a small nearby town that we Royalists had captured earlier.

"That's it?" I asked Bill, who was riding on a large black horse similar to mine. "That's all the action we're going to see? Riding up and down hills in Somerset?"

"Well, Tom, I think that—" He stopped mid-sentence as a cry went up in front of us.

"The enemy! They're coming this way! Draw swords!"

Immediately, we drew our swords, and as we were about to set off and charge the enemy, our commander, Sir Ralph Hopton, signalled us to stop.

"We're not going to charge them head on," he announced. "They've split their forces into two or three groups and it looks as though they're out to ambush us." He stood up in the saddle so that we could all see him. "Colonel Lawdy has just informed me that they're going to try and retake Babylon Hill by going straight through the fields. It looks like they're not going to use the gullies on the sides like we did." He leaned over to one of the captains next to him and sent him off to call back the infantry which had marched ahead. Then he gave orders for us to break up into two main groups, to charge the divided forces of the Parliamentary enemy. "You," he called to Captain Moreton. "You and Captain Stowell will take half of our men, and Captain Lawdy and I will take the rest."

As Richard and I trotted over to join Captain Stowell's forces, I could feel the excitement growing. I noticed our men sitting straighter in the saddle; some were smiling, pleased to be seeing some action at last. Others were more grim-faced, as though they were bent on some form of personal and deadly revenge. I could hear the brasses of tens of nervous horses jingling together as the hooves of our mounts moved along the gravelly terrain.

As we took up our positions, I sensed something in the air. Not just the usual smells of horse sweat, leather, dung, and churned up earth, but something new. Was it the infamous 'smell of fear' that I had heard about, or was it the smell of excitement and anticipation? I didn't have time to find out as just then we received the order to charge.

With my left hand gripping the reins and my right thrusting my sword out in front of me, I charged off in the direction of the enemy. I could feel the air rushing past my face; my hair blowing in the wind. My black felt hat was blown away, to be trampled into the ground by the horses galloping behind me. As I looked ahead, I could see clouds of dust and lumps of earth flying in the evening air as the enemy forces began to charge us.

"Are you ready, Rich?" I yelled.

He shouted something, but I couldn't hear his reply as the terrible noise of dozens of hooves, yells, and clanking armour filled the air. I lifted my sword even higher as I prepared to meet the enemy head on, and out of the corner of my eye, I saw that Richard had done the same.

My heart was beating faster and faster as the small, blurred, yelling, charging mass facing us from a distance grew larger and clearer. As they bore down on us, it was possible to pick out individual soldiers, swords, and muskets. Then, inevitably, the two masses of mounted soldiers met and the ground shook beneath us as both armies crashed into each other.

I was immediately surrounded by the sounds of clashing swords, the screams of fighting men, and the neighing of terrified horses. We pushed, heaved, and twisted as we tried to gain an advantage and overcome them, but as quickly as they had fallen upon us, they were gone. They had stormed their way through our ranks and were now behind us.

"Look behind you!" Colonel Lawdy shouted. "Wheel to the right!"

I did so and saw that we were facing the enemy again, except that this time they were coming from the opposite direction. My horse moved to step over a fallen body, and just as he did, the colonel gave the order to charge. Without thinking, I thrust my sword out again prepared to meet the enemy head on. Whereas before, while awaiting the order to rush them, I had thought about being killed or wounded, now all I thought about was defeating the enemy.

Feeling as though I was a stone being released from a catapult within the body of our charging men and horses, I galloped into the enemy who were still preparing themselves for their next move. Again, I was aware of the exultant shouts, the cries of the wounded men and horses, and the vicious sounds of swords upon men, mounts and armour. Instinctively, I ducked as an enemy trooper swung his sword at my head. A sensation of joy and elation flowed through me as I ran my sword through his chest, and saw him fall from his horse. I had never done anything like it before but I felt no guilt. Kill or be killed. It was as simple as that.

I noticed then that I had become separated from the writhing mêlée surrounding me, but before I could rejoin my men, some other Royalists, including

Richard and Bill, rode up to meet me on the hill where I was standing.

"What happened to you?" I asked Richard, staring in horror at his blood-drenched right hand and slashed sleeve.

"Nothing much," he shrugged. "I was attacked by one of the enemy, but before he could do any more than this…" and he pointed to his sleeve. "…I unhorsed him and left him to die in the mud."

"What's happening now?" I asked. "Aren't we going to attack them again?"

"No, not us," Bill replied. "Colonel Lawdy wants us to go back up to Babylon Hill and reclaim it from those damned Parliamentarians. It's a valuable lookout position, so we need to take back control, and quickly."

Turning around, we galloped back to the hill to meet Colonel Lawdy, leaving the rest of our troops to deal with the enemy. When we reached the foot of the hill, the colonel divided us into two groups, and told us to use the natural ditches in the hillside to reach the top, so that we would be less exposed. Richard and I set off with the rest of our men, all the while making sure that we kept our heads as low as possible.

"Why don't we dismount and walk our horses up there?" I asked the colonel. "That way, it will be easier to stay hidden."

"It's a good idea, soldier, but we don't have the time. I want to get to the top as quickly as possible." He continued to urge to climb to the top as fast as we could. "But keep your heads down," he added.

It was not a comfortable feeling, knowing that, at any minute sitting half exposed on my horse that I could end up dead with a bullet in my head.

Suddenly, the colonel gave the command. "Charge!" he cried, and without thinking about bullets or being shot, I stormed up the last three hundred feet of the hillside.

We had caught the enemy by surprise, and as they ran around frantically trying to grab their muskets and swords, we moved amongst them, slashing, yelling, and riding them down. Within a few minutes, it was all over. The last I saw of the enemy was a motley collection of men and horses running or galloping down the hill as fast as they could, leaving their dead and dying comrades at our feet.

I dismounted with the rest of our men, and Colonel Lawdy gestured for six of us to go to the perimeter of the hilltop and serve as lookouts. The last thing he wanted was for us to be surprised in the same way we had surprised the enemy.

To my astonishment, despite all the noise and violence of our last-minute charge, we had killed only half a dozen soldiers. Another eight were now either lying down or sitting together on the ground. We bound their arms and mounted a guard over them.

"What are we going to do with them, sir?" someone asked the colonel.

"We'll bury the dead ones over there by that tree," he replied. "And we'll keep these others in case there is an exchange of prisoners."

"And if there isn't?" another musketeer asked, his eyes glistening. "Will we shoot them?"

Colonel Lawdy looked at the soldier straight in the eye. "Let's wait and see," he said. "We'll see what happens next."

We spent the night on the hilltop, and the next day, Colonel Lawdy rode off to confer with Sir Ralph Hopton. While ˛we were there, a large group of Parliamentary forces did indeed return. Their leader, Captain Balfour, challenged us to a fight, and as he did so, a shot rang out. Balfour dropped his sword, clutched his chest, and fell from his horse. Later, we would argue over who had shot him. I was convinced it was our own Captain Stowell, but others were sure that it was James Cowell, also one of ours, who had shot him with the gun he used for hunting.

Seeing their leader fall, the Parliamentary forces immediately retreated down the hill. We chased after them. There were a few skirmishes, and I was wounded in the leg by the casual swinging movement of an enemy sword. Fortunately, it wasn't serious, for I was only able to properly attend to it when we eventually reached Sherborne.

"What happens now?" I asked Richard and Bill as we sat down that night to eat a rough and ready meal of beef, carrots, and bread.

They shrugged. "We stay here, I suppose," Richard replied, "and wait for further orders."

In the end, that is exactly what happened. We

waited around for nearly two weeks, until we heard that the enemy had captured Portsmouth.

"You know what I heard?" I told my friends that evening. "We are going to make our way to the coast, to Minehead, and then we'll take a ship to Wales!"

"Why there?" a tall soldier asked.

"Because the king has more support there than here, and it will serve him better as a base."

What I had heard turned out to be correct. We left Sherborne the next day and headed west for the coast. It was one of the most humiliating rides I have ever experienced. Our host of three hundred Royalists were forced to ride through enemy-held country, and the Parliamentary leader, the Earl of Bedford, made sure that we knew this. His men constantly harassed us from the rear, and woe betide any of us who fell behind. In addition, we had sticks and stones hurled at us in every village we passed through. When night fell and we made camp in a quiet spot in the Quantock Hills, many of our men deserted.

"Richard," I said, as we sat around a small fire, cooking some vegetables. "This isn't how I thought it would be, fighting for the king. I feel like, maybe, we should join those that are sneaking off? I feel like I'm an unwanted invader in my own country."

He nodded. "Me too, but what can we do? Let's see what happens when we get to Minehead. I'm sure things will be better there."

He was wrong. Minehead was chaos. Chaos

and confusion. There was no organisation, and no one knew who was in charge. Everyone seemed to be giving orders, but no one was obeying them. When I asked a flustered-looking captain holding a large sheet of paper what was happening, he told me he was very busy and shooed me away.

By late evening, some sort of order had evolved out of the bustling crowds of impatient officers and soldiers. Orders were given that the infantry and artillery were to be loaded onto two boats, but when Richard and I asked an officer what was to happen to us, he shrugged.

"Can't you see, there are only two boats here," he replied, pointing to the shambles on the quayside. "There's no room for your horses. Only for men and cannons."

"So, what are we supposed to do?"

He shrugged again. "Don't know. No one's told me. I suppose you'll just have to make your own way."

"But…" I said, grabbing at his sleeve.

His reaction was to shake me free like an annoying fly as he hurried off to shout at a group of musketeers who were about to board one of the boats.

"What now?" Richard and I asked each other.

"Well, we can't stay here," I said. "Have you seen how the townsfolk are looking at us?"

Richard nodded. "I suggest we find a tavern on the edge of the town, or sleep in a barn somewhere."

That was the best suggestion I had heard all day. We decided to head for a tavern, as we were both in need of a good wash and a good meal. In addition, our horses needed food and water. An hour later found us standing outside the Red Lion, just beyond Alcombe.

"Is your pistol loaded?" I asked Richard.

He nodded.

"Good. Let's just hope that none of the locals want to beat us up."

"Do you think that they'll be prepared to take Royalist money?" Richard asked nervously.

Fortunately, the tavern-keeper was. Indeed, the greedy look in his face suggested he was prepared to take anybody's money. We handed over some coins, which he immediately stuffed into a large pouch as he asked us what we wanted to eat and drink. We decided on rabbit pie, vegetables, and ale, and he told us his daughter would serve us when it was ready. We then moved to a table near the door, in case we had to make a quick getaway. Even though the hour was late as far as we could tell, we were the only customers.

Ten minutes later, the tavern-keeper's daughter approached with our food and drink. She had a pretty face with rosy cheeks and high cheekbones, and her full lips had a smile for us. Bending forward to place our meal on the table, she made sure that I could see down the front of her loose-fitting blouse.

"Are you from the king's army?" she whispered, her blue eyes reflecting the candlelight in a seductive way.

I nodded.

"Good," she whispered again, as she arranged the plates on the table. "I think it's a shame what's happening to his army, but don't let on to my father. I want the king to win, but he's not so keen."

I smiled as she casually ran her fingers along my arm, before turning and walking back to the bar. Before she disappeared into the kitchens, she turned back and winked, her lips smirking invitingly.

"That lass is hungry," I said to Richard.

"Aye, I saw that." Richard smiled. "You can have her if you want. I'm too tired."

"For *that* I'll stay awake. Let's see if I'm right when she comes back."

I was. When she returned to clear away the table, her blouse seemed even looser, and as she turned to go, she gestured with a subtle nod of her head, indicating that I should leave through the back door. Not long after, in a barn behind the tavern, she showed me just how intense her feelings for the king's men really were.

An hour later, I entered our room for the night. I had assumed Richard was asleep, but I was wrong.

"I see you had a good time," he mumbled. "Just remember to remove the straw from your hair before we go downstairs in the morning," he said, before falling asleep.

My thoughts still full of the barmaid, I fell into bed and closed my eyes. I hoped that her father would not find out about our little liaison. He did not look like a very understanding soul.

When we went down early the next morning, neither Sally nor her father were anywhere to be seen. An old woman was sweeping the floor, and told us that if we wanted breakfast, we would have to wait. We decided not to hang around, and taking our horses from the stable, we left. After an hour's riding to the east, we stopped at a small village for breakfast.

"Tom," Richard began. "I've been thinking. According to a milestone we passed a short while ago, Bristol is sixty miles from here. From there, we could do two things. We could either ride back home, or take a ferry and join up again with the king's men in Wales. What do you think?"

My answer was immediate. "I want to go home. I am bitterly disappointed with what we have seen here and I need time to think if I want to continue being a soldier. If you want to go back I will not hold it against you."

He was silent for a moment as he wolfed down a chunk of bread and cheese.

"Tom, you are right," he said at last. "Apart from taking part in the fighting itself, this Royalist army is not really an army. I mean it is an army, but it is so badly organised. Look what happened at Minehead yesterday. It was complete chaos. Yes, I agree with you. Let's go home and if we change our minds later, we can always return. It doesn't look like this is going to blow over quickly."

And saying that, we wheeled our horses around and began to head north.

Chapter 3
Cathy

We arrived at Richard's Lancashire house one week later and were welcomed like conquering heroes. His parents, especially his mother, a plump woman couldn't do enough for us and treated me as one of the family.

"Are you sure your bed was comfortable enough?" she asked me every time I came downstairs on those first few mornings.

"Would you like some more beef or would you prefer the rabbit pie?" she would ask as she hovered over me at the dinner table.

Richard's father was also anxious to make me feel at home.

"Have another tankard of ale, Tom," he'd say. "It's of the best."

Or, "Here, lads, take this and enjoy yourselves down at the Spotted Dog," and he would thrust a handful of coins into our hands before we left the house.

Sometimes, instead of going to the local tavern, Richard and I would go to the local hall in order to meet some of his friends, especially young ladies who thought that it was below them to go to the Spotted Dog.

"It's not that they are snobs, Tom," Richard explained. "It's just that if they went to the Spotted Dog or any other tavern, they'd be thought of as sluts. You should know what it's like in these small towns and villages."

"I know that, my friend," I replied. "It's just

like that at home in Ireland. If a lass enters a tavern, her name will be in the mud forever."

It was while we were at the local hall that I first met Mistress Annie Whitcombe. I had gone there with Richard and his parents to enjoy an evening of folk dancing and she had been sitting there at the table next to ours with her parents. I was immediately struck by her jet-black hair sparkling eyes and full figure. When she got up to dance, the way she moved her hips was truly enticing and I could not keep my eyes off her.

"Tom, you look moonstruck," Richard whispered to me. "There are other young lassies here apart from yon Annie Whitcombe."

"Is that her name? Then you must introduce me when she sits down. She's fascinating and I must get to know her while I am here."

Richard nodded and was as good as his word. When she returned to her parents' table, Richard took me over and introduced me as Thomas Blood who was a fellow soldier.

"I assume you are fighting for the king if you are friendly with our Richard?" Annie's father asked immediately in a gruff voice?"

"Of course," I replied and I saw smiles break out all around.

"Well, that's good news," he said, clapping me on the back. "We cannot have you fighting for the Earl of Essex or any of those Parliamentarians. If they had their way, this country would be a republic. Can you imagine anything worse than that?"

I said I could not and then asked for his permission to dance with his daughter.

"Of course you can. Anyone who fights for His Majesty can dance with my Annie. Isn't that right, my love?" he asked his wife while clapping me on the back again.

She nodded and I escorted Annie onto the dance floor, winking to Richard as I did so. We joined in for three different dances and then she asked me if we could sit down for a while. I agreed and walked over to a quiet corner of the hall where we could sit down and talk without being disturbed. As we pulled up our chairs, I noticed that while we had been dancing, the top two ties of her blouse had come undone but I did not say anything.

At first we talked about our families and she told me that her parents had been friends with Richard's parents for many years.

"Our farms are near each other in the valley," she said, "and sometimes we share the village farm labourers between us during the harvest season."

She told me that she liked to ride and that she had her own mare. "My father bought her for me and I call her, Emma. She's four years old and jet-black in colour…"

"Just like your hair," I said.

"Aye," she smiled and ran her fingers through her long hair which fell like a waterfall to her shoulders.

"And I love going out to ride over the hills

around here. Sometimes I go with my older brother, John, and sometimes I go on my own."

"Well, if you don't object, I would be happy to join you one of these days," I said.

She nodded in agreement and one week later we went for a long ride over the green undulating scenery of south Lancashire.

It was on our third ride, this time along the valley of the River Ribble that she drew alongside and told me that she wanted to rest for a while.

"What here?" I asked. "The ground is a somewhat soft and muddy."

"No, no, over there," she replied, indicating with her head. "I saw that there's a hut near the top of that hill and it should be dry there. I would think that it is probably empty."

It was. It was an old disused shepherd's hut and the only things inside were a broken chair, a table and a bed.

She picked up some pieces of wool and a rusty pair of shears. "I suppose this is where the shepherd used to stay when it was raining or if he had to stay here at night," she said. "Well, I'm glad he isn't here now."

"So am I," and gently pulled her towards me and began to kiss her pretty face. "You know, your eyes even shine here in the darkness of this hut," I continued as I kissed her eyes and then her soft cheeks and the rest of her face.

She kissed me passionately in return and I

moved slightly away from her so that I could undo the ties on her white blouse. She did the same with my shirt and minutes later we were making love on the shepherd's old bed. Fortunately it was strong enough not to collapse from our frantic amorous movements and afterwards we lay still close together, our arms and legs tightly entwined like roots of a tree.

This was the first of many such encounters, although there were also occasions when we rode out together as a group with friends of Richard and his family. By now, people were so used to seeing us together that Richard told me that there was talk in the village of us getting married.

"Yes, Richard, "I said. "Annie and I have also talked about that. In fact, I want to ask her father for his permission. I plan to do so next week, but don't tell anyone yet. I want it to remain a secret for a little longer."

The following week, according to plan, I rode over to Annie's house and asked her father whether I could wed his daughter.

"Of course you can, Tom," he said, clapping me on the back. "I thought that you would never ask. Come, let's drink to it and I hope you'll both be very happy together."

He called for his wife, Annie and her two bothers to join us and we all drank a fine red wine as a toast to our future. From then on I was immediately accepted as one of the family and was at Annie's house almost as much as I was at Richard's. The only time I was not there was when I took a week off to travel back to Sarney to inform my parents of my impending wedding. They too were delighted and I promised I would let them know when the actual date was fixed.

You can imagine how excited I was to return to Annie's house and on arriving there after a day's ride from Liverpool, I expectantly knocked on the front door.

It opened immediately and I was confronted with the tear-filled face of Annie's mother.

"She's gone, Tom, she's gone," she mumbled as she threw her arms around me, her tears wetting my neck.

"What d'you mean, she's gone? Where?"

"She's dead, Tom. She died yesterday. It was the plague or some other fever. We don't know exactly."

She ushered me into the house and there I learned that two days after I had left, Annie suddenly developed a fever – "something like that sweating sickness that used to be" – and became very pale and weak. They had put her to bed and called in the local doctor but his medicine hadn't helped to reduce her fever. Then they called on the old woman who dealt in herbs and lived on the outside of the village. She made up some sort of green-looking poultice and promised that that would restore Annie back to health by the next day or the day after that "at the latest."

It did not. Annie died late that evening and now I had arrived in time to attend her funeral instead of our sitting down and working out plans for our wedding.

I was devastated. I had never been in love with a girl like Annie before and the thought of marrying her and having a life together had filled my head from the moment her father had given me permission to marry her. Now it had all gone. Gone as if it had never happened, but of course it had.

I spent the following month drinking and moping about Annie and the love that I had lost. In the end I must have made myself insufferable and after having nearly beaten Richard up after a stupid argument about horses, he grabbed hold of me and told me it was time that I grew up and stop behaving like a lovesick schoolboy. That did it. I resolved there and then to try and put the past behind me and the next day Richard and I began talking about our army careers and where we should go if we wished to rejoin the Royalist forces.

"You know, Richard, there is another alternative," I said after we had talked about going east to sign up with His Majesty's army near York. "If we decide to continue fighting for the king, we don't have to join Hertford and his men in Wales you know. We could just join Sir Ralph to the south."

"What do you mean?"

"When Sir Ralph left Babylon Hill, he took nearly two hundred of our men with him. I'm sure it'll be easier for us to join him in the West Country. And besides, we already know Sir Ralph. We don't know what this Hertford fellow is like."

After a moment's thought, Richard agreed, and after our much needed meal, we decided that we would set off for the south the next day.

Chapter 4
The Battle of Edgehill

We caught up with Sir Ralph's men three days later, near Tiverton, Devon. By the time we arrived, the men who had been with us at Babylon Hill had already set up camp, and Sir Ralph was putting them through rigorous training, trying to improve their musketry skills. He wanted to know that the infantrymen under his command would hit their targets' dead centre, and not just waste bullets firing into the middle of nowhere. Shooting somewhere near the target was not acceptable to this demanding officer. He also wanted his musketeers to be able and load their weapons at a much quicker than they had been doing so up to now.

At the same time he was training these frontline troops, he also organised exercises for the cavalrymen. He insisted that they charged in organised formations, with a purpose, rather than blindly and with hope that they would defeat the enemy without any previously thought out plans. This method, he explained, allowed them also to look out for their fellow comrades, and make more of an impact on the enemy.

When Richard and I arrived, we asked to see Sir Ralph, who was delighted that we had decided to rejoin his forces. We left our belongings in a tent, and were quickly commandeered to take part in some of the cavalry exercises he had devised.

That evening, we were free to go into the centre of Tiverton, on condition that we returned to our camp by eleven o'clock. It was while we were sitting in the Blue Bell, a small, pleasant tavern between the castle and the River Exe, that we came across our old friends, Bill Radstock and Fletcher Howard.

"What happened to your face?" I asked Fletcher, who now wore a jagged red scar across his right cheek.

"Oh, that. I got that during the battle on Babylon Hill," he replied, gently rubbing the side of his face. "One of those Parliamentary fellows attacked me with a bayonet. I ducked and—"

"Yes," Bill laughed. "But you didn't duck fast enough!"

"Fear not," Fletcher smiled back. "It looks worse than it is, and the lasses over there aren't scared by my face. In fact, they seem to find it fascinating."

"No wonder," Bill grinned as he finished off yet another tankard of ale. "You double the number of enemy soldiers you fought off every time you tell the story of how you sustained such an injury!"

We continued talking about Babylon Hill for a while and what had happened over the last two weeks. Then, I asked whether they knew what Sir Ralph's plans were for us.

"Aye," Bill said. "We're going to join up with other units of the king's army, then set out for London. There, the king plans to oust Parliament and reclaim his palace, and of course, his rule."

"Do you think that will happen?" Richard asked.

Bill shrugged. "I don't know. I suppose it depends on how determined each side is to fight for its cause. I think we have better commanders, and the king's nephew, Prince Rupert, has come over from Germany to join us. According to what I've heard, he's a very good cavalry commander."

"When are we leaving for London?" I asked.

"Soon," Fletcher replied. "But we're not going there directly. We're going to join up with more of the king's men at Worcester and Stratford-upon-Avon first. Then, as a larger army, we'll advance on the capital."

It sounded a good plan to me and, after a few more days training, we headed north towards Worcester, where hundreds of men joined us. From there, we turned east towards Stratford, our Royalist Army by now numbering over fourteen thousand men. It was a good feeling to be riding with so many; we looked like an invincible force which included three thousand cavaliers, one thousand dragoons – mounted soldiers who used muskets instead of swords – and twenty heavy, iron cannons.

I was on guard the night we camped east of Stratford, meaning I was one of those whose job it was to ride around the perimeter of our camp and make sure that none of the enemy decided to sneak in to steal our horses, or kill any of our men. We were also ordered to stop any of our own men deserting. Quite a few had already done so. When caught, these men had claimed that their wives were ill or about to give birth, or that they had to leave to look after their farms. That night, we caught three men who claimed they were farmers and begged to be released so they could go back up north to see to their lands. We tied them up and took them over to a holding tent. They would be dealt with in the morning.

Just as I was returning to my section of the camp, a messenger on horseback galloped into the central area. I made him halt and asked him what his business was. We were worried that Parliamentary troops, disguised as Royalists, would try and penetrate our camp. Several of their spies had already been caught like this and had been questioned, after which they had been shot.

"Here, look at this letter," the man panted, getting off his horse. "It's for your commander. It says that the enemy are blocking our way to London."

"Where?"

"A few miles east of here. At a place called Edgehill. It's between Little Kineton and Warmington. Come on, man," he said impatiently. "Let me give this letter to your commander. I've got to get back to my own camp before the sun comes up."

I escorted him to Sir Ralph's tent and, following a brief discussion, I was relieved of my duties and returned to my tent.

I found it difficult to fall asleep that night. I kept thinking about the battle that must take place soon. I was convinced it would be on a far greater scale than the one at Babylon Hill. There had only been about four hundred men on each side during that fight, and only a few had been killed. This time, it would be very different. Based on the reports I had heard earlier that day, I knew that the Parliamentary Army, whom we now called the 'Roundheads,' had about the same number of men and guns as we had. A battle with nearly thirty thousand men! It was unimaginable. Eventually, I fell into a troubled sleep, only to be shaken awake by Richard.

"Wake up, Tom. We're moving out in an hour. Get yourself and your horse ready, and find some breakfast. Sir Ralph doesn't want any stragglers today."

Even before the sun had fully risen, we were heading east, together with hundreds of our cavalrymen and thousands of our infantrymen. We were about a dozen miles from Edgehill, but our pace was being slowed by our marching infantry. They were all carrying long muskets, forked musket rests, and leather bandoliers full of bullets and gunpowder. Some of them were singing rude songs about the Earl of Essex, the enemy commander. Sir Ralph had insisted that the cavaliers and musketeers all move east together. He didn't want any stronger Roundhead forces attacking us piecemeal.

We arrived at Edgehill in the afternoon, meeting up with the rest of the king's army. I must admit, when I saw the flags, the armoured breastplates flashing in the sun, the bright colours of the uniforms, and the thousands of horses, to say nothing of the many more thousands of musketeers and pikemen, my doubts about the strength of our cause melted away.

My determination to fight was strengthened when I saw the king himself, mounted on a large black stallion, talking to Prince Rupert and two of our best commanders, Lord Astley and Lord Wilmot. To my surprise, the King was quite a small man. He was wearing a highly burnished breast plate over a dark jacket, slashed with gold, and a pair of very impressive black boots, which reached to the middle of his thighs. Across his chest he wore the wide blue ribbon of the Order of the Garter, which made him look even more regal as he sat high in the saddle of his impressive war horse.

Once all the men were assembled, we were ordered to ride as quickly as possible to the top of the crest overlooking the plain. The king wanted us to claim it before the Roundheads could take it, so that we had the strategic advantage of height on our side during the forthcoming battle. From the summit of Edgehill, we would be able to see over the whole area, and avoid being overcome by a surprise attack.

I sat upon my horse and waited. Richard was positioned to my right; Fletcher to my left. We were on the eastern side of our men, waiting behind the king's chief commander, his nephew, Prince Rupert. The prince was known to be a brave and accomplished horseman and I said as much to Richard.

"You know he fought with the Dutch against the Spanish?" I said. "I heard that he acquitted himself well."

"I know, but it is also said that he's somewhat impulsive."

"Well, perhaps it's better to have an impulsive commander rather than a passive and cautious one," I offered. "We'll just have to wait and see."

And Lord did we wait. We did not know it then, but we were going to have to wait for nearly two hours before we saw anything happen. And when it did, it had nothing to do with the fighting. Instead, what we saw was the king, riding along the lines of his troops on his magnificent black charger. When he reached the middle of the first line of troops, to our left, he stopped. It was clear that he was about to say a few words, but before he could begin, someone shouted 'God save the king!' Within seconds, the cry of 'God save the king!' rippled along our ranks, as His Majesty sat there in his saddle in front of us, smiling and waving, acknowledging our patriotic cries. As our shouts faded away on the breeze, he began to address us. I did not catch all of it – the wind blew away some of his words – but I vividly remember how he started his speech.

"Friends and soldiers, I look upon you with joy. It is a privilege to behold so great an army as ever a King of England has seen in these later times, standing with high and full resolutions to defend their king, their country, and all its loyal subjects."

After this I heard only a few phrases. 'Defending the country' was mentioned, as was 'loyalty to the nation' and 'risking our lives for the glory of the realm'. Then he said that he placed his faith in God and that he had wanted to preserve his country without any bloodshed, but it seemed that this was not to be. He added that he had confidence in his army and was sure that we would bring him victory. He finished by saying that our cause was just, and he commanded us to be brave and true to the Royalist cause. He ended his speech saying, "Your courage will bring a victorious end to this conflict."

"I certainly hope so," I muttered to Richard as we stood there, still waiting for something to happen. It wasn't in my impulsive nature to wait about.

"Tom, why are you squirming about so much? Do you need a piss?"

"No," I replied, leaning forward to stroke the neck of my horse. "It's just that all this standing around is making me nervous. That's all."

"Well, I don't think you're going to be nervous for much longer. It seems the enemy are even more jittery than you. Look down there. They've started moving forwards and bringing up some of their cannons. There," he pointed. "Can you see those men on the far left advancing along those hedges?"

"They're Sir Richard Fielding's men," I said, before I was deafened by an enormous explosion as a dozen cannonballs flew in our direction. Fortunately, the Roundheads had shot wildly, and their cannonballs landed some distance away from the troops in front of us, lower down the hill. Immediately, the enemy fired another round, this time more accurately. My thoughts were drowned out by the screams of the wounded and the piteous neighing of the horses that had been hit or panicked by the noise, smoke, and confusion.

As I was standing there, hoping that their next round of artillery would fail to reach us, I saw three of our horses rear up and throw their riders. Blood was spurting from the flanks of the horse nearest me, and I saw the sticky redness splatter over its rider, who had recovered himself and was now trying to calm his beast.

A loud cry rang out as our guns fired a return salvo at the advancing enemy troops.

"Look, Tom!" Richard shouted. "We're answering them!"

"Fire away!" the nearest artillery captain shouted. "Fire away and don't stop!"

"But, Richard," I yelled above the sound of the

crashing cannon. "We're not hitting them. We're firing short."

It was true. Either because of the angle of our fire, or because our cannons were not powerful enough, the battery we were sending their way was having little effect on the enemy. From where we were standing, high above the battlefield, I could see our heavy cannonballs ploughing harmlessly into the soft ground below.

I was beginning to think that we might end up fighting the advancing Parliamentary forces on top of the ridge, when Fletcher tapped me on the shoulder.

"Tom, look to your right. Prince Rupert is getting ready to charge. Prepare yourself. And look, the enemy's falling back!"

Fletcher was right. Our cavalry regiments, positioned at either end of our lines of troops, had begun to leave the hilltop, their swords swirling as they swooped down like vicious birds of prey onto the Roundhead forces below, forcing the enemy to retreat.

"Forward! Charge!" a captain shouted, and we all began galloping down from the top of the crest to where the hill merged with the surrounding lowland. As we charged down the hillside, the cacophony of the battle grew: the shouting, the shooting, the screams of wounded men, the neighing of panicking horses, and the pounding of the cannonballs. All of these terrible noises hammered heavily into our ears, just as the acrid smell of the gunpowder burnt by the cannon and the muskets assailed our noses. Watching the battle taking place from the ridge-top, through the swirling clouds of black smoke, was one thing, but being an active part of it was something else entirely.

We were brandishing our swords savagely, burning to make contact with the enemy, and within moments we were charging after Prince Rupert and his men as fast as we could. I rushed on, the blue-coated Prince racing ahead of me, and within moments we were upon the Roundheads, cutting and slashing through their ranks. It was nothing like the fighting at Babylon Hill. That had been a mere skirmish. *This* was the real thing.

Just as that thought flashed through my mind, a Roundhead tried to push me off my horse with his pike. I lifted up my sword and brought it viciously down, slicing him through his head. As I raced forwards, I saw him fall, holding his bloody head in his hands, gore streaming down his face.

"Follow the prince," one of the captains shouted above the clangour of men, muskets, and cannon-fire, but we did not need his instruction. Instead, we charged blindly on, only thinking of winning the battle and killing the enemy.

"*For the king!*" I yelled, as I galloped forward, plunging my now bloody sword into the chest of an enemy soldier who had been about to shoot at me. Suddenly, above the terrible din, I heard a shout.

"Look ahead! Look what Wilmot's cavalry are doing! They're charging Fielding's men!"

"They're forcing Fielding to retreat. They're

giving way!" someone else shouted.

As the breeze blew the cannon and musket smoke away, I saw the enemy forces ahead of us turn and flee. In an attempt escape faster, some of them had thrown their swords and muskets aside while others tried to hide or duck away from our charging horsemen. Our cavalry were soon among them, slashing and hacking at will, and within minutes those green fields were decorated with blood, dead soldiers, and wounded, writhing bodies.

Instead of being filled with the cracking of musket volleys and the cries of the wounded, the air was laden with the sounds of splintering pikestaffs and the clash of steel and swords. As I looked around, ready to attack more Roundheads, Richard called over to me.

"Tom, look! The Earl of Essex is fighting with his men. There he is! To the right! Swinging that broken pikestaff around like a club!"

The enemy musketeers joined their leader, using their own muskets as clubs and striking at our men. The enemy was too close for our musketeers to shoot them, and so they too, together with our pikemen, tried to force the enemy frontlines to retreat. As they did so, they became tangled up in the lines behind them, and soon, the two separate armies became one mass of soldiers. Each side was trying to force the other to give way. The noise was terrible, a fearful mix of clashing pikestaffs, yelling soldiers, the screams of the wounded, and the neighing of terrified horses. But above all were the shouts of our own men, turning to retreat, trying to escape the enemy's vengeful, pointed pikes.

I was about to turn and run when I saw an enemy musketeer approach Richard from behind. "Richard!" I shouted.

"What?"

As he turned to answer me, the jagged end of a broken pikestaff whistled past where his head had been mere seconds before. We ran then, spurring our horses into a gallop and sprinting like frightened rabbits away from the yelling enemy.

As we ran, we heard loud cheers coming from somewhere on our front lines, and turned to look. A large group of Lord Wentworth's cavalry had gathered in formation, and were mounting a charge on the advancing enemy. They came to a halt, and we knew then that it was time to rejoin the battle. We wheeled around swiftly and surged forward like an angry wave together with the rest of our horsemen. The enemy troops panicked and began to pull back. Advance and retreat seemed to be an inherent part of this battle; just as we had all spun around to retreat a few minutes earlier, now we had turned back, our previous fear and panic already forgotten.

By this point we had completely encircled the enemy. I saw Prince Rupert stand in his saddle and signal for us to attack them from the rear. Hundreds of us horsemen wheeled around in a triumphant arc and rode back into the fray, cutting down and hacking at enemy troops as before. It was late on a cool October evening, but the sweat was pouring down my face, stinging my eyes. With the back of my sword hand, I rubbed my eyes, and plunged on.

Soon we had cut our way through the enemy and joined up with Lord Wilmot's men. As we stopped to regroup, I noticed that several of our cavalrymen had dismounted and were picking through the bodies of the dead and wounded enemy, looking for loot. More of us joined them, and after having a brief moral debate with myself, I joined them. I found some money and jewels, which I stuffed into my pouch. Then, as I was looking for more, I felt someone tap me on the shoulder. Tensing, I grabbed my sword, ready to back away and fight.

"Fear not, man," the Royalist officer said quietly. "It's all over. The enemy are retreating."

I looked up and I saw that he was right. Large groups of soldiers on both sides were moving away in different directions, leaving the dead and wounded lying on the bloody grass. Just as I was about to mount my horse, I noticed a Roundhead musketeer loading his weapon, aiming at me. I rushed forward and ran him through with my sword. My last memory of him was the look of surprise on his face. Returning to my horse, I mounted, and wearily followed a group of our men, heading off in the direction of Radway.

As we rode away, I saw the bodies of soldiers, ours and theirs, lying on the churned-up fields or against the hedges. Many were still, but others were moving, struggling to survive their bloody wounds. I stopped to give a wounded cavalier some water.

He looked at me with desperate eyes, as if asking me to give him back his life. He put my bottle to his lips, but the effort was too much. Suddenly, his body jerked as a spasm overcame him, and he dropped my water-bottle, fell to the ground, and died.

*

That night, lying on a pile of dirty straw in a barn, I turned to Fletcher.

"We threw away that battle today," I said.

"What do you mean?"

"We could have thrashed those Roundheads if we hadn't stopped to loot those bodies," I explained.

"But you joined in—"

"I know, but only after I saw that everyone else was doing so. I'm telling you, Prince Rupert should have stopped us. We should have charged the enemy again. They looked like they were half-beaten, but now they'll have time to build up their strength; they'll be ready to attack us again. This war isn't over yet. Of that I am sure." Just then, it occurred to me that someone was missing. "Where's Richard?" I asked.

Fletcher pointed somewhere to the left. "He's in the barn over there. With the wounded."

"What happened to him? We got separated towards the end."

"A musketeer shot him in the shoulder,"

Fletcher said. "Richard was riding away after that looting business, and an enemy soldier shot him from behind."

"Is he all right? Will he live?"

"I think so. Go and see him. I don't think he's hurt too badly."

I stood up and despite my heavy weariness I walked over to the nearby barn. As soon as I entered, I could smell the foul stink of blood and piss and Lord knows what else. Covering my nose and mouth with my sleeve, I searched for my friend in the feeble light cast by a few lanterns.

"Tom? Tom, I'm over here."

The call had come from the far corner, amongst the groans of the wounded men and the rustling of straw. I walked over and found Richard, lying on a torn blanket.

"How are you? What happened?" I asked.

He repeated the story Fletcher had told me, but with more detail. "Fear not, Tom," he smiled when he had finished. "That enemy bastard didn't get away with it. As he was moving away, thinking that he'd killed me, I got up and ran him through with my sword. I don't know whether I managed to kill him, but even if I didn't, he's sure as Hell going to be feeling rough for a very long time."

"But what about *you*, Richard? Has anyone seen to your wounds?"

He nodded. "A surgeon has. He took out the bullet and bound up my shoulder. He said I won't be able to move my arm for a while but, if I'm lucky, it should heal itself. I should count myself lucky, I suppose, that it's my left shoulder not my right."

I gave him some water and an apple from my pouch and told him that I would come back in the morning. When I returned the next day, I saw him sitting outside on a log. He told me that the groans and cries of the wounded had stopped him from sleeping, so he had crawled outside and slept under the stars.

I asked if he could walk.

He nodded. "I've damaged my shoulder, Tom, not my legs! And to be honest with you, I'd be happy to get away from this hellhole." He stood up, leaned on me for a moment, and then stood up straight on his own. "See, good as new," he grinned. "Let's go and find the surgeon and see if he'll let me go. I'm sure he will. The fewer characters he's got to deal with, the better."

Richard was right. After a quick inspection and a kindly 'good luck', the elderly surgeon, who was wearing a bloodstained leather apron, gave Richard permission to leave.

"Just make sure you change your dressing every day," he added, before turning to deal with a soldier who looked as though half his face had been slashed away.

That afternoon, exploiting the post-battle confusion, we took our horses and left Edgehill. We rode north, setting a gentle pace – the last thing I wanted was for Richard to jolt his shoulder by riding to fast – as we set off towards Lancashire.

Nobody stopped us, and we were pleased to get away. I wanted to distance myself from the place where I felt, despite what several soldiers had said, we had lost the battle. Also, Richard had no desire to remain in the place where he had been wounded. I told him to wear his jacket over his bound shoulder and that we would avoid any places near here where the locals might start asking questions. Regardless of whether they were sympathetic to our cause or not, there was always the risk of attracting trouble. We had no specific plans; after six weeks of fighting, all we wanted was some peace and quiet.

Chapter 5
The Road to Marston Moor

That night we stopped at the Black Pig, a small tavern a mile or two north of Redditch, in Worcestershire. After paying for a room for the night, we enjoyed a meal of beef, vegetables, and ale. As we were eating, I overheard the man sitting behind me say something about the battle at Edgehill. I turned around and casually asked him what he had heard, the excuse for my curiosity being that 'my nephew' had been at the battle.

"Oh, I hope he wasn't," the somewhat portly man, in a dark brown jacket, replied. "From what I hear, hundreds, if not thousands, of men were killed. They say that the king's horsemen slashed their way through the Roundheads like a farmer cutting down his wheat…"

"Aye," his companion interrupted. "But those Roundhead soldiers, especially the pikemen and the musketeers, took their revenge as well."

"So, who won in the end?" Richard asked.

The two men shrugged. "Don't know," the man nearest to me replied. "It depends on who you ask. Someone told me last night that it was the Royalists, and then someone else swore it was the Roundheads."

"Well, whoever it was," his companion said. "Let's hope that this was the last of the fighting. I mean, we don't want a civil war on our hands, do we? We don't want to be like the Scots, or the Irish. They're always fighting each other. Me, I'm all for a peaceful life; I suppose most people are, aren't they?"

The portly man glanced at Richard's shoulder, and noticed the dressing showing under his jacket. He nodded towards the bloodstained fabric. "What happened to you?" he asked.

"Oh, he fell off his horse last night," I replied, quickly. "Landed badly on his shoulder. I told him not to have another drink, but he wouldn't listen."

That satisfied the man's curiosity, and after wishing Richard good health, he turned around and continued his conversation with his companion about the price of mutton.

We decided to stay in the Black Pig for another day, to give Richard's shoulder time to rest. We knew that riding fifty miles in a day would only hinder his recovery. We spent the day sitting outside on a bench, casually asking passing travellers if they had heard anything about the battle we had taken part in. We received a variety of replies.

"The king's men thrashed those Roundheads, y'know. Killed 'em all off," a thin farmer told us.

"No, I heard different," his friend said. "I heard those Roundhead musketeers put paid to that Prince Rupert fellow. I even heard that they killed him. Damned foreigners! What right does he have coming over here and fighting in our country? That's what I want to know."

The more stories we heard, the more we came to the conclusion that neither side had won the battle.

We left the Black Pig early the next morning, and made our way through to Barlaston via Birmingham and Stafford, where we stopped for a meal. Although riding to Barlaston was quite an effort for Richard, he decided that even though it might be hard going for his shoulder, it was worth the risk. Richard had a cousin living in the village, named Lucy, who was married to the owner of the town's largest tavern, the Three Tuns.

"Of course, we'll put you up," she smiled when Richard asked if they had a spare room for the night. "I'll give you the quietest room at the back, the one furthest away from the yard, so you won't be disturbed."

Richard believed that his cousin supported the king, but we decided to remain cautious, and after a couple of careful questions, we learned more about the battle of Edgehill.

"Aye, it were a terrible thing, that battle," Lucy's husband, George, said. He was a huge man who could lift heavy barrels of ale with no apparent effort. "We've heard tremendous stories of how many men were killed. Passing travellers have been saying that at least five hundred were killed on each side, and thousands more were wounded. Poor bastards," he sighed. "To be wounded by a sword or cannonball ain't no good for you. You might live for a while, but probably not for long. I saw that when I was a soldier before I married my Lucy and bought this tavern. There's at least two old soldiers in this village now, and they can't do a day's work between them. Poor buggers. They just get by living on handouts and charity. Ain't that right, love?"

Lucy nodded, before heading into the kitchen to prepare us our evening meal.

We spent three pleasant and restful days with Lucy and George. We bid them farewell after breakfast on the fourth day, but not before Lucy had given each of us a bag full of apples, pears, cheese, and a small loaf of freshly baked bread.

"I don't want you two dying of hunger," she smiled, as she and her husband waved us on our way.

"And make sure you keep off the roads at night," George warned us. "There's all sorts of strange characters about these days, even more than usual. Keep your pistols loaded is what I say, and find somewhere clean to stay."

Fortunately, we didn't have to use our pistols at

all and enjoyed our relaxing ride back north.

Eventually, we arrived back at Richard's house where once again we were treated like conquering heroes. His parents fussed over us as before: his mother did her best to fatten us up like chickens for the Christmas dinner while his father insisted on us joining him on several hunting expeditions.

"Come lads," he said happily. "We're going to join Squire Aldington tomorrow when he goes out to catch some foxes in the woods to the south of the river. I'm sure you'll enjoy yourselves."

Fortunately for us, the next day was bright and sunny, although there were some grey clouds to the west which appeared to threaten our day's sport. When I mentioned this to Richard's father, he dismissed it saying that I, a son of the Emerald Isle, shouldn't be deterred by a few drops of rain.

We, that is, Richard's father and his two brothers and me and four friends of the family, left Richard's house at mid-morning and set off for the wooded countryside some three miles away. At first it was a pleasant ride as we rode along and chatted about past hunting stories and tales of military exploits. Then suddenly, Roger, one of Richard's brothers galloped back from where he had ridden on ahead to tell us that he had seen two foxes in the woodland half a mile to the south. Immediately our gentle ride changed into a furious charge as we galloped south.

"*There! There!*" Roger shouted. "There over to the left." And on we galloped. The two foxes didn't stand a chance. Our dogs raced ahead and within minutes were gathered around the two russet coloured mangled carcasses. The dogs were ecstatic. Their tails wagging as if they would never stop as they barked and jumped around the scene of the kill.

For me in a way, this was all something of a let-down. This was my first hunt and I had been very excited about what would happen. Now it was all over and so quickly. We had killed the foxes and for me it all seemed like a gigantic anti-climax.

"Is that it?" I asked Richard. "Is this what we came for? Just to kill these two foxes?"

"No, no, Tom," he laughed. "Oh, your face. You look so disappointed. You remind me of my youngest brother yesterday when my mother took all his sweetmeats away from him. No, no, Tom. That was just the beginning. We'll stop over there by the river and have a picnic lunch and then continue afterwards. They say that there are some more foxes further south."

My spirits restored, I rejoined the rest of our party as saddlebags were opened and packets of food and bottles of ale were taken out of our saddle-bags and spread out on the grassy river bank. I enjoyed our outdoor meal and happily joined in all the talk about this morning's hunt, previous hunts and of course we talked about the ongoing civil war. Some of the men, especially the older ones supported the king, while I noticed that the younger ones tended to be for the Parliamentary side. However, the political scene was not allowed to disturb the picnic and it seemed that no-one took their own or anyone else's politics too seriously.

As I was telling Richard's uncle about my experiences at Babylon Hill, I casually looked up and saw that the grey clouds I had noticed in the morning were nearly above us.

I pointed this out to Richard and he spoke to his father.

"Fear not, lads," he said. "We'll not let a few clouds spoil our fun. Besides, they don't look too bad from here." And saying that, he told everyone to pack everything up and be ready to start the afternoon's hunt in a few minutes.

We started moving south and ten minutes later, the heavens opened and a heavy rainstorm caught us out in the open. The blue skies of the morning were now dark grey, heavy and threatening. Within minutes we were all soaked through. I could even feel the cold rain which had permeated my clothes and made me shiver.

Just as I was remembering a similar situation when I had been in the army in Somerset, my horse slid on a muddy patch on the hillside and I was thrown off. In addition, my horse landed on me, fortunately on my lower half. I was trapped between the cold soft mud and his warm heaving body. Everybody stopped immediately and within minutes had managed to prise my horse off of me. As soon as they did so, I realised that both of my legs were aching and that the right one looked as if it were lying there at a strange angle.

"I think it's broken, lad," Richard's father pronounced. "Either that or it's badly twisted. I've seen things like this before when I was in the army. I think we'll have to put it into a splint. You cannot ride home with it like that."

"Richard," he said. "Go and find some straight bits of wood in that forest we've just ridden through and we'll make a splint for Tom's leg."

Half an hour later, with both of my legs bound in splints – "We'll do both of them, just to be on the safe side" – I was gently hauled up onto the back of Richard's horse. Sitting behind him, and inwardly groaning at the pain each time his horse started to move quickly, we arrived back at Richard's house.

There his mother took over and sent Richard to fetch the village doctor. He arrived an hour later – he had been attending a childbirth – and told Richard's mother how to prepare a poultice to bring down the swelling on both of my legs. This she did as he gave me some foul tasting medicine to ease the pain.

I did not sleep much that night, but I must confess, that when Richard's mother untied my dressing in the morning, the swelling on my left leg had certainly gone down. The doctor was called for again and after studying my right leg, he said that it was definitely broken and that I should rest for a few days.

"It's the break and the shock what's making you look so pale," he said as he took his fee. "You lie down and drink that medicine I've brought and you'll be as right as rain."

I didn't remind him that it was the rain and the mud that had caused my broken leg and despite Richard's mother's pleas, I didn't take his awful medicine either.

The result was that I spent much of the next week lying in bed reading various news-sheets while being fretted and fussed over by Richard's mother. I also had to listen to Richard's father who was feeling guilty about taking me on the hunt and ignoring the signs of a storm.

"Aye, I shouldn't have done that, Tom," he kept saying. "You were right when you told me about those black clouds coming over."

I told him that it was not his fault and that one fine day, I would like to go hunting with him again.

It was while I was resting and reading that I was shocked to learn about the grim tales of fighting and unrest that were happening in Ireland.

Whilst I had been away fighting for the Royalists, the Catholics in Ireland had started protesting against the English's plans to settle more Protestants in the Emerald Isle. King Charles wanted to control the country and use its men and resources to help him fight the Parliamentary opposition and the Scots. To do so, he had established two major areas: one in Ulster, in the north, and the other near Dublin. But this had not worked as planned. Parliament had sent ten thousand Scottish soldiers to Ireland, defeating most of his troops which left the king only in control of Dublin which he had previously lost.

The result of all this unrest had been the formation of a Catholic Irish Confederacy which now controlled most of Ireland. The only areas it did not control were Ulster, Cork, and the Pale of Dublin.

"You know, Richard," I said one evening, after learning about the Catholic takeover of Ireland. "I think I should go back there and help out on the Protestant side."

"To Ireland?"

"Yes, of course to Ireland. That's the land I know best, my friend, and I sure as Hell don't want those Papists taking over my country, now do I?"

Richard agreed, and a week later, we found ourselves in a Protestant army camp, north of Dublin.

*

"How many men do we have?" I asked the commander the first night we arrived.

"A few thousand."

"And the Catholics?"

"According to what I'm reading," he said, looking at a report in front of him. "They've got a lot more. More than us. And they're spread out all over the country. They've also got a large number around here. Again, more than we have."

However, despite the potentially explosive situation, nothing exciting happened. We went out on patrols, took part in a few skirmishes, but nothing was resolved. In September 1643, we, the Protestants, signed a truce with the Catholics, but this did not change the situation in any noticeable way. We continued with our patrols and skirmishes, and each side kept raiding the other's bases.

One evening, after Richard and I, along with two dozen others, had returned from attacking an enemy base near Balbriggan, some twenty miles north of Dublin, I took Richard aside.

"I've had enough of this," I said. "We go out on raids; we kill a few of them, they kill a few of us, but nothing really changes. I want to go back to England and rejoin the king's men."

"Are you sure, Tom? From what I've heard, His Majesty isn't doing very well. I know his men beat the Roundheads recently at Newbury, and Lansdown, and Adwalton Moor, but those victories didn't amount to much, and they haven't changed the situation. The king is still bottled up in Oxford, and it doesn't look as though he's going to be able to recapture London again, that is, if the people there even want him back."

I sat there for a few minutes, thinking. What Richard had just said wasn't news to me. Some of the men we had been fighting alongside here had told me similar stories, but I hadn't wanted to believe them. Now that my friend Richard had said much the same, I began to think about what was happening 'o'er the water' in a different light.

"So what would you say to joining the

Roundheads, then?" I asked at last. "They are also against the Catholics, and right now, that is more important to me than having this king or anyone else sitting on the throne."

The result of this and similar conversations, was the two of us crossing back over the Irish Sea in a small ferry boat from Dublin to Liverpool. From there we made our way east and met up with the Parliamentary Army outside the city of York.

I had assumed that when we approached the Roundheads and told them we had previously fought for the king, they would turn us away or even imprison us as possible spies, but this was not the case.

"Ach, Royalists who've seen the light," remarked the Scottish commander, Sir William Baillie, when we were taken to him. "And what has made you change your tune?"

"Sir," I began, carefully choosing my words. "We have noticed that the king is splitting the country with his ideas and that his Catholic wife has too much influence over him."

"Och aye," he agreed. "She's even sold some of her jewellery to pay for her husband's troops, and we canna be having that now, can we?"

We both nodded.

"Well, I'll be pleased to sign you on as part of our army, though you should know that there are actually two armies here on our side: the Parliamentary forces, and the Scottish Covenanters. We're fighting together for once. The Scots here have come south to help us with this siege of York; we want to drive that wretched king's man, the Earl of Newcastle, out of the city. Do you follow?"

We nodded again as he continued.

"We've learned through our spies that the king has sent his nephew, Prince Rupert, up from Oxford to reinforce the Royalists. This means we are going to have to deal with him and his men soon, otherwise there's a high chance that the north of England will fall to the king."

Before we could say anything in response, he asked us whether we had brought muskets, swords, and horses with us and which battles we had fought for the King. We told him we were fully armed, and about our experiences at Babylon Hill. We had decided beforehand that if he asked us where we had fought, we would not mention Edgehill. Then he told us to wait outside his tent. Half an hour later, we were escorted over to the Parliamentary camp, where Lord Newark's forces were stationed. There we were taken to the quartermaster's tent and issued with lobsterpot helmets, buff coats, and wide orange sashes.

"There we are," the jovial quartermaster said. "Now you look like our men and not like those damned cavaliers. You should take these shorter muskets, instead of what you have now. They're easier to carry when you're on horseback."

That night, we slept in a tent which we shared with four other horsemen. One, John Wallingford, was a staunch Protestant from London, who hated the king;

another, James Marlowe, was a Yorkshireman from Leeds who, like us, had changed sides. The other two were twins, Robert and Will Maldon, from Sunderland, County Durham. They seemed to have joined the army for the adventure, rather than out of any desire to fight against the king.

"So, why did you join the Roundheads?" Richard asked.

"Because they seem to be doing better," Robert shrugged.

"Aye," his brother, said. "At first we were going to join the king's army, but when we heard about what happened at Cheriton and Nantwich, we decided to join this side. The conditions are better here anyways, or so I've heard."

"That goes for the food and uniforms too," Will added. He patted his dented lobsterpot helmet affectionately. "This helmet saved my life when we were ambushed at Newark."

The next day, we learned that the Parliamentary generals, the Earl of Manchester and Sir Thomas Fairfax, had been asked to break off the siege of York, but they had refused: to do so would have be seen by the enemy as a sign of weakness, or so they assumed. As a result, I was sent out as part of a cavalry patrol, charged with denying any Royalist reinforcements access to the city and to make sure that the Royalists felt our presence,. We were also told to observe whether the city's defenders were making any changes, such as building more defence posts or enlarging their own patrols.

The officer in charge of our patrols was a tight-lipped cavalryman from Huntingdon. His name was Oliver Cromwell. While he seemed to be less authoritative than most of our officers, he nevertheless had a commanding presence about him. He made you believe that he knew what was needed, and that he trusted you to fulfil his orders as best as you could.

After one such patrol, I returned to my tent with news to report. "Have you heard what the Royalist commander in York has proposed?"

"Who, the Duke of Newcastle? What does he want now?"

"He wants to surrender the city so that we won't damage it."

"That sounds very noble," James Marlowe commented.

"Nobility my arse," I replied. "I hear he's running out of food and water."

"So, are we going to accept his surrender?" Wallingford asked.

I shook my head. "Our commanders will refuse to agree to his terms. He wants to leave the city in an honourable fashion and…"

"Save his men to fight us another time," Richard said, finishing my sentence.

A few days later, one of our commanders, Lieutenant-General Crawford, planted land mines outside St Maria's Tower, a strategic site defending the city. Unfortunately, the mines exploded too soon, and in the following firefight, several of our men were killed and wounded. Though we mourned the loss of our troops, it did silence any further discussions about an honourable Royalist surrender. They had killed our men and we were not going to let them get away with this.

However, the situation at York became more complicated when we learned that Prince Rupert, at the head of a very large Royalist force, had long since left the king at Oxford and had recently reached Knaresborough. He was a mere twenty miles to the west, threatening to besiege us, the besiegers of York.

Thus, on the first of July 1644, our Parliamentary Army, led by Lord Fairfax and his son, Thomas, as well as the Earl of Manchester and Oliver Cromwell, marched west. The aim was to prevent the Royalists from reinforcing their troops in the city of York, thereby strengthening their hold over the north of England. In addition, the Scottish Covenanters, led by the Earl of Leven, Lord Newark, and General William Baillie, also marched west with us. I remember thinking that if there were to be a battle, like at Edgehill, it would be a huge one. It would certainly not be anything like the Babylon Hill skirmish. We, in our thousands, were to meet the enemy in their thousands, on a bleak stretch of country called Marston Moor.

As I sat in the saddle that day, looking around at the thousands of soldiers surrounding me, all armed and ready to thrash Prince Rupert and his Royalists, I felt that victory was in the air. Our army comprised of well over twenty thousand men, cavalry, dragoons, and musketeers. I was told that the enemy had about the same number. We also had fifty cannons with us.

"Imagine that," I said to Richard, as we rode. "A battle with over forty thousand men! This is going to be the biggest battle ever, my friend. What we fought in the south will look like child's play."

He nodded and adjusted his helmet. "Just make sure your sword and musket are ready. I've got a feeling that we're going to need our swords more than our muskets this time."

Chapter 6
The Battle of Marston Moor

The second of July 1644 dawned grey and foreboding. A cold drizzle had set in, which felt as if it might turn to a heavy downpour at any moment. Such weather was typical of this wide stretch of moorland and open fields. As we cantered west, I pulled my helmet down and pushed up my collar to keep the wet from seeping down my back. As I did so, I noticed that several of the men riding alongside me were doing the same.

As we passed through the villages of Knapton and Rufforth, small crowds of people came out to cheer us on. Most of them were calling out the name of our commander, Fairfax, while a few others shouted for the Earl of Manchester. I even heard a few people yell 'Cromwell! Cromwell!' which surprised me. I had thought the name of our young cavalry leader was known only within our ranks.

As we continued riding, the low clouds lifted, the drizzle stopped, and the pale sun even made an appearance. A short while later, we were ordered to a halt. We had arrived at Marston Moor, and now stood facing Prince Rupert's loosely formed lines of cavalry and musketeers.

We rapidly moved into the positions that had been previously decided by our commanders, Lord Fairfax, the Earl of Manchester, and Lord Newark. Richard and I found ourselves on the left flank, which was to be led by Cromwell. While sitting on my horse and waiting there, I looked along the lines of men and horses and noticed that both sides had lined up using the same formation: the cavalry positioned at the end of each wing, while the musketeers were in the centre, facing their enemy counterparts. To me, it looked as though we had more men than the Royalists. I could see that they had only one block of musketeers, who now faced our three blocks. Our men were under the command of General William Baillie, together with Sergeant Major Generals Lawrence Crawford and James Lumsden.

Several of our captains and sergeants started shouting at our men, directing them where to place the fifty cannons that we had brought with us. While all this activity was going on, I said to Richard that it looked like we had at least three times more cannon than the Royalists.

"If we fire them all at the same time, that should give us an advantage," I mused, looking at the distance between the two armies: a mere four hundred yards, split down the centre by a ditch.

"Yes, and I think we should fire them soon. We won't be able to move the cannons much once the fighting starts," Richard replied. "Besides, that ditch won't allow us to move them forward any further. It's too deep."

By the time the commanders on both sides had manoeuvred their forces and artillery into position, it was late afternoon.

As I was stuffing some bread and cheese into my hungry mouth, I felt Richard kicking my foot.

"Look over there, Tom. It seems as if those Royalists are standing down to eat something. Now would be a great time to attack them, when they're not expecting it."

Apparently, our Scottish commander, the Earl

of Leven, thought the same, for at that moment, I saw him raise his arm and shout the order to attack. Immediately, our musketeers in the centre fired volley after volley, as we cavalrymen charged forward to catch the enemy unprepared.

It was an exhilarating feeling, galloping as fast as we could with our sword arms extended, ready to cut down anyone in our path. Holding the reins tightly, I clamped my helmet down hard on my head as I felt the wind rush past me. All I could think about was defeating the Royalists casually lined up ahead. As I drew closer, I saw them throwing their food aside, doing their best not to be caught completely unprepared. But they were too late. Many of them realised what was happening, and leapt into the saddle, but those on the front line had no chance. We were upon them like a huge scythe, cutting them down as a farmer works his way through his fields.

As I cut and thrust, I saw many of the enemy go down around me, their faces showing the agony of sharp steel violently slashing through flesh and bone. The noise was ear-piercingly horrendous. The clash of swords; the yells of the charging horsemen; the screams of the wounded, and the heavy galloping thuds of our horses.

I became aware of a pungent mixture of smells: the earthy scent of upturned moorland together with the sweat of men and horses. Perhaps I should have been frightened, but I was too busy searching out Royalists to kill and too pre-occupied with deflecting

[72]

the swords thrust out at me to be concerned about being wounded or killed.

Suddenly, I felt a sharp blow on my back, and turned around to see a Royalist cavalryman using his musket as a club. He had hit me, and was now raising his musket by the barrel, holding it as a club high in the air ready to hit me again. I lunged forward with my sword, ramming it straight through the centre of his chest, just above where his blue sash crossed over his body. I saw his eyes shift from vicious intent to shock as he looked down and saw a red stain rapidly spreading over his sash and jacket. Then, with one final look of disbelief, he fell off his horse. The last I saw of him, he was being dragged away by his horse over the bloody terrain, his foot having been caught in his stirrup.

"Tom! To your right!"

I looked to the side to see two Royalists bearing down on me. Perhaps they were his friends, but I had no time to think about that. Turning my horse to face them, and thrusting out my sword, I charged between the pair and separated them. As I was about to stab the one on my left, his horse tripped over the body of a fallen horse and all I could do was slash his forehead as he fell to the ground. Whirling around, I severely bloodied the arm of the other Royalist as he rushed past me. He immediately turned back in preparation to rush me again, grabbing his musket in readiness to use as a club.

Then, the strangest thing happened. All I was

aware of was this Royalist cavalryman in his plumed black hat, preparing to rush me and club me to death. At that moment, I did not hear the sounds of the fighting around me. All I could hear was the heavy snorting of my horse as I felt my heart thumping like cannon fire. Nothing else in the world mattered. Just me and this unknown enemy horseman. I could have charged him there and then, but for some reason, I didn't. I let him engage me. As he gained momentum and raised his musket high in the air to smash it down on me, his face suddenly exploded in a bright red splash. A stray bullet must have hit him and he crashed to the ground, screaming in agony. He lay there writhing for a few moments and then, with a final spasmodic kick of his right leg, lay still.

Richard appeared beside me.

"Did you see that?" I shouted over the noise of battle and pointed to the dead Royalist. "He almost killed me. A stray bullet saved me."

"That was no stray bullet, my friend," grinned Richard. "*I* shot him. I saw what was happening and as my musket was already loaded, I shot him."

I grinned back in reply. "How can I repay you? You saved my life."

He shrugged, and as he did so, I saw an enemy soldier about to charge Richard from the side. Turning my horse to block the soldier's path, and with my sword still in my hand, I thrust it out and brought my already bloodied blade down sharply into his thigh. He screamed as he galloped away, the blood flowing, forming a huge red stain on his pale blue breeches.

"Thank you," Richard said. "I didn't see him coming."

"Well, it's lucky I did then. I suppose I've repaid you now," I said, grinning, as I turned to see what was happening on our left. Our men were getting ready to charge, so I told Richard to follow me. I then shouted to one of our captains to ask what was happening. Above the surrounding cacophony of battle he shouted back that we were about to attack the cavalier forces in front of us led by Baron John Byron.

Ahead of us I saw Cromwell sitting high on his horse. We also sat ready, tense, waiting for him to give the signal for us to rush the Royalist forces.

"Why don't we charge now?" the Roundhead on my right asked. "Those Royalists don't look ready. We could have them finished off in minutes."

"Patience," I said, despite the fact that I was itching to take on the enemy. "Cromwell wants us to be formed up properly. He doesn't want to attack them like Prince Rupert does. Y'know, disorganised, every man for himself."

I was right. Cromwell spent the next few minutes organising our lines into an orderly formation; only once he was satisfied did he raise his arm for us to charge. We were on the enemy in moments. They must have known that we were going to attack, yet they did not seem to take any defensive action. A minute later we were through them like a hot knife slicing butter, cutting and slashing, forcing those who were not

[75]

wounded to flee the battlefield.

Some of our men, in their desire to finish off the enemy, started to chase them even further, but Cromwell sent some of his men after them and ordered them to return to our new position. He then gave orders for us to regroup and told us, as he rode up and down the ranks, that we would now be attacking the Royalist musketeers, who were currently beating our own musketeers in the centre of the battlefield.

"What about those Royalists who have fled?" someone shouted.

"Forget them," Cromwell called back. "I doubt if they'll be returning. To me, it looks like they've had enough for the day. Now, let us trust in the Lord and pray that He gives us this victory."

As before, we did not move until Cromwell had finished organising us, and it was only when he gave us his signal again that we wheeled around in a wide arc to the right, galloping towards the Royalist musketeers.

We caught them completely by surprise; they were so busy fighting our own men that they did not realise we were coming until we were upon them. We sliced through them again like a scythe cutting through wheat. Although a few of our men fired their muskets, I decided not to bother. My sword was much easier to use, especially on a horse. Why use a weapon that required reloading with black powder and ramming a musket-ball into place when you would use a deadly blade that was always there, ready for any moment?

From the corner of my eye, I noticed that Richard had made the same choice, and was busy thrusting and slashing as we forced the enemy to flee. From time to time, I heard a few cheers coming from the men we were now supporting, as we smashed through the king's forces and helped turn the tables in the centre of the battlefield.

Just as I was beginning to feel pleased with myself, I realised that I had dropped my guard too soon. Standing there in front of me was a determined looking group of six enemy soldiers, all pointing their muskets at me. I was about to take the initiative and charge them when, from my right, I heard a huge explosion. Something round and black suddenly shot from behind, straight into the enemy facing me. It was all over in seconds. The cannonball crashed into them, leaving four dead and two lying there, bloody and wounded. From the looks on their faces I could see that they were desperate to escape from the legs of our galloping horsemen, who were racing in to finish off the remains of the king's once-proud musketeers.

I offered up a quick prayer of thanks, then looked around, staring ahead in horror. The Royalists had received fresh reinforcements: the Duke of Newcastle's regiment. They were called the 'Whitecoats' because of their white uniforms, and having once been assembled at York, they were now supporting the Cavaliers in the centre of the battlefield. Seeing this, Cromwell immediately ordered us to join forces with Lord Newark's men. We were to attack the

Whitecoats from behind.

It was at this moment that the Royalists showed some of the stiffest resistance I had seen all day. Despite the mounting pressure from our cavalrymen and musketeers, they refused to give up. Slowly, brutally, I saw them fall, and by the time Baillie and Crawford's men joined us, the Whitecoats and their fellow Royalists had been virtually wiped out.

"Where's Prince Rupert?" someone shouted.

"There!" another of our men pointed and shouted back. "He fled away through that beanfield. Couldn't get away fast enough."

Now that their commander was no longer in the centre, the Royalist army broke up in chaos. As the sun set over Marston Moor, we mowed down any Royalists who were still standing. Those who were injured but alive, we took as prisoners of war, gathering them up in large groups. They were scattered around the battlefield, amongst the dead men and horses from both sides. From my saddle, it was easy to see that the enemy had been completely defeated.

As I sat there, surveying the grim scene before me, I realised that this was the first time I had seen so many dead men together in one place. I felt Richard's sword tapping against my thigh.

"You alright, Tom? You look shocked."

"No, I'm alright. I was just thinking how lucky I've been today. First, you saved me, then a stray cannonball killed a load of musketeers who were about to shoot me down."

"But your arm and leg…you've been wounded…"

"What? Where?" I said, looking down at myself in disbelief. Richard was right. I had fended off more than one sword attack, but obviously the enemy had managed to inflict damage without me noticing. There were two deep, bloody cuts on my upper thigh, and when I inspected my right arm, I saw that the sleeve of my thick leather buff coat had been slashed through along its length. It was only now after Richard had told me, and a sort of calm had descended over that bloody moor, that I began to feel where I had been wounded.

"I'd get the surgeon to see to those wounds," Richard said, "Or they may turn bad."

I promised I would, but when I saw the lines of men near the surgeons' tents, I turned away and dressed my wounds myself. I did not want to wait there among the crowds of wounded and dying men, groaning, screaming, and praying for the Good Lord to put an end to their agony.

"What are we to do now?" Richard asked me later when he saw that I had dressed my wounds.

"I don't know about you," I replied. "But I'm off to the nearest tavern for a meal and a bed. Nothing else interests me. Are you coming?"

He nodded and we set off east in the direction of York.

After a slow hour's walk, we found ourselves at the Old Boar Inn, in Rufforth. The innkeeper said he was glad that we were Roundheads, but I believe he would have taken Royalist money as readily as he took ours. He sent his daughter to serve us with a late evening meal, and she started to flirt with us. Normally, I would have enjoyed such attention, but after the battle I was too weary to respond to her behaviour.

"Just give us what we ordered," I said gruffly, too tired to even pat her on the behind as she walked away, something I usually did when served by a pretty young wench. By the time I finished half my tankard I felt completely exhausted, and the next thing I knew, I was being shaken awake by Richard.

"Tom, Tom! D'you know what time it is?"

I shook my head and opened my eyes, trying to get the world into focus. I was lying fully dressed, boots and all, on a bed in a small room. Somehow, Richard must have carried or dragged me up to this room the previous night, though how he had managed it without waking me I could not understand.

"No, what is it?" I mumbled.

"I heard the church clock chiming ten! We must go!"

An hour later, after a hurried breakfast and a hard gallop, we found ourselves back at Marston Moor. Some soldiers and local villagers were picking through the bodies to see what they could find, as other soldiers stood around wondering what would happen next. A few officers were shouting out orders, but nobody seemed to be paying much attention to them.

As the sun climbed ever higher in the summer sky, the stench of the dead bodies increased, the horses being the worst. All I would hear was the buzz of flies, as they circled and hovered over the gashed and slashed bodies and spilled guts.

"Come, let's go and find our captain, or Cromwell," I said to Richard. "We can't just leave without permission."

Carefully avoiding bodies and pools of blood-red mud, we made our way to a large tent. After waiting for twenty minutes, a burly sentry with a large moustache motioned for us to enter. Inside, I saw several officers sitting at tables, poring over long lists of names. I went to one table; Richard went to the next.

"Your name?" an officer asked, without looking up.

"Blood."

"Hmm, very appropriate," he muttered, and started searching for my name on one of his lists.

"Ah, here we are, Thomas Blood from Ireland. That's you?" he asked, looking at me for the first time.

"Yes, sir."

"Well, it says here that you fought well. You have been promoted. Congratulations, Captain." He shook my hand and gave me a piece of paper, bearing the seal of the Parliamentary Army and his scribbled signature at the bottom. "Dismissed," he said curtly.

I pushed the flap of the tent aside and found Richard already waiting for me.

"I'm a captain now," I said, showing him my

official proof.

"Yes, so am I," Richard grinned. "Apparently we did well yesterday. Come on, Tom, let's go home. I want to see my family. I've had enough of this place."

I nodded in agreement and we set off to find our horses tied to a small tree on the far side of the battlefield. We untied them, mounted, and without looking back, set out westward for Lancashire. We had a two-day journey ahead of us.

As we made our way through the undulating countryside, I wondered what reception we would receive when we got home. Who was considered better: a Roundhead or a Royalist?

Chapter 7
Cathy

I spent two days in Lancashire, then took a ship to Ireland. To my surprise, when I arrived back home in Sarney, during the second week of July 1644, I realised that I was far more exhausted than I thought. My parents were shocked at my unkempt appearance, and my mother insisted that I see a barber immediately. She was also concerned about the various cuts and bruises on my arms and legs, and made sure that they were dressed daily. However, while I enjoyed her care and attention, after a few days I began to find her constant mothering a little annoying.

"Mother, I am quite capable of pouring myself a tankard of ale," I said one day, perhaps a little too sharply. "And I know how to slice a loaf of bread without cutting myself."

She was rather taken aback by my tone of voice, and I promptly apologised.

Unlike my mother, my father regarded my wounds as badges of triumph.

"Look at them," he remarked one day, after asking me to roll up my sleeves to show one of his friends. "It's plain to see that you were in the thick of it. No wonder they made you a captain. They'll be making you a major or colonel next, you mark my words."

I spent the next few weeks resting and living the life of a country gentleman. I would meet friends from time to time, at my house or theirs, or we would spend a pleasant evening in one of the local taverns, where we would eat and drink to excess. Naturally, we would exchange stories with other local Roundheads who had fought at Marston Moor and elsewhere.

"Say, Tom, your stories remind me of thrashing those cavaliers at Cropredy Bridge and Cheriton," said George, a tubby fellow with a scar down his left cheek. "Those Royalists didn't stand a chance."

"You're right, there, George," his drinking companion added. "But it wasn't all good. That fight at Cheriton cost me two fingers!" He held up his sword hand to prove it.

"And we still haven't won yet," I said. "Much of the north is still in Royalist hands."

"Aye, but it won't be for long," George predicted. "You mark my words."

"How d'you know?" his friend asked.

"Feel it in my bones, lad," he replied, tapping the side of his nose, as though doing so confirmed this.

George must have had very accurate bones, because several weeks later, the Roundheads' northern Scottish allies captured Newcastle-upon-Tyne, and our chief commander, Lord Fairfax, beat the Royalists at Helmsley Castle in North Yorkshire.

It was at one of these social gatherings – an evening of Gaelic dances - at the local hall that I became first became interested in Mistress Catherine McAfee. I had gone to there with Patrick 'Paddy' Gallagher, one of my oldest friends, and he had introduced us before we took part in a reel.

"Meet Mistress McAfee," Paddy had said to me. "She's the prettiest girl around these parts."

"Oh, don't you start flirting with me," she said. "What will your sweetheart say if she hears you say that?" However, I had to agree with Paddy. Mistress McAfee was definitely the prettiest girl there that evening.

"You are newly arrived here, are you not?" I asked.

"Aye," she smiled. "We moved down here just a few weeks ago."

"Why do you say you moved *down* here," I asked while looking at her green eyes and auburn curly hair.

"Because we lived in the north, in Ulster and so by living here now, we moved down to Sarney and…"

"Well, I'll leave you to it," Paddy interrupted,

"seeing that you are getting on so fine," and he moved off to find his own girl, Siobhan, with whom he was due to marry the following month.

"So tell me," I continued. "Where did you live in the north."

"Just west of Belfast in a wee village called Glenavy. It's between Belfast and Lough Neagh."

It was then I picked up a feint trace of her Scottish accent. It was hardly noticeable but it was definitely there.

"But you are Scottish, no?"

"Aye, but I was born here in Ireland. My family moved here from the Scottish Lowlands over fifty years ago."

"You mean when the government moved lots of Scottish Protestants here to live among the Catholics?"

She nodded. "My grandfather was offered a good plot of farming land in the north instead of the bad patch he had near Glasgow."

For some reason, probably because of her flashing eyes, pretty smile and attractive figure, Catherine McAfee intrigued me. I had to know more about her.

"Tell me, Mistress Catherine…"

She held up her hand. "Call me Cathy or Cat like everyone else does. Only my mother calls me Catherine."

"So tell me Cathy, you haven't told me why you are here now living in Sarney. Didn't the Scottish

Protestants remain in the north, in Ulster?"

"Aye, most of them did, but a few of them like my grandfather found out that the land the government had given him was no good and so he moved south, to Rathcoole…"

"South of Dublin."

She nodded. "And then my father moved to here, to Sarney, a few weeks ago."

"Ah, when I was in the army."

"You are a soldier?"

It was my turn to nod. "Yes, I'm a captain," and making a flourish and a deep bow, I said, "Captain Thomas Blood at your service."

She laughed and when we were not dancing, we spent most of the evening talking about our families and my army career. When I told her that I had fought in the Parliamentary army, she smiled.

"Oh good. I'm pleased to hear that. My family are against King Charles and his Royalists, so that means as far as I am concerned, you fought on the right side."

From then on we used to meet frequently, so much so that my old flame, Annie Whitcombe, became a dim memory of the past. As our friendship grew, Cathy brought me over to meet her family and she came to meet mine. After the first time I met hers, I sensed there was a problem. I was right. She said that even though her mother approved of me, her father did not.

"Why, did I do or say something I shouldn't

have?" I asked.

She shook her head. "No, no, Tom, It's nothing like that. It's just that he's against soldiers," she replied. "All soldiers. Ever since my oldest brother, Seamus, who had joined the army and was killed fighting the Catholics, he's been against soldiers and armies. And then, two years after that, some Catholic troops burnt his fields and stole his cows and sheep. That was ten years ago and that made him even more bitter. So since then he's never had a good word to say soldiers and armies – whichever army, Catholic or Protestant, English or Irish."

"But he's rebuilt himself since then, no? I mean he moved from the south of Dublin to the north of the city and his fortunes have improved, have they not?"

Catherine shook her head. "No, Tom, they've worsened. The land he thought was good here turned out to be even worse than what he left in Rathcoole, and to make matters worse, nearly all his cows died last year from some disease or other. I don't know what it was, but sometime last summer he lost more or less all his milking herd. Now he's got only half a dozen left and two of them aren't much good, either."

"Yes," I said. "As a countryman myself, I can understand why he feels so bitter about life. Farming's hard enough without having poor land and your herd dying on you."

This meant that whenever we met, it was either at my parents' house or somewhere such as the local hall where Paddy had first introduced us. In addition, when we wanted some privacy, she would climb up onto the back of my horse and we would ride away to a sheltered wood or ride through the countryside and then go for a walk along the bank of one of the tributaries of the Liffey.

On one particularly hot June day, we stripped off our outer garments and jumped into the cool waters. It was then that I saw that her figure was even better than I had imagined. After she came out of the water and saw me admiring her, her wet clothes sticking to her body showing all her curves, she suddenly took off all her clothes, laid them out flat on the grass to dry and lay down. I followed suit. Then seeing no-one was around and after some initial caressing of each other, we made love. It was the first time that I had ever done so in the open and doing this among the trees, grass and the river certainly heightened the experience.

Afterwards we lay there gently caressing each other again and then made love again. We only stopped when the sun began to set behind the woods. Feeling somewhat chilly in the evening breeze, we reluctantly but hurriedly got dressed and I took her back home.

This became the first time that we made love in the open as we happily repeated this joyous experience many more times that summer. But our joy was not to last.

One afternoon in September, when I rode over to take her for a ride – I loved the way she held on to me from behind – she greeted me with a long face and signalled for me that she had something to tell me, "but not here."

As soon as we had left the village and stopped to sit on a fallen log in a nearby wood, I asked her if she was with child.

She shook her head. "No, no, Tom. It's worse than that. This is the last time I am going to see you."

"What? Why?"

"We are leaving Sarney," she began as the tears welled up in her eyes. "My father has had enough here. He's sold the farm for whatever he could get for it and we're moving to Scotland – to be near my father's cousin south of Glasgow. I..." but she couldn't say anymore because of her tears and shaking shoulders.

I pulled her closer to me but she gently pushed me away.

"No, no, Tom," she said quietly. "What was is over. You and I can never be close again. We have to live with that," and saying that, she burst into tears again.

"But I can come to Scotland," I said. "It's not so far away."

She looked at me and then buried her face in her hands. "Take me home," she said. "I want to be on my own for a while."

I took her home and she was right. I never saw her again.

For the next two weeks, I drank too much, argued with my parents and in the evenings, took it out on two of the local lassies. Then after a severe dressing down from my father, I pulled myself together and decided to go 'o'er the water' again and rejoin the army.

Chapter 8
Manoeuvres in the Dark

Piece by piece, the Royalist north began giving way to the superior Parliamentary forces, sometimes through a quick, decisive victory, but other times after an apparently endless, long, drawn-out battle.

"Y'know, Tom," my father reported to me one evening, after seeing his nephew, Edward, off to rejoin his regiment. "My friend, Sam, told me that it took Fairfax ages to capture that castle at Helmsley. The governor, Sir Jordan Crossland, held out for three months. Just think of it, three months being cooped up in that old castle before he surrendered."

"And afterwards, did we use it for our own defences?"

"No, Tom. Sam said Fairfax blew up much of it, so the king's men wouldn't be tempted to try and win it back. He destroyed the walls, the gates, and most of the rest. Only the East Tower has been left standing."

"Why didn't he blow it up completely?"

"So that we could use it as a look out, I suppose."

The next news we heard of Royalist defeats came from nearer home. I had taken the ferry to

Chester and back on some family business, and when I returned home, I told my family what I had learned there.

"Prince Rupert was on his way to Chester as I was leaving," I began. "I hear that he wants to join up with his younger brother, Prince Maurice, who is stationed there with Baron Byron."

"But wasn't it dangerous for you to be there, son?" my mother asked. "We'd never have let you go there if we'd known about this."

"Fret not, mother," I said. "No-one there knew I was a Roundhead. I just looked like an ordinary businessman. Besides, I am twenty-seven years old. I'm not a child anymore. I've decided I am going to rejoin my regiment, like Edward did. I told Richard to expect to see me sometime next week."

Despite my mother's protests, but supported by my father, I left Ireland again as planned, and met Richard at his family home. His parents welcomed me warmly, and that night we sat in the parlour and discussed the latest news about the war.

Richard's father, a blunt and stocky fellow who limped and always walked with a thick stick, was of the opinion that the war was a very bad thing. "Thousands are being killed and wounded," he began. "And it's dividing families across the country. Why, just last week I received news that one of my cousins in Weymouth is for the king, while another cousin in London is for this Fairfax fellow. And that's not all. Even here in the village, the tavern-owner's two sons are on different sides. What would happen if one of them killed the other in a battle?"

Neither of us had an answer for that.

"Just be thankful, Father," Richard said. "In our family, we're all on the same side."

"Aye," his father nodded. "And where is the next fight going to be? Up here or down south?"

"I think it's more likely to be in the south," I said. "After beating the king once at Marston Moor and twice at Newbury—"

"And beating him at Cropredy Bridge, and losing places like Helmsley Castle," Richard interrupted. "It looks as if the king has given up the north completely."

His father nodded in agreement. "I reckon you're right. The next fight will have to be in the south if His Majesty wants to get back to London."

Our assumptions were proved right. The next major battle took place at Naseby, in Northamptonshire, some ninety miles north of the capital. But before that battle took place, Richard and I were involved in a few small fights and skirmishes. We had rejoined the Roundheads and placed ourselves under the command of Lord Newark, whose main task was to prevent Princes Rupert and Maurice from trying to bring the north back into the Royalist camp.

In parties of about fifty men, we would ride out at night and raid the enemy camps, under cover of darkness. This usually meant cutting down their tents, killing a few enemy soldiers, and most importantly, stealing their horses. This meant that we reduced their mobility and made it more difficult for them to raid us in the same way.

In general, I would say that our Parliamentary forces were far more disciplined than the enemy. To me, it seemed that Prince Rupert's way of fighting was to charge the enemy in a more or less organised fashion, then after the charge was over, it was every man for himself. His soldiers would ride off as individuals, with no co-ordination between them. This of course made it easier for us to defeat them. I had observed this at Edgehill and at Marston Moor. Although several of the men in our army were not pleased with Cromwell's insistence on discipline and planning, I saw that Cromwell's tactics were paying off. Indeed, we were beating the Royalists in nearly all the raids, skirmishes, and larger battles that were now taking place.

As time passed, and summer turned to autumn, then to winter, the weather became increasingly unpredictable, and fighting on both sides came to a standstill. I returned to Ireland for a while and spent the time helping my father on his estate. The Catholic Irish Confederacy still controlled most of Ireland, apart from the north and the areas surrounding Dublin and Cork.

"Those stupid Confederate fellows wasted the opportunity they had to take over the whole country," my father said one evening, as we were sitting in front of the hearth enjoying one of our favourite whiskeys.

"How?"

"They signed a truce with the Royalists and now they spend all their time negotiating who controls what and where. And that James Butler, the Royalist Duke of Ormonde, is the most pig-headed of them all. Whatever you do, son, make sure you never cross his path. From what I've heard, if he ever decides you're worthy of his wrath, he won't let up until he's done you some serious damage."

Soon after this conversation, I returned to Lancashire, to stay with Richard and his family. We spent a pleasant three months riding, hunting, and joining Roundhead raiding parties when we were called upon. I enjoyed this last activity the most; the possibility of being wounded or even killed added a certain zest to the proceedings. We would leave the village in the evening, armed with our muskets and swords, meet up at an appointed place and from there, swoop down like a flock of eagles onto an unsuspecting and poorly guarded Royalist camp. We would inflict as much damage as we could before riding swiftly off, with the horses we had stolen in tow. When I asked a senior officer why a man as strictly religious as Cromwell permitted us to kill and steal, he told me that since we were fighting in the name of the Good Lord, our actions were permissible.

But, unbeknownst to us, things had not been going as smoothly for the Parliamentary Army as we had supposed.

"You know, Thomas," a captain said to me one

night after we had returned from yet another raid. "Cromwell and the Earl of Manchester are going to come to blows soon unless someone stops them."

"Why?"

"Cromwell doesn't trust him. Cromwell believes that although we beat the Royalists at Marston Moor, our victory would have been greater if the Earls of Manchester and Essex had been better commanders. He thinks those two would fight for the king if they had half a chance. In fact, someone heard Manchester say that regardless of how many times we beat the king, we would still be his subjects. And, if the king beats us just once, then we will be hanged as traitors."

"Can Cromwell do anything about them?"

"Aye, he wants those two earls and several others to resign from the army. He reckons all the army commanders who are also Members of Parliament should resign their commissions. He has called this his Self-denying Ordinance."

"But, sir, Cromwell himself is an MP."

"I know, but it looks like that he's trying to find a way around that one. In the meanwhile, he has become one of the most important leaders in the Parliamentary New Model Army. Sir Thomas Fairfax has been appointed the new Commander-in-Chief, and Philip Skippon is to be his Major General."

I heard the next instalment of this saga one April night, when I was in the tavern with Richard and his two cousins, John and Matthew.

"Have you heard, Tom? The Earls of

Manchester and Essex have been persuaded to resign their commissions?" Richard said.

"That Cromwell fellow is even more important now," Matthew added. "He and Lord Fairfax are going to be our new chief commanders."

"Aye," John nodded. "That Oliver Cromwell is a strict and religious man. Any soldier caught swearing, drinking, or wenching is going to be in deep trouble."

For a second I thought of Cathy and then I asked, "Speaking of wenching, what do you think of the one who served us earlier? She's one I could happily wrap my arms around."

And that night, I did.

"What's your name?" I asked the barmaid when we were lying on a cot together in a small outbuilding behind the tavern.

"Juliette, sir, but you can call me Julie. What's your name?" she asked, as I started to undo the ties on the front of her blouse.

"Er, Rob."

She looked down at my busy fingers.

"What are those scars you've got on the back of your hands? Were you in a fight?"

I nodded. "I was in one of those battles you've heard about, but I don't want to talk about that now."

"I see," she grinned. "You're like all the others, you just want to feel my tits and have your way with me."

She didn't hear any clear response as my mouth

[98]

was too busy sucking her nipples. But she was right. I didn't want her for conversation. That I could have with Richard and my other friends. For the rest of the evening, we spoke very little, just a few hurried instructions, the sound of clothes being roughly removed, all followed by grunts and moans of ecstasy. I left her behind the tavern an hour later, and spent the night sleeping off my drinks and exhaustion in the room Richard's family had given me.

The next morning, Richard and I received a message that we were to report to our local commander on the morrow. We were to meet up at the Black Lion tavern, two miles south of Bolton, fully armed with swords and muskets. We were to bring as much ammunition as we could, as well as food, warm clothes, and bedding. This was not going to be an ordinary raid.

Richard and I woke early the following day, and before leaving, I wrote a short letter to my parents. This I gave, together with a few shillings, to a young businessman who was going to Dublin, with the request that he deliver it to my parents. In the letter, I explained that I was off to the south, and that I hoped to see them again, God willing, by the end of June. I did not mention that I would probably be taking part in a major battle.

As we started off on our journey to the Black Lion, we noticed more and more Roundheads joining us at every town and village we passed through. It was like being part of a human river that became stronger and stronger as tributaries joined it from all sides. As I looked around at the crowds of soldiers with their shining helmets and breastplates, and buff coats, I confessed to Richard how wonderful it felt to be part of such a major military campaign.

We arrived at the Black Lion on time, and found even more men waiting there, who had arrived from Burnley, Rochdale, and the other surrounding towns. It took the senior officers and commanders well over an hour to sort everyone into their various regiments. Once our troops were organised, each regiment recorded the name of each soldier and their military status. For instance, Richard and I were listed as horsemen; others were recorded musketeers or artillery gunners, and so on. It then took another hour or more for everyone to eat and check their horses and personal equipment, so it was not until early afternoon that we began our journey south.

Our aim was to reach Oxfordshire, some sixty miles north-west of London. There, we would be able to prevent the King's forces from marching onto the capital, if indeed that was their plan. Unfortunately, when we arrived a few days later, we discovered that the king had eluded us. Instead of heading towards London, as our leaders had assumed, he had taken his army north, presumably in an effort to regain his influence there.

Though this turn of events was more than a little frustrating, the king soon chose to abandon his conquest of the north and, advised by Prince Rupert, turned south-east, fiercely attacking Leicester before heading back in the direction of Oxford.

"You know, Richard," I said one evening, as we sat around a campfire at the end of a long day's riding. "We're going to have to meet up with those Royalists soon. It doesn't make sense not to."

"You're right," he said. "Our spies report that they are stationed just north of us in Northamptonshire, near Daventry. It seems to me that if they're hoping to return to Oxford we must stop them before they reach there."

"Aye," I nodded. "But when, and where?"

My questions were answered the following Tuesday, when we found ourselves spread out along an upland ridge just north of Naseby, a small village in Northamptonshire, facing the vast Royalist Army.

"Look, Tom," Richard said, pointing to the north. "There must be thousands of them. It's like Marston Moor all over again."

"I know." I screwed up my eyes in an attempt to see through the light fog, scanning the opposing ridge. "But look carefully, I'm sure we have twice as many men as they have. Our ranks look much thicker."

He nodded. "Aye, and our lines extend further along than theirs."

We would both turn out to be right; our army of some fourteen thousand men was double that of the Royalist forces. But we did not know that at the time. Indeed, we would have to wait until after the battle to find out.

Chapter 9
The Battle of Naseby

I woke first the following morning, and gently punched Richard on the shoulder to wake him. After checking on my horse and weapons, I ate a hurried breakfast, by which time the sun was up, and any remaining wisps of fog had disappeared. Shortly after this, I found myself looking out from the top of the Huntingdonshire hills waiting for the battle to start.

As I waited there, I wondered how I would acquit myself in my third major battle once the fighting started. Like every soldier before a battle, I also asked myself whether I would end the day dead or alive; wounded or not? My horse had picked up on my nervous anticipation and was straining at the bit, his reins and harness jingling as he stepped forward out of line. I reined him back in and saw that several other horses nearby were behaving the same way. My horse now under control, I took the time to look over my musket and ammunition again, and to check that the straps of my helmet were tight.

Suddenly, to my left, I heard a cacophony of shouting, followed by the sound of hundreds of hooves galloping together and the crack of hundreds of muskets opening fire. As I looked to Cromwell, my commander, I saw him hold up his gloved hand for us to remain where we were. Lord Fairfax had ordered Cromwell's son-in-law, Henry Ireton, to use his horsemen to charge the opposing Royalists, led by Prince Rupert, while Fairfax himself led thousands of musketeers to overcome Lord Astley's men on the other side.

As I saw all this taking place, I shouted to Richard, "What are we going to do? Just stand here?"

He shrugged and shouted back, "We have to wait for the signal…look, Tom! Ireton's falling back! He's retreating!"

Richard was right. Our right wing was being swamped by a wave of Prince Rupert's Royalists, and I saw our men and horses falling, the wounded musketeers throwing their muskets into the air and stumbling for their lives. Mixed in with this chaos were cries of 'For the King!' and 'For Fairfax!' along with the clash of swords and volleys of muskets being fired by both sides. Clouds of smoke blew over to us: the lighter grey-white of the muskets, and the choking black of the artillery.

As I was trying to understand what was happening, I saw Cromwell raise his hand and shout 'Forward! Forward, for the love of God!'.

Seconds later, we were charging ahead as fast as we could, our hands gripping our swords as we smashed into Commander Langdale's Royalist forces. We had an overwhelming advantage as they had been caught in an area of marshy ground and so presented us with an easy target.

With flashes of memory from Marston Moor interweaving with the scene before me, I cut and slashed my way through Royalist lines, my body dripping with sweat; my face bright red with heat, and my sword sticky with blood. I heard shouts and groans all around me, and hoped that most of these were coming from the enemy.

Just then, I caught sight of Richard, fighting off a group of Royalist horsemen. Turning my horse in his direction, I urged it forward, but nothing happened. I looked down and found the ground coming up to meet me. Before I could understand what was happening, I found myself half-trapped underneath the heaving body of my horse.

After a moment of shocked paralysis, I managed to wriggle free, noting the bloody bullet hole in my horse's forehead. Sad though his death was, I did not have time to pity the poor beast, for Richard was still in danger. Leaving my dead horse behind me, I ran towards Richard, who was still wildly slashing away. I jumped up onto the back of the nearest enemy horse and hit the creature's Cavalier rider with the hilt of my sword, throwing him to the ground. As he scrambled up to attack me, I slashed him across the face, and he fell to the ground once more, screaming in agony. By now the pressure was off Richard, and I was pleased to see three of the enemy riding away. Two of the others now lay on the ground, writhing and groaning.

"Thanks, Tom," Richard panted. "Just like old times."

"You're right there, my friend. Come on, let's go and find Cromwell."

Taking my newly acquired horse, we galloped off towards the rest of the army, but as we did so, I caught sight of a dozen Royalists trying to tow away one of their cannons. If we attacked them with sufficient force, they would be no match for us. Employing my status as a captain, I rounded up thirty or so horsemen and we were soon ready for the attack. The Royalists were so intent on hitching up the cannon to three of their horses that they did not notice us approaching them. In true Prince Rupert style, we charged the surprised enemy, slashing and hacking them down. Some of them tried to fight back, but they were on foot and had no chance of defending themselves against our flashing swords and galloping horses.

It was all over in minutes. Only six of the enemy were left lying still alive on the ground near the cannon. The others had been killed or had fled, on foot or on horseback. I gave the order for those who were still alive to be tied up as prisoners and taken to the large oak tree where we had rounded up other enemy prisoners. Then I ordered our men to hitch the now abandoned Royalist horses to the cannon and tow it over to where I had heard Cromwell say he wanted to place his artillery. I decided to join the artillery men and tell our commander about his extra artillery piece myself.

"You're Captain Blood, aren't you?"

"Yes, sir."

"And was this your doing?" Cromwell asked, looking at the cannon.

I nodded.

He took out a piece of paper and wrote something down. "Leave this cannon here and prepare your men to join my men here. We are going to reinforce Whalley and Rossiter's men, who are dealing with Langdale's troops."

A few minutes later, together with several hundred Roundheads, we set off to the east at a swift trot. Seeing Cromwell's signal, we broke into a charge, storming into the Royalist forces on the eastern side of the battlefield.

Looking back now, our charge had been somewhat pointless. The Royalist commander, Baron Marmaduke Langdale, had seen that he was not succeeding and as we approached, we saw him leading his men off the field of battle. To him, it was clear that they had been beaten; there was no point in any further killing.

We drew to a halt before we reached them and I turned to see Cromwell talking to Fairfax, probably discussing what to do next now that most of the Royalists had fled. Then just as I was looking at Cromwell, I saw Richard suddenly lurch forward in his saddle and fall to the ground, his foot still caught in his stirrup. His horse managed to drag him a few yards before I caught up, leaned over and grabbed the reins to stop him.

I jumped down. "Richard, what's the matter? What happened?"

He looked up, his face pale as milk pudding.

"What happened?" I asked again, before I noticed the large bloodstain spreading across the front of his jacket.

"It didn't hurt at first," he gasped. "But now, now it…"

He never finished his sentence. Looking on in horror, I saw my friend writhe on the ground for a few seconds before becoming completely still. I bent over, whipped out my pocket watch and placed it to his lips, praying that the shiny case would fog over with his breath. But it was too late. My best friend, Richard Cavendish, the man who had fought by my side at Babylon Hill, Edgehill, Marston Moor, and now here at Naseby, was dead. Never again would we go riding out over the Lancashire hills; drink in the taverns; laugh and joke with each other; spend hours talking by candlelight. No more would I visit him and his family, and no more would we fight as brothers in arms.

I leant over him, closed his now useless eyes and covered his face and chest with his cape. There was nothing else I could do but weep quietly. I wiped my eyes, went quickly through his pouch, and took out his personal possessions, which I stuffed into my own pouch. I promised myself that I would give these to his parents when I next went up north. There was no more time to grieve now; I had to rejoin my men and hear what Cromwell wanted us to do next.

With one last look at my best friend, I mounted my horse and rode off to where Fairfax, Cromwell, and the two other commanders, Edward Whalley and Edward Rossiter, were talking, discussing what had happened to Cromwell's son-in-law, Henry Ireton.

"He's a prisoner, I tell you," Fairfax was saying to Cromwell. "I saw some of Prince Rupert's men go for him and tie him up."

"Then we must get after them now and free him," Cromwell said. "We owe him that."

Fairfax lifted an arm. "I've already sent off a party. It shouldn't be long before he's free, considering how many prisoners we've taken today."

I looked around and saw, huddled in large groups on the ground, hundreds, if not thousands, of dejected men, guarded by armed and mounted Roundheads. Some of them were wounded and clearly in agony, but the only help they received was from their fellow Royalist prisoners.

Just as I was revelling in having fought on the

winning side, I heard an outbreak of hysterical screaming and cries for help. Several hundred yards away, a large band of Roundhead soldiers were moving about the Royalist camp, killing all the remaining womenfolk. Some of the women tried to defend themselves with kitchen knives and other sharp tools, but they were no match for the incensed soldiers. This group of Roundheads was made up of strict, Puritan men who could not abide these women. They called them 'whores' and 'prostitutes'. Massacring them was the only solution in the Roundheads' eyes.

I tried to say something to Cromwell, but I was silenced. Half an hour later, the screaming stopped. But not for long. As it started up again, I overheard Fairfax informing Cromwell that his men were branding those women who still lived, so that they would 'never be able to practise their sinful, whoring ways again'. I felt sick. I had joined the army to fight men, to fight the king, not to murder women. Most of these women were simply following their menfolk, making their lives easier by cooking, cleaning, washing, and darning for them. Admittedly, some of them, especially the younger ones, offered their bodies as well, but surely that did not matter now? Besides, we had women camp-followers on our own side as well, and none of our men objected to that. The battle was over, and in my mind, such violence towards these innocent women at this stage could not be justified.

Feeling disgusted by what I had witnessed, I quickly gave my name to a senior officer, who registered me as having taken part in the battle. I then examined my new horse for wounds and seeing that it had none, quietly stole away. Hidden by the oncoming darkness of the night I left the battlefield to begin my return journey north. I spent that night at a small tavern south of Leicester before heading for Lancashire the following morning. Every joint ached, but I was determined to put the battlefield, the death of my best friend, and the senseless killing of the Royalist womenfolk far behind me. My journey of one hundred and fifty miles would take me through Coventry, Stoke-on-Trent, and Warrington, where I planned to stop to visit an old friend, Liam O'Neill from Ireland, for a few days.

I arrived at Liam's house a week after Naseby, and naturally, as we sat in his parlour that evening, we talked about the battle. He felt guilty that he had not taken part in it. As he explained to me, he had broken his arm during a skirmish against Prince Rupert at Loughborough, a few days before Naseby and had been sent home to recover.

"It sounds like what you went through was hell," Liam said. "The fight I was in at Loughborough sounds like child's play compared to what you have just told me," he continued as we finished off a bottle of wine.

"I can't disagree with you there," I replied. "You know, it's a strange thing. When you're in the middle of a fight like I was at Naseby or Marston Moor, all you can think about is your next move. You don't see what's going on around you. You are too busy fighting to be scared. It's only afterwards, when you look back, that you realise what you were doing and how you could have easily been killed."

We sat in quiet contemplation for a moment. I thought about what I hadn't told Liam; about the massacre of the women after the battle. Should I tell him? Just as I opened my mouth to speak, he broke the silence, saving me from repeating that particular horror.

"So, what's happening now?"

"Well, I heard that Prince Rupert has joined the king at Leicester; I suppose they've decided to return to Oxford. Whatever happens, I'm sure they aren't going to be returning to London."

Liam refilled both our glasses. "I heard the Royalists lost at least one thousand men at Naseby, and Cromwell took over five thousand of them prisoner."

"Aye, I heard about that," I interrupted. "The best part was that among those five thousand men, many of them were officers."

Liam grinned. "Good, that should set them back for a while, especially since we captured their artillery and a carriage full of the king's private correspondence."

"Why is that so important?"

"Because, Tom, we now know what the king's intentions and battle plans were. They can't possibly use those plans now, they'll have scrap all that and start again."

I grinned. "If I were the king, I'd give up."

Liam shook his head. "No, Tom, not this king. He truly believes in his divine right to rule the country, and nothing except his own death will stop him."

We spent the rest of the night drinking strong red wine and catching up on more personal news. Then, over a late breakfast the following morning, we discussed the situation in Ireland. The Catholics and Protestants were still caught up in a continuous war, where neither side was able to gain the upper hand. The Protestants had fled to Cork, Derry, and Dublin, and each side was burning their enemy's farms, killing cattle and other livestock.

After a restful week with Liam, spent trying to put the death of Richard and the massacre of the women out of my mind, I bade him farewell, and a few days later, I crossed the Irish Sea to Dublin. From there, I rode straight home to Sarney, where I was greeted warmly by friends and family, who all spent the next few days questioning me endlessly about my military exploits.

All too soon, I decided it was time to head back to England, and I journeyed south, to rejoin Sir Thomas Fairfax's forces, camped out near Oxford. There, I met one of my first army friends, Fletcher Howard, who filled me in on what I had missed.

"Tom," he said one evening, as we were sitting around a small campfire. "This war is coming to an end. The Royalist forces surrendered at Chester, and our men who were besieging Stow-on-the-Wold…"

"Near Gloucester?"

"Aye. They surprised Lord Astley's men, and took His Lordship prisoner."

I smiled. This was all excellent news. "But what about the king himself?" I asked. "Is he still in Oxford with his army and Prince Rupert?"

"No, not anymore. The king is a prisoner of the Scots."

"*The Scots*? How did *that* come about?"

"It seems His Majesty was carrying out secret negotiations with them and, according to the stories I heard, he sneaked out of Oxford at the end of May."

"And no-one caught him?"

"No. He disguised himself as a servant and managed to meet up with the Scots that way. But Tom, I'm not sure that he's very pleased about that arrangement now that they're holding him prisoner. Apparently, they want to use him to bargain with Parliament in London. You know, something like, give us more independence and we'll give you back your king."

"Did Prince Rupert go with him?"

Fletcher shook his head. "No. He surrendered Oxford to our men. Then Bristol, Pendennis Castle in Cornwall, and Raglan Castle in south Wales surrendered." He smiled. "This accursed war is all but over."

"I'll drink to that," I said. "That's the best piece of news I've heard for a long time."

We spent the rest of the night discussing what

would happen now. Would Lord Fairfax become the country's ruler? Would we negotiate with the Scots to get our hands on the king? Suddenly, everything seemed possible.

Chapter 10
Rainsborough and Marriage

It was during this time, in 1645, that my father, also called Thomas, died. Fortunately, I was home at the time, so we were able to arrange a simple but dignified funeral for him. His death meant that I was now head of the family, and although this title forced responsibilities upon me that I might not otherwise have chosen to take on, it did give me far more financial security.

I stayed in Sarney for the next three years, looking after my newly acquired estates in the east and west of Ireland, and enjoying playing the role of a country gentleman. Then, in 1648, I received an order to rejoin the Parliamentary Army in Lancashire.

Owing to the stormy weather, I had to delay taking the Dublin-Liverpool ferry, such that when I eventually met with my commander, Oliver Cromwell, towards the end of August 1648, the battle of Preston was over. Cromwell's New Model Army had thrashed the Royalist forces serving under the Duke of Hamilton. Even though the King's men had outnumbered the Parliamentarians by three thousand, fewer than one hundred men of Cromwell's men had been killed, whereas the Duke had lost over two thousand soldiers. In addition, nine thousand of the Duke's troops had been taken prisoner. Fortunately for me, Cromwell too had suffered because of the terrible weather, so he forgave my absence from the field.

"It was hard going, Blood," he told me. "The Scottish Army had come down from the north; General Lambert and I had to stop them before they could reach London. Although most of them faced us on the battlefield, many of them didn't take part in the fighting."

"Is that why you won, sir?"

Cromwell gave one of his rare smiles. "It certainly helped, as did their disorganisation. I don't think the right flank knew what the left flank was doing. To cut a long story short, it looks as though my reorganising and retraining of our army has paid off."

I saluted, and was just about to leave the farmhouse he was using as his headquarters when he stopped me.

"I want you to take half a dozen men and ride over to Pontefract to reinforce the men guarding Sir Marmaduke Langdale," he said

"Is he one of your new Royalist prisoners, sir?"

Cromwell nodded. "He was one of the commanders we took prisoner at the Battle of Preston. We want to use him when it comes to a prisoner exchange. Make sure no harm comes to him, is that clear?"

"Yes, sir," I said, saluting again.

Fortunately, two hours later, the rain stopped, and I set out with my small army of six men towards Pontefract, in Yorkshire. The journey took two days, and as soon as we reached the Pennine Mountains and began to climb 'over the tops' the air grew cold and damp, as heavy mists started swirling about us. I urged my men to keep within sight of one another as we had almost lost one of our number in the mists earlier and I wanted to avoid any more potential accidents.

We spent that night at the Three Tuns, a mile outside Huddersfield, all of us relieved to see the welcoming lamp shining by the front door. We entered the warm room and divested ourselves of our damp hats and coats, ordering six hot meals and rooms for the night. It was here, in this most unlikely spot, that I was unintentionally promoted. That evening, after our meal, Peggy, the buxom lass who had served us our beef and vegetables, came over and sat on my lap.

"Colonel," she began, caressing my thigh. "You're not from these parts, are you? You have a strange accent."

"I'm from Ireland."

"Are you a colonel, sir?" one of my soldiers

asked. "I thought you were a captain."

"Of course he's a colonel, Will," his tubby friend said. "I heard one of the officers call him that before we left Preston."

I had no idea which of the officers had mistakenly called me thus, but I was more than willing to be addressed by my new rank.

"Your friend is right," I told Will. "But now I think it's time for you and the others to go to bed. We had a long ride today, and we've still got a good way to go tomorrow."

The men looked pleased as they got up to leave.

"G'night, colonel," Will said.

The others nodded in agreement.

In truth, I wasn't at all concerned for their health. I just wanted to have Peggy to myself. As soon as the others had gone, Peggy turned herself around on my lap and kissed me deeply, caressing the inside of my mouth with her tongue. As she pushed her soft face against mine, I could smell her intoxicating scent, a mixture of woman and ale. Then she pulled her head away and looked around.

"Good," she said quietly. "My master's gone up to his bed. Let's go round the back."

She took my hand and led me to a small shed behind the tavern; it was clear that she had done this many times before. Without hesitating, she pushed the door open, and I noticed a somewhat crumpled blanket lying on some straw on the floor.

"This is where one of the other girls sleeps, but she's not here tonight," she grinned. "I believe she's ailing with a cold so no-one's going to disturb us."

Three cheers for sickness, I thought to myself, having already decided to exploit my good luck.

"I hear Irishmen make good lovers," she whispered in my ear as she pushed the long fingers of her right hand down the front of my breeches.

"Aye, they're very good," I smiled and rose to the occasion as she pushed her hand deeper.

I undid the ties on her low-cut blouse and began to fondle her full breasts. It was clear that neither of us wanted to waste much time whispering and caressing each other, so it did not take long to achieve what we wanted. Afterwards, we slept beside each other on the soft blanket and straw, calm and relaxed, our arms and legs intertwined. We separated as the sun's first rays poked their thin beams through the small window, and just over an hour later, after a warm breakfast, my men and I were on our way east.

We reached Pontefract in the early evening, and after seeing my men to their billets, I went to find my new commander. As we were discussing my immediate duties, one of my men came in, interrupting us.

"Excuse me, Colonel?" he asked. "Who did you say was on guard duty first tonight? Will and me, or Jim and Nate?"

I told him it was Jim and Nate, and he left.

"Ah, so you're a colonel," Colonel

Rainsborough said, looking at me oddly. "Isn't it unusual for a man of your rank to be carrying out such a task as this? No-one told me they would be sending another colonel here."

I nodded. "I also thought it strange, but as I was the only officer around at the time, they had no choice but to send me. I hope you don't mind. I promise you that I will not question your authority, you have no need to be concerned."

He nodded back and I hoped that my new rank would not present me with any further problems.

"Well, I wish you a good night, Colonel Blood," he added, turning to leave.

Unfortunately, his wishes were in vain. That night, a party of twenty Royalist soldiers, under the command of Captain Paulden, set out to free Marmaduke Langdale from the house where he was being held prisoner. When they reached the house, four of them pretended to be Roundheads, claiming that they had been sent by Cromwell with a special message for Colonel Rainsborough about his Royalist prisoner. Their bluff worked. Rainsborough let them in, and the four Royalists immediately overcame the Colonel and his lieutenant.

Just as the Royalists were about to mount their two captives on waiting horses, Rainsborough, despite the gag over his mouth managed to shout out '*Arms! Arms!*' in a desperate attempt to awaken some of his soldiers. Unfortunately, at the time, I was at the back of the house, warning my men to be on their guard, so none of us heard this cry of desperation. It was only later that we found out what had happened.

We also learned, from one of my men who was on guard at the time, that the four Royalists were not joined by their fellows for some unknown reason. When Rainsborough saw that there were only four men who had kidnapped him, he started to fight back. His lieutenant tried to fire the pistol that Rainsborough had dropped, but he was cut down before he could do so.

Rainsborough, now on his own, fought back as vigorously as he could, but to no avail. Badly wounded from a stab wound in the neck, sustained whilst trying to drive his attackers away, he was run through with a Royalist sword and died on the spot. At this point, the Royalists fled.

On hearing this news, I immediately divided my men into two groups. One group was to remain behind in Pontefract to guard Langdale, whilst the second and smaller group rode back with me to report to Cromwell about what had happened. We made the whole journey in one day, without stopping at any taverns along the way, and by the time I stood in front of Cromwell, I was exhausted. My clothes were heavily spattered with mud and it did not take much for me to convince my commander that I had come to report to him as soon as I could.

"Thank you, Blood," he said. "Since you were the most senior officer present, aside from Colonel Rainsborough, I have no choice but to hold you responsible for this. However, you posted guards, and fulfilled your duty to the best of your ability, so I cannot be too strict with you. I will make some further enquiries and let you know of my decision later. You are dismissed."

Two days later, I was called before Cromwell, and informed that although I had been present at the time, he was not going to press any charges against me for negligence of duty.

"I will take into consideration your military record at Marston Moor and Naseby," he said. "And as I don't wish to lose a good officer, I will not reprimand you any further. Since I have no further use for you at the moment, you are free to return home, but prepare to be called upon at a moment's notice, understood?"

"Yes, sir."

He nodded. "Dismissed," he said, turning his eyes back to the document he had been studying when I had entered his office.

I cannot tell you how happy I was when I left the camp that afternoon. I had fully expected to be severely punished, but had got away almost scot-free. Fortunately for me, in the end, despite the Royalists initial success in trying to free Langdale, they had not succeeded. However, sometime later, he was transferred to Nottingham Castle and from there managed to escape disguised as a milkmaid, before fleeing to France.

I spent my last night near Preston celebrating with my fellow officers in the local tavern, enjoying both the drink and the women. The following morning, despite suffering from a fearful headache, I set off to stay with my aunt and uncle in Lancashire. There, I met up with my Uncle Conor and his wife, Roisin.

"Tom?" Aunt Roisin asked that evening as we were sitting around the table in their spacious parlour, drinking a fine red wine. "How old are you?"

"Thirty-two, why?"

"Isn't it time you settled down? Found yourself a wife?"

"But, I…"

"Let me finish," she said, holding up her hand. "Your father died over three years ago…"

"Yes?"

"So you are not exactly poor, are you? On the contrary, you are the owner of your father's house and a nice plot of land or two. Admittedly, you don't have as much as some people, but still. Your uncle and I think the war in England is drawing to a close and the time has come for you to end your soldiering days. So tell me, Tom, have you thought about settling down and raising a family?"

I told her that I had thought about it, but not too seriously.

"Well," joined in Uncle Conor. "You had better start thinking about it, because we have someone in mind for you."

"A local girl?"

"No, lad. A lass we know in Lancashire. From near where you studied years ago."

This sounded interesting. I refilled my glass

and asked my uncle to tell me more.

"First of all, Tom, the Holcroft family is one you should get to know. While not aristocratic, they are certainly very influential around south Lancashire, and I wouldn't exactly define them as poor, in terms of lands or money. Secondly, from what I know, and have seen, they have a very comely daughter."

My uncle had me hooked. "Tell me more," I said. Of course, I had enjoyed more than a few flings with wenches in taverns, but they had been more to do with lust and proving myself as a man than anything else. "What do you know about this young lady? What's her name? How old is she?"

"Her name is Maria, and she's about fifteen years younger than you. Her father is Colonel John Holcroft; his wife's name is Margaret."

"How do you know them?" I asked.

Aunt Roisin took up the thread. "Social occasions and the like. I think that you may have met Maria's brother, Thomas, in the past."

"Thomas Holcroft? From Newchurch?"

"Aye, that's him," my uncle replied. "He told me he'd seen you once before when you'd fought together in that battle in Yorkshire when you thrashed the king's men."

"Ah, Marston Moor. I remember talking to an officer of that name, but as he told you, I met him only once. All I can remember is that he spoke with a strong Lancashire accent and he knew his horseflesh. But tell me more about his sister, Maria."

"She's a very attractive young woman, wouldn't you say, dear?" my uncle asked his wife, who nodded. "Well endowed, and she has a pretty face; rosy cheeks, dark eyes, and dark brown hair, slightly curly if I recall correctly."

"As well as a pleasant temperament," my aunt added. "If you wish to meet her, I would be very happy to arrange it. Her family is having a party at the end of the week and, since you are a family friend, I will of course be able to take you with me."

I agreed wholeheartedly, and the following Saturday evening, dressed in my finest blue satin doublet and breeches, silk shirt, white lace collar, and dark calfskin boots, I made my way with my uncle and aunt up the long curving drive from the Warrington road to the imposing entrance of Holcroft Hall. The Hall's crenelated roof made it look more like a medieval castle than a three-hundred-year-old manor house.

About halfway along, I put my hand out to stop my uncle.

"What's the matter, Tom? You don't want to meet this young lady?"

"No, no, it's not that," I replied. "It's that I've only just realised that although you have told me about Maria, you haven't told me very much about her family, especially her parents. You said the other day that they are not aristocrats, but if that is the case then what are they? I don't want to say the wrong thing."

"Colonel Holcroft, or rather, his father and

grandfather, did well out of the dissolution of the monasteries. King Henry the Eighth granted them lands at Preston, Warrington, and Lancaster, as well as in Lancashire and Cheshire. In addition, the Colonel's grandfather had connections at court. He even took part in the coronation ceremony for Henry the Eighth and Anne Boleyn. His grandson, Colonel John Holcroft, the one we are going to meet, is a notable man. He's very interested in local politics, and there's talk of him becoming an MP for Liverpool soon."

Satisfied that I now knew enough not to make a fool of myself, we continued up the driveway. I had high hopes for the evening; Maria sounded like a cut above the other women I had so far been involved with. I could only hope that my aunt and uncle's descriptions of her were correct.

I was not disappointed. As soon as we entered the spacious wood-panelled hall that had been set aside for the night's party, I saw her standing at the far end between her parents. We walked up to them and presented ourselves.

"Ah, yes, Conor and Roisin," the Colonel said. "Good to see you again. I trust you are both well? And you, young man, are you perhaps the brave nephew that I have heard so much about?"

"Yes, sir. I believe I am. I was born in Ireland, but at the moment I am living here in south Lancashire. I went to school just down the road from here."

He nodded. "Ah, so that's where your accent is from. Let me introduce you to my wife, Margaret, and my daughter, Maria."

I bowed to each in turn, and while my uncle was talking to our host about some local political event, I studied Maria. My uncle's description of her had been correct. She was very pretty, with a pale round face contrasted against rich brown eyes. She had a small, upturned nose, and soft, pale pink cheeks. Her full lips gave an attractive smile, and I smiled back, taking her hand and bowing low.

"It is a pleasure to meet you, sir," she said. "Your aunt speaks very highly of you. She tells me you are a good horseman, and she also says…"

Maria was interrupted by her father. "My apologies young man, but I have urgent matters to discuss with my neighbour who has just arrived. Maria, would you show this young gentleman to the tables across the hall? I can't imagine he wishes to stand around talking all day. I'm sure he would like some refreshment as well."

We made our way over to the far side of the hall and sat down. Knowing that Maria knew I liked horses, I asked her if she liked riding as well.

"Yes," she smiled. "I have my own horse, a light brown palfrey. She's very gentle, but can canter quite quickly if I let her. Do you have any horses at home?"

I told her about my horses back in Ireland, adding that while I was living here in Lancashire I borrowed from friends when I needed to go anywhere. I then asked her if she would like to go riding with me the following day, as the warm weather looked as though it would hold. She nodded, and we arranged to meet the following morning at her family's stables. From there, our friendship grew, and a few months later I sought out Colonel Holcroft to ask for permission to marry his daughter.

"Of course, Thomas," he replied, shaking my hand. "I was just saying to my wife this morning how surprised I was that you had yet to ask me for Maria's hand. Come, let us celebrate." He called for his wife and Maria to join us, and we began discussing possible dates and churches.

Maria and I were married in nearby Culcheth on the twenty-first of June 1650. In March of the following year, our first son, Thomas, was born. That same year, 1651, I travelled back to Ireland, with Maria and my son joining me a few months later. I learned then that switching sides from the Royalist to the Parliamentary Army had paid off, as I received a grant of land instead of the back pay the army owed me, and was promoted to Parliamentary Commissioner. This unexpected promotion came about due to me having apparently impressed Henry, one of Cromwell's sons, who was now Lord Deputy of Ireland.

"Listen to what he's written about me," I said, showing the letter about my promotion to Maria. "He says I'm a man fit for employment and promotion, and that the main use I made of my authority was to assert and uphold Protestant values within the kingdom."

"But what does it mean?" Maria asked. "What does a parliamentary commissioner do?"

"It means, my love, that I now have the power and authority to make sure that those rebellious Catholics obey the law."

"And if they refuse?"

"Then I shall send them to prison."

This was a state of affairs that lasted for a few years. In addition to acting as a local authority who represented the government in London, my role as Parliamentary Commissioner enabled me to establish myself financially. Unsurprisingly, I was not at all popular with the Catholic majority, so I always made sure that I armed myself with a sword or pistol or both whenever I left my estates to go to Dublin.

As my finances grew, so did my family. Maria bore me five sons and two daughters and I grew to be very pleased and satisfied with my lot in life. But, all too soon, the cracks began to show, though for a time I was too busy in my little green corner of Ireland to notice them.

Chapter 11
Plans for the Duke of Ormonde and Dublin Castle

"What are you reading there?" I asked Clancy, as I walked into my office.

"The latest news sheet from London," my estate-manager replied.

"Anything we should know about?" I asked, as he passed it over to me.

"It says that Cromwell died two weeks ago. His son, Richard, will be taking over as the country's new ruler."

"What? Tumbledown Dick?"

Clancy nodded and grinned at my use of the Protector's son's nickname.

I scanned the closely printed page quickly to see if I could find anything about Richard Cromwell, but there was nothing significant. It was only over the winter and during the spring of the following year that I learned the truth. Tumbledown Dick had no real supporters from the military or within Parliament, and as a result, in May 1659, he resigned his position and exiled himself to France. His resignation was followed by a period of parliamentary chaos which was not resolved until February 1660. This was when General Monck, who, like me, had fought on both sides during the civil war marched on London from Scotland with an impressive number of troops. He took over the capital and began working towards the restoration of the monarchy.

"Does that mean he wants King Charles' son to become king?" Maria asked me when I told her about this new situation.

I nodded. "Yes, my dear, though I doubt his plans will have anything to do with us here. We're too far away across the sea. If Prince Charles does become king, he'll have more things to worry about than us."

Unfortunately, I was sorely mistaken in my assumptions. Prince Charles was crowned King in April 1661, and one of the first things he did was to take revenge on anyone who had either condemned his father to death or had benefitted from fighting against his father's army. Of course, preoccupied with my estates and judicial activities in the north of Ireland, I was too busy to fully appreciate the way the wind was blowing in London.

When I first heard the vague rumours about the

newly-crowned king seeking revenge, I ignored them, shrugging them off as merely the wishful thinking of the local Catholics. But later that year, when the Irish Parliament passed the Act of Settlement, everything changed. This new Act meant that settlers like me, who had gained from fighting for Cromwell, would have to surrender the lands they had been granted to loyal 'old English' Royalists.

"What?" my oldest son asked. "We're going to be thrown off our land?"

"No, Tom, not all of it, just everything Cromwell's government awarded us. Fifteen hundred acres or thereabouts."

"But that's not fair."

"I'm afraid it's not a question of 'fair'. It's more a question of 'to the victor go the spoils'."

"Can we fight this?" Maria asked.

I shrugged. "I don't know. It looks as if they are going to establish a Court of Claims, but I don't know whether that will help us or not."

Maria insisted that I at least attempt to resolve the issue, so I visited the Court of Claims office in Dublin.

"Listen, Colonel Blood," the overweight official with a heavily pock-marked face and a London accent said to me, "Don't think that you are the only Irishman to come here with some sort of claim. Since we opened this court, hundreds of your compatriots have filed cases. I'm afraid you're going to have to wait patiently until we can deal with your matter."

[133]

Looking down his long nose through his piggy eyes, he continued, "Just leave your name, address, and other details with the clerk in the room at the end of the corridor. We'll be in contact with you shortly. Good day."

I went to the office he had referred to and gave all the necessary information to another mean and pasty-faced individual, who duly recorded it in a large black ledger. Twenty minutes later, I found myself back on the street. I was not feeling particularly optimistic.

That night, in the local tavern, my pessimistic thoughts about my visit to the court were confirmed by another local landlord, Seamus McConaghy. He, like me, had fought at Marston Moor and Naseby and had been awarded land in Ireland after the war.

"It's going to be a dirty job, Tom," he said, as we sat there drinking in the oldest tavern in Sarney. "You'll see. Those English Royalists will be fighting for their plots of land and the government will just take ours away from us to appease them."

"But there's other lands that we don't own. Can't they give them those?"

He shook his head. "No, my friend, it's not like that. The king wants to take *our* land, not only because we fought against his army and his father, but because we're Protestants. The fewer there are of us around here, the better. At least, that's the way I understand it."

Several months passed and I received no

communication from Dublin, I returned to the Court of Claims and saw the same pasty-faced clerk as before. I told him my name, and he looked it up in his black ledger.

"Ah, Colonel Blood. I don't hold out much hope for you. You see, since you first came here, half a year ago, over five thousand of your lot have applied for restitution of their property and—"

"*Five thousand*!"

"That's right, you heard. Five thousand. If you ask me, I don't think you'll be getting your property back. After all, you did fight against the king, which just so happens to be a treasonable offence. Now sir, I have a lot of work to do, so I will bid you good day." He closed his ledger with a bang and pointed to the door of his office.

Three weeks later, on a grey and dreary day, I was asked to appear at the Court of Claims. My friend, Seamus, was also asked to appear so we went together. Neither of us felt very hopeful and the cold drizzle that permeated our coats did not help.

"I've heard of only one or two fellers who got their land back," I said. "And even then, they didn't get it all. When they protested, they were told they should be grateful for what they had been granted. It'll be a bloody miracle if they give us anything."

After waiting for nearly two hours outside the clerk's office, we were called in to hear what had been decided.

"No, not both of you," he said. "I'll deal with

Colonel Thomas Blood first."

Seamus stood up and walked out.

"Please close the door behind you," the clerk called out. "This is official government business," he added pompously. "We need privacy in here."

I sat down on the other side of the wide desk, which was piled with neat stacks of papers and documents.

"Colonel Blood," he began, as he picked up his quill pen and he leafed his way through his black ledger, his bony fingers slowly turning the large pages. "Ah, here we are. Thomas Blood, Colonel, I believe, from Sarney, north of Dublin. Is that correct?"

I nodded.

"Born in 1618 in County Clare," he continued. "Ah, this was what was decided by the Court of Claims." He pushed his ledger over to me so that I could read what the seven-man court had decided. I was to lose all the lands that Cromwell's government had awarded me and no other land would be given to me in compensation. I would be allowed to keep the land that my father had farmed, but nothing more. I stood up and walked out. There was nothing to say. It was clear that appealing to this functionary would be a waste of time. If I wanted to appeal, I would need to do so at a higher level.

I opened the door and gave a thumbs-down signal to Seamus as he walked into the court room. He reappeared five minutes later with an equally long face.

"All five thousand acres," he said quietly. "Every single one of them. I have been permitted to keep only my farmhouse and the ten acres surrounding it. I can't believe it. The rest of my land is to be given to those damned Royalists. English as well. Not even good sons of Eire like you and me, Tom."

We decide to drown our sorrows in the nearest tavern. We knew the drink could only do so much, and would no doubt only make us feel worse later, but we felt that we had to do something. We both ordered a large whiskey, instead of our usual ale, and even when the big-breasted barmaid thrust herself at us I simply told her to go away. Neither of us were interested and just ordered another couple of large whiskeys instead.

Early the next morning, despite a throbbing hangover, I sat down and worked out what I had lost. The government had confiscated nearly fifteen hundred acres of the land that Cromwell's government had given to me, leaving me with only two hundred and seventy acres at Brittas, and a few hundred more at Sarney. The land at Brittas was very poor, and was virtually useless for anything other than grazing. Although my land at Sarney was of decent quality, there was not enough acreage there to make much money. At least I still had *some* land and farm buildings left to my name. Some of the poor sods I had met and talked to over the past few months had lost everything including their land, farmhouses and outbuildings.

But no matter how much I consoled myself, the

fall from being a successful Roundhead officer and owner of a large estate to becoming a landowner of just a small parcel of land was indeed a mighty fall. It was not one that I could easily live with. How would I be able to live in the manner to which I aspired, and what would I have to bequeath to my sons one day? These thoughts kept hammering through my head, day and night. I had to do something. But what? The more I thought about my situation, the angrier and more desperate I became.

One May evening, in 1663, while sitting in the White Hart, a small tavern on Patrick Street, Dublin, I exploded in front of a small group of my family and friends. I could contain my anger no longer.

"My blood is boiling! What that accursed king and his government in London have done to me is beyond outrageous!" I shouted, as I pounded on the table. "They've stolen my land! Land that was given to me in recompense for the battles I fought for this country. I fought to keep that useless King Charles off the throne, and now his wretched son has taken it back."

"Well, it wasn't his son who took your land, Tom," said William Leckie. "It was James Butler, the Duke of Ormonde, who did that."

My brother-in-law was right, but his point did not help to cool my rage. The duke had sent his men to clear me off my estates and I felt that he should pay. I could not get to the king but I could get to the duke. He should not be allowed to get away with what he had done, even if it was in the name of the king.

"You know, I've been thinking about this for some time now," I said, looking around at the men sitting at my table. "That bastard of a Royalist duke needs to die."

"You mean...we should kill him?" James Tanner, a close friend asked.

"Aye, man. You've just taken the words right out of my mouth."

"Wouldn't taking him hostage be safer?" Tanner asked.

"No," my brother-in-law replied. "If he escapes, it'll be the hangman's noose for the lot of us."

"You're right, Will. *The Duke must die!*" I almost shouted. "There's no other way. That accursed duke must die!" I said, pounding the table with my fist.

"Tom's right," Colonel Alexander Jephson, a friend I had known since my army days, nodded.

"So, you all agree with me?" I asked, looking around. "Ormonde must die?"

"Yes, but when?"

"When his castle is in our hands."

They all nodded vigorously, and I was pleased to see that no-one had raised any objections to this plot, a plot that could potentially cost them their lives. I raised a toast to our venture.

"My proposal is this. The duke, as Lord Lieutenant of Ireland, spends most of his time in the castle, here in Dublin. He feels safe here, which means he will be less careful. He will rely on his men to guard him and be less vigilant himself. Do you agree?"

A round of heads nodded in confirmation.

"This is what I propose. A plan that I've been thinking about for some time."

My friends all moved their heads closer to me to catch every word.

"I propose," I began, "that six of us disguise ourselves as workmen, y'know, dress ourselves like Jenkins the blacksmith or the local baker and enter the castle in the usual way through the Great Gate and—"

"No-one will suspect us," William Leckie said, finishing off my sentence.

"Right," I continued. "We'll walk to the gate, up from Sheep Street and pretend we are waiting to deliver our goods or whatever. Then, the one disguised as a baker will drop his basket of loaves, and the others will all start shouting and cursing him for his stupidity. Of course, the guards will come over to see what is happening and, in the confusion, some of our men, who will be carrying arms under their coats, will overcome them. Then, while this is happening, our remaining men, who'll be waiting outside, will rush in and deal with the other guards. Once they have succeeded, they'll give us a signal—"

"D'you think six men will be enough to act as a diversion?" asked Richard, an old soldier.

I nodded. "If there are more than six, the guards may become suspicious, which is the last thing we want to happen," I replied. "Then—"

"Tom," interrupted Philip Alden. "You talked

about 'us' before. Who is 'us', and where will we be while all this is going on?"

"Us will be me and the rest of you who'll be disguised as workmen together with other men hidden outside, ready for the signal," I replied.

"Who will be the other men?" Alden asked, looking around the table."

"Fear not, Philip. We'll have another hundred men who fought with us on Cromwell's side," I added. "Men who are used to fighting and getting what they want, and this time, what they'll want is Ormonde's head."

"But won't the duke's men, his guards, fight back?" Jephson asked.

"Of course they will, but I've planned for that."

I took out a sketch map of the castle and pointed to the room that the duke used as his office. "Ormonde will be sitting in here…"

"What happens if he isn't there?" my brother-in-law asked.

"Fear not, Will. He will be," I answered. "I'll bribe Crawford, one of his men who doesn't care for the duke, to lure the duke to be in his office when we want and so he'll be there when we rush in. I've also been talking to William Warren, Colonel Abel Warren's brother. He'll round up some of the cavalry at Trim and they'll support us. We'll have armed men on both the inside and the outside of the castle. How could we possibly lose?"

I sat back and finished off my tankard of ale. I

knew these men hated the duke, and blamed him for their misfortunes as much as I did, so I expected to hear them shower my plan with praises.

They didn't. They asked questions instead.

"Who's going to enter the castle first?'

"Can these men be trusted?"

"Who's going to be the baker?"

"Are they going to be armed?"

"Can Crawford be trusted?"

"What if the Captain of the Guard doesn't move his men out of the way?"

I carefully answered each question as exactly as I could.

"What will you do with the castle and its arsenal once they're ours?" Alden asked.

"Huh, that's easy," I replied. "We'll raise the flag on the main tower, and the rest of the men will rush in and join us."

"All of them?" Alden persisted.

I nodded. "They'll be fully armed, and they'll put down anyone in town who still supports the Duke. That way, other folks in town who hate the Duke will join our side. I'm sure there are a fair few of them."

"Is that it?" Richard Thompson asked.

"No. After we've stormed the castle, we'll take all the men in town who agree with us…"

"You mean, those who have also had their lands and property confiscated?" Thompson asked again.

"Yes. We'll all head north to Ulster, and get rid

of the Catholics and those who support the King there." I leaned back in my chair and smiled at everyone. "Not a bad plan, is it?"

Alden signalled that he was just about to ask another question when one of the landladies, her apron stained with ale, approached me. Anger was written right across her plump face. She stood there facing me, threatening, her small eyes black and sharp, her fat arms akimbo.

"Listen here, Mister Whatever-Your-Name-Is, and listen good. Me and Martha have heard all about what you've been planning here, and we want no seditious talk in our tavern. You get out of here quick fast, before the duke's men or the constables come along. You'd better count yourselves lucky we haven't already gone and reported you to the duke or the constables."

We were all outside within two minutes, finding ourselves crowded around the base of the wide trunk of an old oak tree on the far side of the tavern's courtyard.

"Well, that's the end of that," my brother-in-law said. "They'll probably go to the law and tell them what they just heard."

"No they won't, Will," I assured him. "They won't want to get mixed up with anything against the duke."

"What makes you say so?" Alden and Ford asked together.

"Because if they report us to the authorities,

they'll have to go to the castle and also become involved in this. They don't want to get caught up in politics. From what I know of tavern-keepers, the only thing they want is a quiet life and lots of money."

"Tom's right," Will nodded. "Those two old biddies don't want to be known as tale-bearers in the town. It would kill their business."

After going over the plan in more detail, we decided to put it off for a week or two. Alden was keen to move forward as quickly as possible. He was worried about word getting about and us all being arrested before we could even make the first move.

"And you know what that means?" He drew a long finger across his throat.

"Fear not," I said. "We're better putting it off; if we leave it a week or two, those tavern-keepers will assume we were just talking a load of hot air and forget about it."

How wrong I was.

Chapter 12
The Attack on Dublin Castle

Three days later, I met up with that same group of men from the White Hart, only this time, we gathered in a barn on my brother-in-law's land. Here there would be no meddlesome landladies to overhear our plans. We sat around a large table on an assortment of chairs and benches. I asked them whether they had heard any word of our plans leaking out in the town. They all shook their heads.

"You see," I said, looking around. "I knew those two old biddies would keep their gobs shut. They didn't want to get involved with Ormonde and his men. They probably love him as much as we do."

"Tom," said Philip Alden. "Have you called us here for a special reason? Have you any more news or details to tell us?"

"Aye, that I have," I replied. "Since we last met, I've been asking around, discreetly that is, and I believe that once we've taken the castle, another five hundred men from town and the surrounding area will join us."

"*Five hundred*!"

"Yes, colonel," I said to Alexander Jephson. "Five hundred. I'm not really surprised at that number at all. Lots of people around this area hate Ormonde because he confiscated their lands or had them fined for other offences. If you ask me, there'll be even more than those five hundred wanting to join us once the word gets out."

"Are you sure?" Alden insisted.

I nodded. "Now, let's get down to working out the details." I unrolled a large map of the castle onto the table and, as if they didn't know the features already, I pointed out the Great Gate and the Record and Bermingham Towers. "When the first six men enter, the rest of us will be hiding around here." I pointed to various buildings and clumps of trees where our reinforcements would be waiting for the flag to fly from the tower: the signal to rush the castle.

"Aren't they too near the centre?" Alden asked. "Surely they'll be spotted by the guards?"

I shook my head. "They can't be hidden any further away or they won't see the flag fly from the tower."

"I can't help but think you're being too optimistic about all this?" he persisted. "I mean you're talking about our motley group of men overcoming the duke's guards who are almost certainly stronger and better armed."

I assured the hesitant Alden that all would be well on the day and that seemed to satisfy him. I continued going over the details with the others and answering questions for another hour. Then we wished one another luck and had a celebratory drink. As we were wishing ourselves success, Colonel Jephson admitted that he had informed Sir Theophilus Jones, the former governor of Dublin about our plans. He too had lost a lot of land and hadn't had any luck when he had petitioned of the Court of Claims. The Colonel said that he had sworn Sir Theophilus to secrecy, so we had no reason to worry.

After that, with a general feeling of great optimism and many slaps on the back, we dispersed. I took my brother-in-law back to my house for another drink and the others returned to their families or friends. Later, I found out that the only one who did not do so was Philip Alden. Making sure that he was not followed, the quiet-spoken loner of a lawyer made his way to Colonel Edward Vernon, one of the Duke of Ormonde's men, who had been appointed to note any signs of non-Catholic sedition. Colonel Vernon wasted no time. He immediately rode to the castle and passed on the information that Alden, a double-agent, had told him.

I was informed of this devastating news when my brother-in-law woke me early the next morning.

"Tom! Tom! We've been betrayed!" he panted. "More than two dozen of us have been arrested and—"

"Slow down, man. Catch your breath," I said, as I hitched up my breeches and fastened the ties on my shirt. "Tell me what happened, slowly. Who betrayed us?"

"I don't know who betrayed us, Tom, but two dozen of us were arrested early this morning and taken off to the castle."

"How do you know this?"

"Lieutenant Richard Thompson's servant escaped out of the back door and ran over to tell me and—"

"Are you sure about this?"

"I'm certain of it," he nodded vigorously. "Ford himself rushed over to tell me, and now I'm telling you. Our men are being held under heavy guard. We must get away now, before Ormonde gets his hands on us."

"We can't abandon our men now! What will they think of us?"

"Where the devil are we going to hide then? We can't stay here, *that's* for certain."

"Why not? I for one am planning to stay right here," I said. "It's up to you whether or not you want to join me."

Will sighed. "I'll see what's happening and let you know later."

I remained in Dublin for a few days, sleeping in a different place every night. Some days, I would disguise myself as a workman and on other occasions I would wear the cassock of a Catholic priest. This was a particularly good idea as I could hide my sword within its dark voluminous folds. In addition, while wearing a large black hood and cloak, I could move about but remain hidden at the same time. Although a few of my friends urged me to leave Dublin for my own good, I felt that I should stay in the city, at least for now. This way, I could learn what had happened to my fellow plotters and also find out what steps the authorities, especially the Duke of Ormonde were taking against them.

One evening, a week after our attack was to have taken place, I was staying with Brendan O'Connor, a good friend of my brother-in-law, and his wife, Bridget. As I sat at the table with Brendan discussing what had happened and speculating how the duke had discovered our plot, a very out of breath Bridget rushed inside.

"Brendan, Tom, I've just heard some terrible tidings," she gasped. "I…I…"

"Well, what is it, woman? Out with it!"

"T…T…Tanner, James Tanner, you know? Henry Cromwell's old secretary…he's told everything he knows to the duke!"

"How do you know?" Brendan and I asked together.

"You know Fat Dermot, the guard? The one who's had a soft spot for me since I fixed his broken arm and—"

"Aye. What did he say?"

"He was one of the men who brought Tanner in to face the duke. Dermot said that Tanner was like a jelly, and once the duke had threatened to torture and then hang him, he broke down and confessed to everything he knew."

"Did Dermot say if he mentioned my name?" I asked.

Bridget nodded. "Aye, he did that. He said that you were the leader, or at least one of the leaders. He told him that Philip Alden and a man called Ford were also involved, and he mentioned two others called Thompson and Jephson."

Brendan looked at me. "Tom, you're going to have to leave Dublin now. You've got no choice. Besides…"

"Yes," Bridget continued. "Dermot told me that once Tanner had told everything to the duke, the duke gave him a pen and paper and made him write down there and then everything he had just confessed. Dermot said that Tanner filled up about three pages, and when he finished, the duke made him sign his name on it."

"And then what?" I asked. "What did he do to Tanner?"

"The duke made him read what he'd written aloud and Dermot told me that your name, Tom, came up a lot. At least a dozen times."

I sat there quietly, wondering what my next steps should be.

"I'm sorry, Tom, but you can't stay here after tonight," Bridget said. "The duke knows too much and now it's in writing as well."

Brendan nodded. "Bridget's right, my friend. I don't feel good saying this, but after tonight, you'll have to be on your way. I'll give you all the help I can, but you *must* be out of here by early tomorrow morning." He shrugged. "I'm sorry, I truly am, but I can't risk my family."

Brendan was right, and I fully understood his attitude. I left early the following morning after Bridget had given me a pouch filled with fresh bread, cheese, a few apples, and a tightly closed flask of ale.

"That should keep you going for a while," she smiled. "At least till you're clear of Dublin."

However, although Brendan and Bridget assumed I would leave Dublin, I remained in the city, spending that night in an abandoned cowshed on the outskirts. The straw wasn't too fresh, but beggars couldn't be choosers. At least I had some food and drink, and was still a free man.

Once the sun had gone down, I crept out and washed my hands and face in an old stone trough, then I lay down with my sword by my side in the darkest, least smelly corner of the shed and hoped that I would not be disturbed.

I wasn't.

The next morning, heavily disguised in my priestly garb, I set out to discover whether anything had happened since Tanner had been forced to confess all he knew. Being hungry and thirsty, I walked into a small tavern by the side of the Liffey, and after finishing my breakfast, I sat down near a couple of talkative soldiers. Pretending to read a Catholic news sheet, I listened to what they were saying, and learned that they were based at the castle. They were complaining about the extra duties they had been assigned.

"Can't the sergeant find someone else?" the smarter-looking one whined as he sawed through a chunk of cheese. "I've got a wife and four wee ones who need me at home."

"Just think of the extra money we'll be getting," his friend replied.

"What money? We're not going to be getting any more for looking after them seventy new prisoners. We'll be lucky if we get a day off instead, and that won't be before the hangings, *that* I can tell you."

"What hangings?" the curly-haired one asked.

"Don't you know anything? They're taking some of them, the leaders, I think, to court tomorrow, and then there'll be some hangings. How many, I don't know, but you can be sure that they'll want to swing at least a dozen of them."

They were silent for a few minutes as they continued with their meal. Then, the curly-haired one looked up. "Kevin, you seem to know a lot about all this. D'you know who they'll hang?"

"Aye, that I do. They'll likely hang that Leckie fellow and his friends, Jephson and Thompson.

They're the ones I've been guarding. The sarge told me to keep my wits about me. He said that they are very slippery fish. He said their leader, that Colonel Blood fellow, might try and rescue them, but I reckon he said that just to keep me on my toes."

"I reckon the same. No one in their right mind would try and break into the castle now," his friend added. "Especially since they've doubled the guard."

Their conversation completely changed my plans. I had previously considered disguising myself and worming my way into the castle to rescue my brother-in-law, but on hearing that they had doubled the guard, I realised that this would be impossible. All I could do for now was remain in Dublin, and try to find out what had happened to James.

Two days later, disguised in a high-collared brown coat and a wide-brimmed black hat, I made my way into the courtroom where Leckie and the others were to be tried for insurrection, attacking the Crown, and similar offences. As I entered, I noticed a creased and abandoned handbill lying on the floor, detailing the reason for our attack on the castle. I did not need to read it. After all, I had organised the attack, hadn't I? But curiosity got the better of me, and I bent down and picked it up.

Having long expected the securing of our lives, liberties, and estates as reasonable recompense for that industry and diligence exercised by the Protestants of this kingdom in restoring His Majesty to the exercise of his royal authority, instead, we find ourselves, our wives, and our children, without mercy, delivered as prey unto these barbarous and bloody murderers, whose inhumane cruelty is registered in the blood of one-hundred-and-fifty thousand innocent Protestants.

Just as I was stuffing the handbill into my pocket, a guard gave me a push.

"Can't you wash yourself, man?"

To make his point, he even pinched his nose and waved his arm dramatically, making sure that everyone near me could see him.

"Aye, he smells like a herd o' cows," added the man behind me.

I was pleased to hear this; it meant people would avoid standing too close.

After waiting for another quarter of an hour, my brother-in-law Will, Colonel Jephson, and Lieutenant Thompson were all brought in. The three of them were chained together, and every time they moved, I could hear their chains clanking against the stone floor. In addition to the chains, there were two armed guards responsible for each of them. The Duke and the authorities were taking no chances.

Not wishing to be recognised, I fixed my gaze to the floor, only raising my eyes for a second to see James' hands being chained to a long bar facing the bench. I was shocked by his appearance. The strong, upright, suntanned fellow I had known was gone, replaced by a bent, gaunt, grey-faced man, who looked twenty years older than his true age. During a second brief glance, I noted the black shadows under his eyes, and that my normally well-dressed relation now looked like the poorest beggar in all of Dublin.

I snatched another glance as the judges entered. I recognised all of them. The first to step up was the stout Sir Audley Mervin, the Speaker of the Irish House of Commons. As he surveyed the courtroom before sitting down, he was joined by John Clotworthy, First Viscount Massereene from Londonderry. It was only once they had settled themselves, adjusted their robes, and placed some papers on the bench in front of them, that Baron Santry, the Chief Justice, entered. He was a frail, white-haired old man, and even though he walked with a black, knobbly walking stick, he still had to be helped up the three wooden steps to his maroon upholstered seat.

The proceedings were rushed, as though the judges were concerned that something might happen which would prevent them from arriving at their desired verdict. Each of the three accused were asked in quick succession their names, occupations, and addresses, before being questioned about their roles in the planned attack on the castle.

It was clear that Sir Audley, who seemed to be senior to Viscount Massereene, had been instructed to run the proceedings, and every so often he would look to the Chief Justice if the pace seemed to slow.

Following a nod from his superior, Sir Audley asked the 'learned counsel,' as he called Patrick Darcy, if he had anything more to add. Darcy shook his head, and the judge then asked my brother-in-law if he had anything to say in his defence.

"No, Your Honour," Leckie said. "Like my other fellows here, I pleaded 'not guilty' before, and I repeat this plea now."

The other accused men were asked the same question, and they repeated what my brother-in-law had said.

"Very well, since you are all insistent on your innocence," Sir Audley stated pompously. "I will now ask the jury to retire and reach their verdict."

The jury left the courtroom for a mere ten minutes. In their eyes there was nothing to deliberate. During that brief period I tried to catch my brother-in-law's eye and had just managed to do so when the jury returned and took up their places.

"Have you reached your verdict?" Sir Audley asked, his voice barely audible above the rustling of the crowd.

"Yes, Your Honour, we have," a tall figure in a black coat and breeches answered.

"Would you please reveal this verdict to the court."

"Guilty, Your Honour."

"All of them?"

"Yes, Your Honour. All of them." The man smiled at his fellow jurors and sat down.

"It has been decided then," the Chief Justice said. "You three men, William Leckie, Alexander Jephson and Richard Thompson are to receive the appropriate punishment for those who have committed high treason." He paused for a moment or two, coughed, caught his breath, and continued. "Each of you will be drawn by a horse to the gallows, where you will be hanged by the neck, cut down while you are still alive, and quartered. This will be arranged within the week. That is all," he wheezed.

"Guards, take them out," Sir Audley ordered. "This court is now dismissed."

As my brother-in-law was led out, he passed me and, hidden by the wide sleeves of my dirty coat, I managed to sneak a quick squeeze of his arm. He winked briefly in reply before being hurried out back to his cell.

Later, I learned that Will had tried to cheat the hangman by repeatedly knocking his head against the wall of his prison cell, but to no avail. Several sorrowful days later, my brother-in-law and his fellow plotters were brutally sent off to meet their Maker. I stood at the back of the crowd in the city's square, and noted the sullen looks of the people there. A few called out 'death to the traitors' whilst others shouted words of encouragement to Leckie and the others. I wanted to do the same, but I thought it best not to draw attention to myself. There were a few constables mingling with the crowd and having stayed one foot ahead of the law so far, the last thing I wanted was to be caught out here.

I did not wish to see my brother-in-law die. It was enough for me to know that, within minutes, his soul would be winging its way towards Heaven. As the hangman placed the noose around his neck, I sneaked away from the crowds, leaving the sound of screams and jeers behind me. I returned to the abandoned cattle shed, retrieved the horse I had acquired and my meagre possessions and prepared to leave Dublin. I was in a foul mood and feeling extremely guilty. It was because of my failed plan that my brother-in-law and two other good men had died and many others were destined to follow them.

Chapter 13
On the run

I rode ten miles south of Dublin, before stopping at a wayside tavern for a meal. The tavern was clearly frequented by travellers, for the tavern-owner offered me provisions for my journey should I need them. I took up his offer gladly, knowing that the less I ate in taverns, especially near Dublin, the better. I could not risk being recognised.

My plan was to continue heading south until I reached Wicklow, some fifteen miles away. Donovan McCarthy, one of the junior officers who had fought with me at the Battle of Naseby, lived there. This good-natured man had once told me he made his living in this small coastal town legally as a fisherman, and illegally as a smuggler. I just had to hope that his inclination for illegality would convince him to help me.

I arrived just as the last orange rays of the sun were fading over the Wicklow Mountains. After crossing the River Vartry, I made my way over to the Bridge Inn and asked the landlord where I might find Donovan McCarthy. I recalled Donovan telling me that there were only a few thousand people living in his town and that if I ever wanted to look him up, I should ask for him at this hostelry.

"Ah, you're after Donovan McCarthy are you? The Donovan who fought against the king?" the landlord replied. "Of course I know where he lives. Who doesn't?" Stepping outside, the landlord pointed to a row of cottages. "Walk over there, past that blackthorn tree. His house is the third on the left. You cannot miss it. It has an old saddle nailed to the front wall."

I thanked him and followed his instructions. Five minutes later, I was banging the heavy iron knocker on Donovan's front door.

"What the devil…who the hell wants a word with us at this time of night?" I heard him say to his wife. "Stay here, love, I'll go see who it is."

As he opened the door, I removed my scarf from my face.

"Lord Jesus and all His Saints!" Donovan gasped. "Thomas Blood? Bloody hell, of all the people I expected to see tonight, you've got to be the last. Come on in, man, out of the cold."

I followed him into his roomy cottage as he

called out for his wife.

"Fiona, love, see who's just arrived! My old officer from the army! The one I was talking to you about just the other week."

Fiona, a short, plump bundle of a woman, wearing a white cloth cap and a dark green dress, entered the room. Her sharp eyes were simultaneously welcoming and suspicious.

"Colonel Blood?" she asked. "The one who saved my husband from being trampled underfoot when he was in the army?"

I nodded.

"Well I never. It's an honour to meet you, good sir. You saved my Donny's life, you did. I can't thank you enough," she smiled, looking up at her tall, moustached husband, before turning back to me. "You're most welcome."

I smiled back and then asked where I could stable my horse.

"Round the back," Donovan answered. "Follow me, I'll show you." He stepped outside and then stopped. "Colonel," he asked warily. "Was it you, or another fellow with the same name, who was involved in that planned attack on Dublin Castle?"

I sighed. I had hoped we could build up to this slowly. "Yes, it was me. I…"

To my surprise, Donovan slapped me on the back. "I knew it! It's high time someone stood up to that Duke of Ormonde, good on you! It's a damn shame you were betrayed. I suppose you're on the run

[161]

now then?"

I nodded. "You needn't worry though, no one knows which direction I took. As far as the authorities are concerned, I could be o'er the water in Liverpool by now. Still, I have to ask. Will it be all right with your wife if I stay a night or two with you? She won't go blabbing to everyone?"

"All right?" He grinned. "Of course it'll be all right. Fiona can't stand the duke. She hates him, perhaps even more than I do. That bastard hanged one of her nephews. Trust me, you don't have to worry there, she'll keep her lips tightly closed, as will I."

McCarthy and his wife were as good as their word. I stayed with them for four days, hiding inside the house during the day and only going out at night, usually to the local tavern with Donovan. He introduced me as Liam, his nephew, a carpenter from Cork. Having deliberately stained my face with nut oil I also made a small cut in my left cheek – 'a war wound' I explained – no one guessed who I really was. Besides, I soon found that the main subjects of conversation were fishing and smuggling. Dublin Castle and the duke were a world way.

On my third night, after we had enjoyed a fair few pints of ale down the tavern and a rousing discussion about our past adventures in the army, Donovan beckoned me to follow him outside. For once, his jolly round face was not smiling.

"What is it?" I asked. "Is someone on to me?"

He nodded. "I think so. When I was at the bar,

ordering drinks, I heard Skinny Flynn saying something to his pal, Black Niall, about Colonel Blood."

"So?"

"Those two are known in the town for doing anything to get their filthy hands on easy money. I wouldn't be surprised if they go to the mayor or the constables and say that they think you're here. After all, there's a hundred pounds on your head, and that's a goodly sack full o' money. A real fortune for those two thieving bastards."

"Aye, you're right there," I agreed. "That's certainly a lot of money for anyone. I suppose I best be on my way then. I don't want to put you and Fiona in danger."

"Where will you go? You can't stay around these parts."

"Don't you worry yourself about that," I said. "I'll go to Antrim. My wife has a cousin there, James Holcroft. A merchant. You know I'd prefer to stay here with you, but now it seems that's impossible. Fear not," I said, laying my hand on his shoulder. "I'll be out of here within the hour. I'm sure I'll be all right with my wife's folk."

We swiftly returned to Donovan's cottage, and I packed my things and gratefully accepted a bag of food and a bottle of ale for the journey. After a round of hugs and thanks, I set off for the north. The one-hundred-and-fifty-mile direct route took four days, but I wanted to stay well clear of Dublin, so I took a day or so longer, keeping to the west of Dublin and travelling north via Newbridge, Dundalk, and Cookstown.

Fortunately, my fears of being recognised and arrested came to naught, though I did have a rather tense moment when I stopped for a drink near Maynooth, some twenty-five miles west of Dublin. I was sitting on a bench, just outside the tavern, when a small posse of half a dozen horsemen entered. I assumed they had come to refresh themselves so didn't pay too much attention to them, that is, apart from pulling my black woollen cap down further over my face and turning away. A few moments later they came out, and the officer walked over to me.

"You, what's your name?" he asked, standing in front of me, his hand on the hilt of his sword.

"John. John Hogan," I replied. "Why?"

"Let me ask the questions," he continued. "D'you live here?"

"Here, in Maynooth? No, sir. I'm from Wicklow." I gave him Donovan's address.

"So, what are you doing here?"

"I'm on my way to Antrim, to visit my cousin. He's sick and he wants—"

"You're going a long way out of your way," the officer interrupted. "You'd have been quicker going through Dublin."

"I know. I wanted to visit an old friend who was in the army with me on the way."

"I see." He started walking over to his horse, then turned back. "By the way, what's the name of your cousin in Antrim?"

"James Holcroft, sir. He's a merchant."

The officer looked around to his men. "You," he said, pointing to a horseman who was just finishing off a meat pie. "You're from Antrim. Do you know of a James Holcroft?"

"The merchant, sir? The one who deals in horses and saddles?"

Hearing this, I was relieved that I had mixed my lies with the truth. The officer grunted something, and they went on their way. To my relief, they were heading south, and after waiting a few moments, I continued my journey north.

This incident convinced me that if anyone, be it a passer-by, an innkeeper, or a local constable, asked me questions, it was essential that I had a story ready. 'Yes, I'm a merchant rushing north. I'm in a hurry to meet a client who is due to sail to England at the end of the week'. I repeated this sentence to myself as I galloped along, but fortunately I didn't have to use it, apart from when a friendly old man asked me when I stopped for a rest at Castleblayney. Offering him a free drink and discussing the damage caused by the latest storm soon distracted him from further questions.

I reached Antrim one June evening and, as I had done in Wicklow, made my enquiries at the local tavern, this time asking if anyone knew where my wife's cousin, James Holcroft, lived.

"Will that be Bald Jimmy?" a red-faced man asked. "The horse trader?"

"Aye, that's him," I replied. "If he has family in Lancashire."

"Aye, that he has. You'll find him at his stables near the castle. He's there all hours of the day and night."

I thanked him and set out in the direction of the castle. It was a new building, that is, about fifty years old. It looked nothing like the old Norman or medieval castles that I knew of, and James later informed me that it belonged to the Massereene family who had built it as their country seat.

"But we're not here to talk about that, I suppose," James said, when we sat down later for a meal in his cottage. "I understand from what you've just told me that you'd like to stay here for a while."

I nodded.

I spent most of my time in Antrim helping James – 'call me Jimmy' – in the stables or fishing in Lough Neagh. I showed James a couple of saddle tricks I'd learned in the army, and he was pleased to add this information to what he already knew. We talked about my family and he told me that my wife was getting along well enough back in Lancashire.

"Aye, as soon as she heard that they were looking for you, she returned home to her parents. She was scared they'd come to her, looking for you. As far as I know, they haven't been to ask her questions there so, hopefully, the government has no idea where you are."

"Long may it stay that way," I grinned, raising

a glass of his home-brewed ale to my lips.

During the two weeks I spent with James, I almost forgot that I was a fugitive on the run with a hundred pound prize on my head. But I knew that I had to move on soon, else the risk of the authorities finding me would only increase. So after a two-week stay, I bid farewell to James and as I swung myself up into the saddle he told me that I was welcome to return whenever I wanted. Just as I was about to tell him something, he put his finger to his lips and said that he did not want to know where I was bound for next.

"Why not? I trust you."

"If they ever catch scent of your trail and start asking me questions, I want to be able to honestly say that I don't know where you are. Now be gone with you." James smiled and gave me one final wave before he disappeared into the smoky confines of his smithy.

From Antrim, I went south-east, to stay with another army colleague near the edge of Belfast Lough. Joseph Boyd, a retired Roundhead captain, had been badly wounded in the leg at Naseby. He must have heard me coming as I cantered up the gravel driveway to his large, mansion-like house, for he came out of the front door and greeted me even before I could dismount.

"Captain Tom!" he called out.

I quickly placed a finger to my lips and hissed, "Shh!"

"What's up? Why all the shushing?"

"My name's not Tom, at least, not here," I

replied quickly. "Come, let's go inside and I'll tell you what's happening." After dropping the reins over a nearby bush, we entered his house. There, I told him what I had been doing over the past month, and why it was important that Captain Thomas Blood did not exist. At least, not here, so close to Belfast.

"Shame your plans didn't work out," he remarked once I had finished my story. "I could never stand that Ormonde feller. He'll do anything to keep the king happy, and if that means hanging a good few Irishmen, he'll do that as well."

I nodded in agreement.

"Tom, you're lucky your head is still on your shoulders. They've been looking for you, or so I've heard. But fear not, you'll be safe here. I'll just tell the wife and my servants that you're an old army friend, staying here while they finish off your new house in Coleraine. How does that sound?"

I said that that sounded like as good a story as any and he grinned, limping out into the corridor to call for his wife to join us.

"Maurene, I'd like you to meet another old army friend of mine, Thomas Pilsen. Captain Thomas Pilsen," Joseph introduced me as his wife entered the room. "He fought with me at Naseby and did very well there."

I nodded. Although I enjoyed being known as a colonel, I thought it best for the moment to be a mere captain. Joseph went on to tell her that, as I'd be staying with them for a week or two, she should instruct the servants to prepare a room and a bed for me.

She smiled and bade me welcome, saying, "Any friend of my Joseph is a friend of mine," before hurrying out to do her husband's bidding.

My sojourns at former colleague's houses were becoming much the same, and in keeping with this pattern, I spent a pleasant two weeks with Joseph Boyd and his wife. We passed much of the time sitting in his well-trimmed garden, when the weather allowed, or in his light and airy living-room, reminiscing about our past glories as Roundhead cavalrymen. On other occasions, when I felt I could not possibly remain cooped up anymore, we went for rides in the countryside, making sure that we rode through open land or small villages which were scarcely populated.

The only time I became concerned was on my third day there. Joseph approached me with another man close behind him, a short fellow wearing some sort of dark blue uniform and a wide brimmed hat.

"Captain Thomas Pilsen," he said, winking at me. "Meet Chief Constable O'Sullivan. Apparently, he's heard some rumours that Colonel Blood, you know, that feller who was involved in that Dublin Castle plot, is staying here. I told him the rumours were a load of old nonsense, but he insisted on seeing you for himself."

I stood up and thrust out my hand to O'Sullivan. "Captain Pilsen, at your service, sir. Captain Thomas Pilsen," I said, shaking his hand vigorously. "Do tell me, which idiot told you that I was the famous Colonel Blood? You ask anyone here. They all know me as Captain Thomas Pilsen. Ain't that right, Joe?"

My host nodded. "Aye, that's right."

"Er, yes, sir. I understand that," O'Sullivan said, looking me up and down and then reading the description of me that he was holding. "But you see, sir, it is my duty to check all of these stories out and see —"

"Well, you just continue doing your duty, Chief Constable," I said, clapping him on the back. "And if you catch that dastardly Blood fellow, make sure you hang him as high as you can."

"Er, yes, Captain," O'Sullivan muttered, playing with the rim of his hat. "You can be sure of that." And with that, he was gone.

"That performance calls for a celebratory drink," Joseph grinned. "What an actor you are. If the Chief had stayed for a few more minutes, you'd have had him polishing your boots. Come, let's go in and eat. I can smell Maurene's delicious cooking from here."

My stay with the Boyds came to an abrupt halt one afternoon.

"Tom," Joe began, even before he had taken off his riding cloak and boots. "You're going to have to leave. The government's men are on to you."

"What do you mean?"

"While I was in town this morning, I heard

stories that Colonel Thomas Blood was still free, and that he was planning to kill the Duke of Ormonde."

I smiled. "I wish."

"This is no joke, Tom. The duke is travelling around heavily guarded, and they're arresting all sorts of people." He paused and looked down. "I'm sorry, Tom, but you have to leave now, before they start searching all the houses. I'll get Maurene to pack you some food and then I suggest you make yourself scarce. I'm sorry, but I've got no choice. I can't afford for Ormonde's men to catch you here." He shrugged. "I'm sorry, my friend. I truly am. We really enjoyed having you stay with us."

I was on the road within the hour, heading south at a quiet pace so as not to attract attention. Then, as soon as I was a mile or two outside of town, I began galloping as fast as I could. I spent the night in an old tumbledown barn and continued south early the next morning. I planned to head for the Wicklow Mountains again, where I would be able to stay with another old friend, Cox. He had served in the army for a while before finding religion, and was now a minister, of sorts.

This time, I did not have to ask around for where Cox lived. His past description – 'I'm right next door to the Old Oaktree inn' – was enough to go on. When I arrived at the edge of Aghavannagh, I saw that there were only two inns, the Old Oaktree, and the Black Horse. It did not take me long to find my old army friend. As I had hoped, he was very pleased to see me, and was even more impressed when I told him why I was on the run.

"You'll be safe, here," he grinned. "No-one comes up here apart from us locals and a few farmers. Nevertheless, you shouldn't stray too far. There's always a wicked feller who will turn you in for the price of a tankard of ale."

After two weeks with Cox, I decided once again that it would be best to move on, only this time, I decided to risk my neck and go back to Dublin. Someone had mentioned in the local inn that they had heard Colonel Blood's wife had returned home from England, though they could not be sure whether it was true or not.

"Aye," his drinking partner had said. "Maybe she's there, maybe she isn't. But I bet that Ormonde feller is putting out stories like that to entice her husband back. I mean, it makes sense, doesn't it? The spider and the fly. But I'm telling you, if I was the colonel, I'd be very careful."

I was determined to go back, but I knew the man in the tavern was right. I needed to tread very carefully. The last thing I wanted was to get caught up in the Duke's sticky and far-flung web.

Chapter 14
I return to Dublin

As the crow flies, the distance between where I was staying in the Wicklow Mountains and Dublin was only about thirty miles. On a normal occasion I could easily have done this journey in a day. But this was not a normal occasion. I was knowingly riding into a possible trap, a trap that could cost me my head. I wanted to make sure that I entered the city in the early evening when the skies were grey and threatening, and most sensible and respectable people were tucked away in their homes.

   Wearing a priestly garment and having trimmed my black flowing locks, I rented a room for a few nights at the Red Crown inn, on the south side of the city. I had chosen the inn carefully; I wanted to stay in a place that had at least two entrance doors on the ground floor. The Red Crown, for some reason, had three. If Ormonde's men came looking for me, I would have a fair chance of escaping.

"Will you be wanting a room facing the street or one facing the back, Lieutenant Payne?" the landlord asked.

"The back, please," I replied. "That one you have over there, if it's free." I pointed to the room next to one of the inn's back doors.

"It's a wee bit noisy that one, sir. Are you sure you wouldn't prefer a quieter room upstairs?"

"No thanks," I replied, leaning forward a little, cupping my hand to my ear. "I'm somewhat hard of hearing, so the noise won't bother me."

Stabling my horse round the back, I chose the stall nearest the door and pushed a couple of barrels against the front of the inn's back door, before dropping a few shiny coins onto the ground. These, I hoped, would warn me if anyone came sneaking up in the middle of the night. The barrels would prevent them from rushing in and the coins would surely stop an ordinary soldier in his tracks. What poor soldier would continue carrying out his duty when the price of a drink sat gleaming on the ground in front of him? I smiled to myself. My days as a soldier had certainly taught me a few things.

Before I turned in for the night, I wrote a quick note to my wife, and found a young street urchin just outside the inn.

"Boy, d'you fancy earning a few pennies?" I

asked the thin, scruffy lad.

He nodded vigorously.

"Do you know your letters?"

"No, sir. I never went to school. You see I…"

"Never mind," I said. "D'you know where the Jameson family live, on St George's Lane?"

He nodded again. "Yes, sir. They live next door to a butcher called Kelly. Why?"

"Take this note to the Jameson house. Make sure you deliver it within the next half hour, and they'll give you some extra coin. And listen," I added. "If the lady of the house isn't there, bring this note back here and give it to the landlord of the Red Crown. You understand all that?"

He nodded vigorously again, took the note and a few coins and immediately ran off towards the centre of town.

Early the following morning, after seeing that the landlord had not received my note to my wife, I set out for St. George's Lane where I had discovered that Maria and my family were staying with some of her good friends. Fortunately, the house was a few streets south of the river so I wouldn't have to cross and risk being caught by Ormonde's men on one of the bridges. The only passing place that gave me concern was St. Nicholas Gate. This was usually manned by a toll-keeper and a guard or two. From past experience, I knew that the toll-keepers could be bribed if you 'accidentally' dropped a few extra coins into their ever-open hands. I also knew that the guards were normally old soldiers who just wanted a quiet life. I hoped it was still like that now.

I decided to present myself as an ageing priest, leaning on a strong walking stick and wearing my hat down low over my face. I approached the gate, my left hand holding the knobbly end of my stick, and my right, hidden in my black robes, gripping my dagger.

I muttered, "A good morning to you," as I walked past the two guards and the toll-keeper. Fortunately, they were more interested in eating their early morning hunks of bread and cheese than questioning an old man of the cloth. I passed through the stone archway without any hindrance, and from there, it was but a few minutes' walk to St. George's Lane.

As soon as I arrived, I was whisked inside. There were no joyful reunions while the front door was still open that would have aroused the neighbours' attention. The door was quickly closed behind me as I hurried inside. After the longed-for hugs and kisses with my wife and children, we sat down and began to talk about what had happened. Of course, the children were told in no uncertain terms that they were not to tell anyone – 'and that includes your best friends, Patrick and little Annie' – that I had returned.

It was good to spend that night in bed with Maria, though for the first few minutes we were like a newly married couple on our nuptial night. But soon enough, our desire for the delights of the flesh overcame any such nervousness and we spent the rest of the night holding, caressing, and pleasuring one another. By the time the sun cast its first beams on the bedroom wall early the following morning, I was quite exhausted. But I knew I could not stay here, so after dressing quickly in my clerical garb and fuelling myself with a quick bowl of pottage, I sneaked out of the house and rode out of the city as quietly as I had entered.

My first stop was Balbriggan, a hamlet between Dublin and Drogheda. It was while I was sitting in the dark corner of a tavern, enjoying my first proper meal of the day, that three workmen entered. They ordered some ale and sat themselves down at the table next to mine.

"Excuse me, Father," the tallest one asked. "But may I take this chair?"

I nodded and he returned to his friends with the chair. My ears pricked up when I heard them talking about me.

"Why?" the one called Keenan asked. "Did you think that Colonel Blood would come and rescue those other poor souls in prison? Y'know, his friends?"

"Well, I thought it was a possibility," replied the one who had borrowed the chair. "It's been rumoured that he's still in Dublin, just waiting for the right moment."

"Ah, get away with you. That Blood feller is far away by now. Of that you can be sure," the third man said. "D'you think he's going to risk his neck rescuing his friends now, after all this time? If he had wanted to, he'd have done it by now. Of that you can be sure."

"Aye, you're right there. Those that were hanged, they were a grand bunch of men. I mean, that Colonel Jephson. Did you hear him make his final speech afore they strung him up? I'm telling you. Fine words they were, an' all. Blamed the Papists, he did. Said they were behind all this."

"That's right, Flynn, and then that Warren feller started to give *his* final speech."

"Aye, but the sheriff wasn't having any of it, oh no. Even when Warren called out that a man about to die should have the liberty of speaking his conscience."

"Yes, and then the third man, Thompson, was next."

Keenan nodded. "Aye, he also had things to say. He said it was Colonel Blood's fault. It was him, he said, who had drawn him into the plot."

"But that didn't help him," Flynn commented. "And if I were Colonel Blood, I'd be as far away from here as I could be. That Duke of Ormonde isn't going to let up until he, himself, sees that man on the gallows. If you ask me, the duke wants to pull the damned rope himself."

The other two nodded in agreement, and their discussion drifted towards less interesting matters.

Getting up, I gave the three men a quick nod and left the inn. What I had heard reinforced the feeling that the sooner I left Ireland, the better. The question was, where should I go? Surprisingly, my answer came to me the following day.

I was walking down the road when a torn news sheet blew against my leg. I bent down, picked it up, and started reading about the situation in England. On the top half of the page was an article about the spread of uprisings in the north of the country. It said that dissentions were being caused by 'malcontents' who were against the widespread blasphemy and drunkenness of the English people. This descent into sin, the article said, was due to the Anglican Church's worship of idols as well as unfair taxation. Two of the chief instigators of this evil situation were the Dukes of Buckingham and Albemarle. According to the rebels, they were turning the peaceful land of England into a land of Sodom and Gomorrah.

England was where I should go, I thought. To take part in this rebellion against the government of King Charles the Second. After all, wasn't it because of the king and his rule that I had lost most of my property? Without giving the situation too much thought, I took a ferry to England, after paying another urchin to take a message explaining my plans to my wife. Once I landed in England, I rode hard to the home of Margaret Holcroft, my mother-in-law, in Lancashire.

It was there that I learned I had arrived in England too late. The king's agents had infiltrated the rebel group and had captured many of its leaders before they could bring about their rebellion.

"I heard about two of them," my mother-in-law, a stocky, well-dressed woman, told me. "Captain John Mason, and John Atkinson. They say that Mason was caught while hiding in Newark-on-Trent, near Nottingham, and that he and Atkinson were then arrested by the king's men and taken to Clifford's Tower in York."

"So, that's the end of it," I sighed. "I've met that Mason fellow in the past. He's a good man."

Margaret shook her head. "Maybe…maybe not. Word is they've managed to escape, and the government is worried that they will try to start another rebellion. You know, the person who told me about Mason and Atkinson also mentioned your name."

"Me?"

Margaret nodded. "They said you were one of the leaders, and that the king's men are looking for you as well." She looked at me straight in the eye. "You weren't one of the leaders, were you, Tom? I know how much you hate the king's government, and I can't say that I blame you, but…"

I shook my head. "No, I had nothing to do with it. I've been in Ireland this whole time, but I'm glad that you told me. It seems as though I'm going to have to be on my guard just as much here as I was in Ireland." Instinctively, I looked around. "I wonder when they'll realise I'm here. I didn't think my name had crossed over to England."

It was not long before I had the answer to that question. The following night, we were all woken by a loud hammering on the front door. Cautiously pulling the curtain aside, I looked out from the top floor window and saw a posse of ten horsemen and an officer standing outside. Immediately, I dived into the priest-hole at the back of the house and prayed that, although it had not been used for many years, it would now serve its purpose. As I crouched there amongst the old papers and rags that had accumulated over the years, I peeked out through a crack in the door. I could see the officer talking to my mother-in-law.

"Please excuse me for disturbing you, madam, at this late hour of the night." He bowed slightly. "But I must ask, are you Mistress Margaret Holcroft, the mother-in-law of Colonel Thomas Blood?"

My mother-in-law, who was normally a most forthright and upstanding person, now seemed to shrink, acting the role of a feeble old lady. "Why, yes, sir," she said quietly. "But I haven't seen that rascal for years. Not since he left for Ireland with my daughter. As far as I know, he's still there, sir." She trembled for a minute. "Oh, it is cold out tonight, sir. Would you like a warm cup of wine?"

"No thank you, mistress. We'll be on our way now. If your son-in-law does turn up here, you must know that it is your duty to report him to the authorities. Is that clear?"

"Yes, sir," Margaret replied quietly. "I don't want any problems, especially at my age, and in my present state of health." She pulled her shawl more tightly around her and started coughing.

After wishing her 'Goodnight and good health'

[181]

and apologising again for disturbing her, the officer and his men departed. I waited in my hiding place until Margaret tapped on the door and whispered that it was safe to come out.

"You were wonderful," I said, putting my arms around her. "You really played the part. You would have had me fooled if I had been that officer."

She waved her hand dismissively. "Come, Tom, I wasn't so good. The important thing is he's gone now, and that's all that matters."

We decided that it was not safe for me to remain, so early the following morning, I set out for Yorkshire, where the rebellion was to have taken place. I knew it would be a long and arduous journey; I decided to stay off the beaten track to reduce the risk of running into any curious officials. This meant I would have to cross the snow-topped Pennines in the mist, rain, and unending wind. The first two days were the hardest as the routes heading east were steep and the rarely-used tracks were tough going for my poor horse. On a couple of occasions, he missed his footing, slipping on the slimy wet stones that made up the mountains' surface. On the evening of the second day, just as I was approaching Colne, a small market town on the Lancashire-Yorkshire border, my horse went lame. Fortunately, the weather had improved, that is, the wind had dropped and the rain had ceased, so I slid off the saddle and walked us to the nearest tavern. Looking back, this eventuality may have been something of a blessing, as I arrived at the tavern looking nothing at all like the elusive Colonel Blood.

I told the landlord that I was a cloth merchant named Richard – 'you can call me Dickon' – on my way to York on business.

"Did you *have* to come out on such a bad night as this?" he asked.

I shrugged. "Business is business. If you want to make an honest living, you have no choice but to go where the trade takes you. I must get to York within the next couple of days, or I'll lose my customers. I'll be off as early as I can in the morning."

The landlord kindly arranged to exchange my horse for another, and early the next morning, after a bowl of thick porridge and some thick chunks of brown bread, I set out on my way. The weather had improved tremendously, and as I rode in the direction of Bradford, the skies began to clear and the narrow Pennine tracks became less treacherous. I spent the next night at the White Lamb in Morley, a village half-way between Bradford and Leeds. I thought it was best to avoid the larger towns; I assumed the people in the villages would be less knowledgeable about rebellions and rebels, such as myself.

I was right. No-one asked me any awkward questions. All they were interested in was talking about the weather, sheep farming, and the extortionate price of woollen cloth. The only one who showed any interest in me was one of the barmaids at the tavern. As she cuddled up to me in bed that night, in her small room at the back, she asked me about the city of York.

The furthest she had ever been in her young life was Leeds and Bradford. In between cuddling and caressing her soft, warm body, I made up stories about York, a city I had only visited once, briefly, on route back from the Battle of Marston Moor.

As before, I left early the following morning, and arrived at Pontefract late in the evening. There, I learned more about the rebellion that had never happened. Still pretending that I was a cloth merchant, I began chatting to a couple of customers in the inn where I was staying.

"It's like this," the larger one said. "There was this band of men, plotting an uprising against the government up here in the north."

"Right," his friend nodded. "But the government's men got to hear of it. There's this man called Williamson, *Sir* Joseph Williamson, and I heard he planted a couple of spies among the rebellion's leaders."

"Is that why it failed?"

"Yes, sir. And they also say that this Colonel Blood was involved in it, but they never caught him. He's a lucky sod, I'm telling you. If they had caught him, he'd be in the Tower by now. Ain't that right, Ned?"

Ned nodded. "Aye, or they would have hanged him up here in York. Me, I heard that he's wanted here in England *and* over in Ireland. Lucky will be the bugger that catches him, or tells the authorities where he's hiding. There's a hundred pounds on his head.

What I wouldn't do for a hundred pounds. I could really use that money right now."

"So could I," Will and I said together.

That night, as I lay in bed, I came to the conclusion that England was no safer for me than Ireland had been. While I was flattered to think that my name was being linked with the English rebellion, it meant that Sir Joseph Williamson and his network of spies had not given up looking for me.

There was only one thing left for me to do. I would have to leave England and go abroad. But where? France was no good, I didn't know the language and the same was true for Spain and Portugal. Besides, I didn't like the sound of their methods of torture or their Inquisitions. That left me with the Lowlands. I'd heard that Dutch was similar to English, and although the Dutch were Protestants, they were now busy fighting the English in a series of naval and trade wars. I could not imagine the Dutch authorities handing me over to the English if they caught me. Nevertheless, I reasoned it would still be best if I continued my travels in disguise, using false names and identities along the way.

The following morning, I rose early and left for Hull. I was bound for the docks, where I hoped to find a ship that would take me to the Netherlands and a new life.

Chapter 15
The Netherlands and the Plague

The ship I caught from Hull to Amsterdam was far larger than the ferries that sailed between England and Ireland. These ships needed to be, as the North Sea was a damn sight rougher than the Irish Sea. I must admit, I spent much of the voyage leaning over the side of the ship, vomiting into the swirling grey-green waves below. It was a relief to reach Amsterdam, and sail into Damrack harbour, the line of wharfs near the Dam Square, in the centre of the city.

As I shakily stepped down onto dry land, I looked around to catch my bearings. I could hear a lot of English being spoken, a reminder that although I was in a foreign country, I was not completely safe. As I went looking for a stable, to buy or hire a horse, I decided that I was to be Thomas Hogan from York, a dealer in animal skins and leather. Admittedly, I did not know much about the leather business, but I hoped that, if necessary, my knowledge of farming and my time as a cavalryman would allow me to bluff my way through any awkward situations.

As I walked across Dam Square, I noted the tall houses with their narrow frontage, and the impressive-looking town hall, an edifice I later learned was only fifty years old. I found myself a tavern which looked out onto the square, and bought some bread, cheese, and a tankard of ale. Halfway through my meal, a tubby red-faced man in a maroon coat and beige breeches sat down opposite me and pulled out a news sheet.

"Excuse me, may I ask you a few questions?" I asked him slowly, in English. "My name is Thomas Hogan. I'm from the city of York in England. I have just arrived here, and this is my first time in Amsterdam."

"*Ja, mijnheer*, er, yes, sir. You may ask me. My name is Heer Jan Bakker. I speak your English quite good."

"Ah, so you are a baker?" I smiled.

"*Nee*, I'm a merchant. I supply things for ships. What do you want to know?"

I looked around. "Tell me, Heer Bakker, are all the houses in Amsterdam built of stone? In York, many of them are made of wood and plaster."

"*Ja*, all the houses now must be made of stone. This is er… a rule after the *Groot vuur*, the big fire two

[187]

hundred years ago. It burned down much of the city. It was very sad."

I looked around again. "And why do they have these big hooks sticking out of them at the top? They're not for hanging people, I hope."

"*Nee, nee.* You see, the houses are very er…narrow and so if you want to have something big in your house, like a table, you bring it up with a rope on one of those hooks, *ja*?"

I nodded. "Fascinating. Tell me, sir, is there anywhere close by where I can stay for a few days? I am meeting a business friend here at the end of the week."

He wrote down an address on a piece of paper and explained to me how to get there. "*Ja*," he said. "Amsterdam is good for *bedrijf,* er, business. Look over there. You will see ships from all over the world. They even come here from the New World, from America."

I looked impressed, and indeed I was. It was obviously much busier here than in Dublin or Liverpool.

"But be careful when you walk outside at night," Heer Bakker warned me. "There are sometimes not good men who will try and steal your money, and yes, there are also some not good ladies, *prostitutees,* who will…"

I said that I understood him, then stood up, thanked him and set off for the address he had given me. I found it easily enough, and after paying for a room and going for a walk around the centre of the city, I turned in and went to sleep. The next day, I decided that I would buy a Dutch style coat, hat, shirt, and breeches so as not to attract any attention to myself.

That morning, while I was buying my new clothes, I asked the tailor why so many Dutchmen spoke English so well.

"You see, *mijnheer*," the tailor explained. "We are a small country and we buy and sell all over the world. Also, many people come here from your England and also from France and other places, so if we want to trade with them, we must know how they speak, no? Tell me, do you know any Dutch?"

I shook my head.

"So you see, if I want to sell you these things," he said, pointing to my new clothes. "I have to know your English. *Ja*?"

I nodded.

"We also fight with your country, but this is at sea. We fight about trade, so no-one is hurt here in the city," he added. "But for us, *ja,* trade is very important and that is why we speak your English and other languages."

My sojourn in the Netherlands was one of the most peaceful periods of my life. My only concern was being recognised, and apart from one occasion at the coastal port of Vlissingen, the winter months I spent in the Netherlands passed uneventfully.

One day, while I was walking alongside the

harbour wall in the spring, I saw several warships being made ready. I watched as the sailors loaded them with barrels of water and ale, boxes of food, cannons and the spare parts that ships always seemed to need. As I was idly watching this scene, a man approached me.

"*Pardon, mijnheer, maar zo heet u niet Captain Blot?*"

Although by then I could understand what he was saying, I decided to play dumb with him. "Sorry, I don't understand. Do you want to know the time?"

"*Nee, nee*. I ask you if you are Captain Blot?"

I shook my head. "Who is this Captain Blot? My name is Thomas Hogan. I'm from York, in England."

"Oh, *het spijt me*," he said in his heavy accent. "I'm sorry. I thought you were this Captain Blot."

I smiled. "No, sir, never heard of him. Who is this Captain Blot?"

"He is a bad man. That's what the English think. He fight the King of England."

"No, no. That's not me," I said, perhaps a little too quickly. "I'm a man of peace. I don't like fights. I'm a trader in animal skins. By the way," I continued, wishing to change the subject of the conversation. "Do you live here? This looks like a nice town."

"*Ja, ik woon hier*, er yes, I live here," he nodded and held out his hand. "My name is Andreas Janssen. I am also trader. Trader in food for ships. But come, you should meet my friend, de Ruyter. He is in the navy and he is good for my trade. He like to talk to English people. He talk English better from me. Come, I take you to his house."

An hour later, I was sitting in Michiel de Ruyter's fine house near the sea-front, eating a goodly portion of beef and washing it down with a fine glass of red wine. Andreas was sitting opposite me as our host and his wife, Anna, a comely lady dressed in a white cap and a bright blue dress that matched her eyes, came to join us at the table.

"Ah," de Ruyter said, his dark eyes smiling. "My friend, Andreas, tells me you like our town."

"Ja," I replied, using the little Dutch I had picked up. "It is a very nice city. *Het is een heel leuk stadje.*"

"Ah, so you have learned some Dutch. This is good. *Zeer goed.* Very good."

From that day on, our friendship only grew, even though later, as an admiral in the Dutch navy during the Anglo-Dutch wars, de Ruyter became one of England's worst enemies. This was especially so after the events of June 1667 when he sailed his fleet up the Medway River, almost entered London and captured and burned several of the king's ships.

But that was all in the future. Over the next few months, I continued to visit Michiel whenever I was in Vlissingen and it was on my last visit that I told him I was returning to England.

"All my business deals here are finished," I explained, "and I miss my family."

In reality, my reasoning was that the government and the Duke of Ormonde would have forgotten about me by this time, or so I hoped.

I sailed for England in the spring of 1664, and very quickly became involved with another group of men who were plotting against the monarchy and the establishment. This was a Puritan group known as the Fifth Monarchists, so named because they hoped that, if the monarchy in England proved good and true, the Second Coming would occur. Apart from their hating Catholics, I did not agree with the Fifth Monarchists' religious ideology. But since they also hated the Restoration government that had stolen my land, I decided to throw in my lot with them anyway.

I was first made aware of their group one evening, a few days after I had returned to London. I was sitting near the Tower of London, casually talking to a chubby young man and his friend. He said he owned a small butcher's shop and was complaining about the lack of trade. He blamed the government, and the king.

"I'm telling you," he snarled. "If they hadn't killed my father, I'd be in a much better position today. As soon as I say my name is Venner, everybody turns their back on me."

"Keep your voice down," the other fellow, Arthur, whispered urgently. "You never know who's listening. For all we know, that chap behind you could be one of Williamson's spies."

"Williamson," Venner said more quietly. "If I

had the chance, I'd challenge that bastard Sir Joseph to a duel and finish him off. I'd shoot—"

"Shh!" pleaded Arthur, putting a finger to his mouth. "You'll get yourself hauled into the Tower if the wrong person hears you. Speaking of which, we haven't properly been introduced…" He looked at me suspiciously.

"Fear not," I said quietly. "I'm on your side, and I'm certainly not one of Williamson's spies. I'd have arrested you already if I were. The name's John Hogan. I'm a merchant, visiting from York. Now, tell me, why did the king kill your father?"

Venner looked at Arthur as if to ask whether he should answer my question. Arthur looked me over and then nodded.

"Tell him, James. It can't do any harm. Your father's dead now anyway. They can't hang him twice, can they?"

I moved closer to him as Venner began to talk.

"Have you heard of my father, Thomas Venner?"

"Wasn't he one of those rebels who rose up against the king?" I asked. "I remember hearing about him when I was in Amsterdam."

"Yes, sir. He led a movement against the king and was hanged for it."

"That's right," Arthur added. "Hung, drawn, and quartered two years ago."

"I swear to you, there's no justice in this country anymore. He was a good Christian man, my father. All he wanted was to purify this sick and debauched country."

"What do you mean?"

Venner looked around to check that nobody else was listening, before continuing his story in a low whisper. "My father was one of the leaders of the Fifth Monarchists, you know, the Puritans who first tried to overthrow Cromwell and then the monarchy. He didn't succeed against Cromwell so he waited a few years and then tried to get rid of the king."

"Why? Did the king reclaim your father's land?" I asked.

Venner and Arthur both shook their heads.

"My father believed that this country's new king was sinful and immoral and leading the country away from the true path of the Christian faith," Venner explained.

"I'm guessing he wasn't too impressed with the king carrying on with all those mistresses behind his wife's back?"

Venner's friend nodded. "Yes, and we all reckon that the king is a secret Catholic as well."

"Aye," Venner nodded. "My father thought that this accursed King Charles was a bad example to the people, so he decided that the king would have to die. After all, we'd already gotten rid of his father, so why not him as well?"

"So your father led a rising against him?"

Venner nodded. "At the beginning of January, 1661, he gathered a group of men about him, good

Christians who agreed with him, and they led a rising against the King. They tried to obtain the keys to St. Paul's Cathedral and when that failed, they broke in. Then, the king sent in his troops—"

"But your father held them off," Arthur interrupted. "Allowing him and his men to flee to Highgate, y'know, north of the city."

Venner continued. "My father returned a day or so later, together with me," he added with pride. "And we attacked the king's guard near Threadneedle Street, forcing them to retreat. We thought we were making progress and had a chance of victory. But then everything went wrong. The king's men attacked us again, shooting at us from the roof. That's when they overcame us. My father was wounded nineteen times. *Nineteen* times, can you believe it? Several other men were shot and some even died there."

"I suppose they took your father prisoner?"

"Aye," Venner nodded and looked down. "Two weeks later, he was tried at the Old Bailey, found guilty of treason and hanged. Him and ten others."

"What happened to you?"

"My father told me to run away and be ready to fight again in the future. 'No point in both of us dying today' he said. Those were his last words to me."

I paused before asking my next question. "Does your group, the Fifth Monarchists I mean, still exist? Are they still trying to fight the king?"

Venner and Arthur both looked at each other and nodded.

"We are a much smaller band of men now," Arthur explained. "Only a few dozen. To be honest with you, I'm not sure we are going to be able to do anything. But we're going to damn well try."

Within a few months, I had become one of the leaders of this extreme, Protestant sect, alongside the escaped prisoner and my friend, Captain John Mason, and a stocking-weaver from Durham called John Atkinson. I knew both of these men from my time in Cromwell's army. We used to hold our meetings at a small house in Petty France, Westminster, coming up with a multitude of plans to overthrow the monarchy. But in the end, all our revolutionary planning came to naught. Atkinson had grown weary of forever looking over his shoulder, and one day, after being apprehended by Williamson's men, had disclosed the names and addresses of many of the sect's members, in exchange for his own freedom.

This was the last nail in the coffin for the group and we split up and fled London. I spent some time hiding in the north of England and also paid a visit to Ireland. These travels included a brief visit to see my wife and family. However, I could not stay with them for long as I knew that Sir Joseph Williamson and his agents, as well as the Duke of Ormonde, were still keeping a watchful eye on my house. In the end, I decided that the safest place for me to return to was London. There, I thought, I would easily be able to hide amongst the capital's four-hundred-thousand inhabitants.

*

In the spring of 1665, something completely unexpected happened. The Great Plague struck the city of London. It crept up on us quietly, without warning, like an early morning fog. Suddenly, people were dying and going missing in vast numbers.

"Where's Lord Brondesbury?" I asked one day, referring to a member of the aristocracy I had met casually in the past.

"He's fled the city with the king and his courtiers. They've all gone to Hampton Court."

"And Lady Charlotte Finchley?"

"She's gone with them, like most of the doctors and gentry. Aye, some of them have even fled as far as Salisbury and Oxford."

"Why?"

"For fear of catching this accursed plague. That's why they've been killing off all the cats and dogs. To stop them spreading it and that's why they're lighting these huge bonfires in the streets. They've got to burn off the foul fumes from this evil miasma that's causing it."

From further discussions with friends, I learnt that the plague had first been recorded at St. Giles-in-the Fields, west of the city, and had since spread like wildfire. Some thought it had been sent by the Good Lord to punish the country, especially the king and his court.

"All that dancing, drinking, and debauchery…it's shocking, the king, a married man, carrying on with his mistresses like that. And his courtiers are just as bad. That randy John Wilmot, the Duke of Rochester, never stops! And now we have to pay the price for their wickedness. Shame on them!"

As the weeks went on, the call of 'Bring out your dead!' became an everyday occurrence, and we all became numb to the sight of plague victims being flung into huge death-pits. No burial services were held for these unfortunates. They were simply thrown out as unceremoniously as mouldy potatoes, often having been robbed of their worldly possessions just before death, by those willing to take advantage of their inability to fight back.

I did what I could to survive, wearing a mask whenever I left the house and staying well clear of the houses that bore red crosses upon their doors. The advice given by the few remaining priests and physicians left in the city was to eat powdered unicorn's horn and drink wine, if you were wealthy, and to take opiates and eat toads, if you were poor. From what I could see, none of this helped. As a result I continued to distance myself from infected places as best I was able.

As the plague wore on, the city itself changed its appearance. Fewer people were about and clumps of grass grew up in the cracks between the paving stones. The once bustling capital of England had fast become a ghost town.

The plague grew worse and worse, and in the September of 1665, over seven thousand Londoners had died from the disease. Several times a day, I checked my body for the dreaded buboes, large dark swellings that appeared on the armpits and groin, and looked in the mirror to check that my skin had not broken out in foul-coloured blotches.

"When will this end?" I asked a local baker one weekday morning.

He shrugged. "Either when the Good Lord feels he has punished us enough or when the winter sets in. I remember my grandfather telling me that the last plague, some forty years ago, started to die out when the weather grew colder. Let's pray the same thing happens this time."

Fortunately, his prayers were answered. As winter approached, the weekly death toll decreased, and the king and his court returned to London. People scrubbed the red warnings off their doors, the public bonfires ceased and the mass burial pits were covered over. Later, I discovered that a quarter of the city's population – over one hundred thousand people – had succumbed. But I had not. I had survived.

I took my survival as a sign that God approved of my efforts in trying to rid the country of its wicked leaders and being convinced thus, I travelled north to Liverpool. There, I met Captain Browne, a man who was in the process of planning a whole new series of uprisings against the King and his government.

Chapter 16
Persuading Edmund Ludlow

Captain Browne had been part of my failed plan to attack Dublin Castle, all those years ago, and though our ways had since parted, it was good to see the old soldier again. He had grown stockier and his bushy brown beard of the past was now completely grey. However, his sharp eyes, bulbous nose and ruddy complexion had not changed.

We met on my first evening in Liverpool at his home in the centre of the city. After settling down in his spacious parlour with a glass of port in our hands, we spent at least two hours chatting about old times and how determined we both were to exact our revenge on the Duke of Ormonde.

The following day, Browne introduced me to his friends and fellow-plotters. One of them,

Lieutenant-Colonel William Moore, was another old friend of mine. I knew him from the time when I had tried to capture the Duke of Ormonde at Dublin Castle. As we all sat drinking together in a tavern later that evening, I was surprised to see Philip Alden, another past plotter, join us.

"I heard you were working for the King," I said to him. "You know, telling the authorities about our attack on Dublin Castle."

He shook his head vigorously as he swallowed a glass of claret. "Perish the thought, Tom. What do you think I am? One of His Majesty's agents?"

"Yes, and I—"

Browne interrupted me. "Come, Blood," he said. "Forget your suspicions and let us proceed with our plans."

"Which are?"

"I want to send you and George Ayres – you'll meet him in a day or so – to Dublin. There, you are to make contact with another Irishman, a brewer by trade, named Cooke. You three will be responsible for attacking Dublin Castle again and getting rid of the Duke of Ormonde."

I smiled when I heard this. I was delighted to have the opportunity to complete the task I had set myself years ago. "And what are you going to be doing whilst I am ridding the world of that bastard Duke?" I asked.

Browne pointed to the hand-drawn map on the table in front of him. "We have two agents in Scotland who will prepare the way, by reviving our party up there. Once that's done, the rest of us will march from England up to Scotland, and combine our two groups. Then, when we receive the signal, we will start our uprising in Edinburgh."

"And then what?" Alden asked. "Start more uprisings?"

"Aye, and once we have finished in Scotland, we'll cross over to the north of Ireland to join Tom and his men there."

"Do they know about this in Scotland?" I asked.

Browne nodded. "You'll be supported in Ireland by Captain Sands and a Master Price. I'll tell you where they live later. They've already discussed this revolution at great length and have assured me that they will be fully ready when the time comes. It is time, my friends. A toast, to our success."

We raised our glasses, wished ourselves good fortune and downed more of the captain's fine claret.

Browne continued. "Blood and Moore, as you two are so well-known to the authorities, I suggest that you both travel in disguise."

"I think we can manage that, captain," Moore grinned. "I'm best known for my bald pate, so all I need is a wig. What about you, Tom?"

"Me?" I grinned back. "I like the idea of disguising myself as a priest again. As I recall, not many people refuse a request from a man of the cloth. Especially in Ireland. And besides, a priestly cassock is a wonderful garment in which to hide a sword or a pistol or two."

Captain Browne chuckled. "I like that idea. Disguising yourself as a Catholic priest has a nice sense of irony about it, especially since you'll be attacking the Catholic establishment both here in Britain and in Ireland." He rubbed his hands together as he grinned like a gleeful schoolboy who had just been given an unexpected half-day's holiday. "Yes, now is the time. The Dutch are behind us as well, and may be willing to provide additional funds, troops and ammunition."

"Why would they want to help us?" Moore asked.

"Because they are in the midst of a naval war with our government. They reckon that if we make problems for the king now, he won't be able to use all of his forces against them."

"Ah, so the king will be caught in the middle: attacked from both sides," I concluded. "By us and by the Dutch."

Browne nodded, and we continued to plan the details of our future uprising long into the night.

However, sadly for all our hopes, plotting and planning, our uprising was not to be. Roger Boyle, the Earl of Orrery, and a rival in many ways to the Duke of Ormonde, discovered what we were up to. His spies reported our meetings to him, and he in turn reported them to Sir Henry Bennet, one of the king's closest advisors.

From *my* spies, I learned that Bennet's men thought I was hiding out in one of two places: the home of Colonel Gibby, an old friend who lived in the north of Ireland, or in Dublin with my wife and children. My spies also fed Bennet another story that I was living under a false name somewhere in the south of Dublin.

It was during this time that I learned I was to lose a further five hundred acres of my land, in the mountainous area of Glenmalure, County Wicklow. The land was to be given to Captain Toby Barnes, a man who had served both King Charles the First and the present king 'in Ireland and abroad'.

Knowing this, on one of my brief visits home, I said farewell to my wife, my final words to her on that occasion being 'I don't know where I'm bound, or for how long, and even if I did know, I wouldn't tell you as I don't want you to be forced to lie to anyone'.

I then took the ferry to England, and met up with Browne and his men in Liverpool. After a great deal of discussion, we formed a new plan of action. As a result, I immediately headed south for London. Again, I reckoned that it was easier to hide myself, disguised in the sprawl of London, than remain permanently on the move among the smaller towns and villages of northern Ireland and the north of England.

However, I did not stay in London for long. Soon after arriving there in the spring of 1666 I returned to the Netherlands with a friend of mine, John Lockyer. Our aim was to recruit Edmund Ludlow, a well-known critic of the king and his government. This man had fought on the Parliamentary side during the Civil War and had been one of the judges at the trial of King Charles the First. He had even signed the king's death warrant. After the Restoration, Ludlow had exiled himself to Berne in Switzerland and was now living there under the name of Edmund Philips.

However, when we arrived in the Netherlands, a nasty surprise awaited us. As soon as we left the safety of our ship, Lockyer and I were arrested.

"*Wat is jouw naam*?" a fat official in a dark blue coat and black hat asked us.

"John Hogan," I replied quickly. "And my friend here is John Locksley. We are from York, in England."

"*En waar zijn uw documenten, uw paspoorten*?"

I shrugged. "We don't have any documents or passports, sir. We didn't know we needed them. We will be here in your country just for today. Tomorrow, we are travelling to Switzerland."

He held up his hand and I nudged John to keep quiet. *"Je wacht hier. Ik ga met mijn kapitein-officier praten,"* he said.

He left us standing there under the guard of two soldiers while John asked me to translate for him. I told him about the request for passports, as I watched the fat officer waddle off and then disappear into a quayside office to speak to his superior officer. He returned within five minutes, with his superior.

This time, it was the officer's superior who spoke. He was also wearing a blue coat and a black hat, but they were made of a much finer material than his underling's. In addition, his hat and the sleeves of his coat bore gold rings, showing that he was of higher rank. He had clearly been informed that we were English, for he questioned us in our own language this time.

"My name is Captain De Friess," he said. "What are your names?"

I repeated our names, and where we were from.

He asked us why we had come to Amsterdam.

"We are on our way to Switzerland, for business. We will be leaving here tomorrow," I replied. "We are just passing through your lovely country on the way."

"Where are your travel *documenten,* er, documents? You must be aware that our two countries are at war."

John looked at me and we both shrugged.

"You didn't know you needed them?" the Captain suggested.

"That's right, sir," I replied. "We don't travel much, do we, John?"

John nodded vigorously.

"Him, he doesn't talk?" the Captain asked.

"Yes, I can talk," John said. "But my friend, er, John, can understand Dutch better."

The captain turned to me as he scribbled something down in a large dark brown ledger. "How do you know Dutch?"

"I was here once before, a long time ago, and I have a Dutch friend in York," I smiled. "He's a very nice man of course, and knows all about gin and cheese."

"Hmm, I don't know if I believe your stories. They smell a little," he said, looking at his junior officer. He turned back to us. "You will come with me, until I learn the truth."

"But this *is* the truth," I protested.

"You come with me," he repeated, sternly.

Ten minutes later, we found ourselves locked in a dismal room with only a small, barred window high up. We stayed there for the rest of the day, and as night fell, a guard entered with some hard yellow cheese, two chunks of rough bread, some weak ale, and a blanket for each of us.

"Tom, do you think there's any way we can escape from here? It's dark outside. If we're lucky, nobody will see us." John whispered, after we had finished our evening 'meal'.

"Perhaps," I replied. "You climb up onto my back and see if you can reach the window."

I bent over and Tom clambered up onto my back, but his hands could only reach the lower part of the bars. He tried rattling them but they had been set too deeply into the wall to move. He jumped down and shook his head. There was no escape.

The following morning, after an uncomfortable night's sleep, we were awoken by a loud banging on the door, followed by the sounds of jangling keys and our prison door scraping open. A thin soldier with a drooping black moustache handed us our breakfast, a meal that was almost identical to the previous night's supper.

"*Jouw eten,*" he said. "*Wacht hier.*"

I couldn't help but chuckle when he said '*wacht hier*'. Wait here. Where else were we going to go? When I explained this to John, he frowned.

"It's not funny, Tom," John said. "I don't want to rot in a stinking Dutch jail. Don't forget, we're at war with them now, and if that captain fellow decides we're spies, *this* will be our fate…" He crossed his grubby finger across his throat, signalling death.

"All is not lost, my friend," I said. "They haven't done anything to us yet. We've just got to pray that I've still got the luck of the Irish with me. Remember how I survived Marston Moor? Trust me, we'll survive this as well." I gave John a pat on the back.

We spent what I estimated to be an hour playing a children's game with some stones that we found on the floor. Then we heard the sound of approaching boots, followed by jangling of keys and our prison door scraped open again. Facing us was the officer who had first arrested us, accompanied by three, rifle-bearing soldiers. He ordered us to come with him to his superior's office.

A short while later we stood facing Captain De Friess across his wide desk. Another man, who I thought I had seen the day before, was standing at the side of the room. He winked at me, but said nothing.

"I have made inquiries about you two," the captain began. "And I have learned that you are not English spies. This man here, Master Josiah Arnold, tells me that you are his friends, and that it is true what you told me. He said that you are on your way to Switzerland. To Lausanne, or somewhere near there. You are free to go."

Ten minutes later, I was sitting in a tavern, facing the harbour, with John and Josiah. As we raised our tankards in a toast to our release, I asked Josiah what had happened.

"I come here fairly often," he explained. "And I know Captain De Friess quite well. He told me about you, and I realised that I needed to get you both out. Fortunately, the Captain believed my story. So, now you are free. But come," he said, draining his drink. "Let us leave Amsterdam now, before De Friess or anyone else changes their minds. After all, we are on the enemy side at the moment."

It took the three of us well over two weeks to reach our destination in Switzerland, passing through Cologne, Frankfurt, and Stuttgart along the way. We had no more problems with passports or officials, and were very pleased to arrive at Edmund Ludlow's comfortable house in Lausanne.

Even before he greeted us, he told us to call him Edmund Phillips. "I don't use the name Ludlow here, it's Phillips or Edmund, nothing else. Now that's out of the way, welcome to my humble home."

That night, as we were enjoying the first good meal we had eaten for some time, we talked about our mission. We wanted to persuade our host to return to England with us to take on a leading role in our next uprising against the king.

"We'll return home via Paris," I said. "All of us, together with Algernon Sidney, who we will pick up on the way. Then, afterwards—"

Ludlow shook his head. "No, no, colonel. I cannot do that," he said. "I'm fifty years old and I don't need any more adventures in my life. I fought at Edgehill, as you did. I fought at Newbury, and I was present at the siege of Limerick."

"So I've heard," I answered. "But—"

"And in case you didn't know," Ludlow continued, now looking at Josiah. "There's still a royal warrant out for my execution. The king has not forgotten that I was one of those who, like you, Master Arnold, signed the warrant for his father's execution. I know that all happened more than fifteen years ago, but His Majesty has a long and vengeful memory."

"But, Edmund, don't you think that we should at least try—"

"No, I don't, Tom," he replied. "I doubt if Sidney will join you either; His Majesty is still after *his* blood as well. Master John Lisle, who also had a hand in the king's execution, was killed not far from here two years ago by three Royalist agents. Knowing that, I wish to keep my head down and I have no desire to be next on the list."

I said that I understood his feelings and was about to try another way of persuading him, when he held up his hand.

"Besides, gentlemen, I am now busy writing my memoirs and several other pieces. I don't have time for such dangerous escapades. Do you understand me?"

We all nodded in resignation. Our mission had been in vain.

"I'm living here now in Vevey," he explained, now somewhat more forcefully. "I like it here very much and at last I have found peace and quiet. I believe I have done my best for England, and if that didn't achieve anything, then so be it. So, gentlemen, let us change the subject of this conversation as this discussion about my returning to England is over. Now," he continued, looking straight at me. "Let's settle down. I will ask Martha to bring in our evening meal."

The three of us left Vevey the following morning, feeling disappointed that we had not succeeded in our mission. I had expected so much more from Edmund Ludlow, especially given all the glowing tributes I had heard about him. His rejection of our cause had wounded me greatly.

We decided to head back to England and arrived in London one week later. I assumed my false name, John Hogan, again; trimmed my hair and moustache and wore a wide brimmed hat and high collared coat whenever I ventured out into the city. After spending a mere three days in London, John and I made our way back to Liverpool, to report our failure to Captain Browne.

Browne was less downhearted than I had expected. "Not to worry, gentlemen," he said. "When I sent you, I had already considered that I might be sending you on a fool's errand. I knew that Ludlow was living quite happily abroad, but I was hoping that you, Blood, would be able to use your silvery Irish tongue to persuade him to join us."

I smiled at this expression of faith in my abilities.

"We shall have to go down a different route," he continued. "I reckon we are better off trying to start an uprising in London itself rather than up here in the north or over in Ireland. There, in his own capital, I believe the king will feel the threat of our power more keenly."

But our plans to take over London were destined not to be, for fate, in the form of an unexpected fire in a baker's oven, would soon put an end to our present plotting.

Chapter 17
The Great Fire

Sunday the second of September 1666 was a regular ordinary night in London...until it wasn't. On this night, Thomas Farriner went to bed as usual, in the room above his bakery on Pudding Lane, having assured his wife, as he did every night, that he had raked out the last of the glowing embers and had closed all the oven doors.

But something was not as it should be. A couple of hours later, he and all of his household were woken by choking fumes, and within the next half-hour, Thomas, his family, and his neighbours were all standing in a line outside the bakery, throwing buckets of water at the ever-increasing flames. Their brave efforts were to no avail. Soon, the fire had reduced the houses in Pudding Lane to piles of glowing ashes and it did not take long for the remains of the fire to ignite the whole area. The wooden houses, packed back to back, were an easy target for the voracious red and orange tongues of flame. The densely crowded dwellings, together with the nearby warehouses full of tar, wood, oil, and pitch, were all the same to the fire. They existed to be consumed.

I was woken at three in the morning, by shouts coming from the street below. As I groggily tried to understand what was happening, I became aware of the smoke and the sounds of the flames crackling outside. As I got out of my bed I saw a bright orange light flickering across the walls of my room. I had rented lodgings near St. Paul's Cathedral, several hundred yards to the west of Pudding Lane. Here, I had thought that my disguised self would be safe. I had not expected to be threatened by an ever-growing blaze, but rather by the king and his agents.

I dressed quickly, grabbed my money pouch and some counterfeit papers – showing that I was John Hogan, a merchant from York – and rushed out of the house. Downstairs felt like the inside of a furnace and panic was spreading as quickly as the flames.

"All my jewellery is in there!" a fat lady in her nightdress wailed, pointing to a burning house.

"My son! My son! Where is he?" screamed another woman.

"Look over there! St. Catherine's is on fire!" someone shouted.

"So is St. Laurence's!" someone else yelled.

"Everyone listen," I shouted, using the tone I had used in the army. "We need to try to stop the fire. Everyone fill as many buckets with water as you can. There have been fires before. We must not give up!"

But it was no use. The roaring fire and the heat eventually forced us to retreat. We could not get close enough to the flames to throw our buckets of water. I could smell my singed hair and I realised that my clothes were also beginning to burn as I tried to lead my bucket brigade. I swiftly threw some water over myself and stepped back behind a wall, where I thought I would be sheltered from the flames. My safety was short-lived. Within moments, I heard the wood-and-mortar wall crack and quickly I ran away from the approaching blaze.

"We need to pull down the houses and use the gap as a barrier. That should stop it," a man in some sort of uniform declared. "You," he shouted at me. "Go and find some long bars and hooks so we can pull down those houses over there. Quickly man! Get to it!"

Feeling that I was doing something useful at last, I rushed down to the river, grabbed some long hooked poles from a moored ship, and ran back to the man in uniform.

"You can't pull down that house," a man shouted at me over the noise of the flames. "It's mine!"

"Too late," I shouted back. "Either we pull it down or the fire will burn it up."

"But all my goods and—"

I never heard what he was going to say, for he

was quickly pushed out of the way by a burly sailor carrying another long-handled hook.

I spent all night pulling down houses and throwing water at blazing buildings, never once worrying that someone might recognise me. Not that anyone did. There was too much smoke to see people's faces easily. I did my best to fight the fire, shouting out orders and organising the panicked crowds into efficient teams of bucket wielders. But our efforts were in vain. The fire continued to burn, consuming the city, and there was so much smoke that it was impossible to tell whether it was night or day.

Eventually, I slunk away, exhausted, heading west in the direction of Whitehall. When I could walk no further, I threw myself down under a shady tree, and promptly fell asleep. I woke up hours later to a sky that glowed an unearthly orange. A thick black pall of smoke hung over the city and I could still hear shouting and the crackling of flames. Then, as I looked back towards the city, I noticed something strange. Something was missing. I stared in horror at the vast blank space on the horizon. St. Paul's Cathedral, that once massive church with its famous square tower pointing up to the heavens, was no longer there. It had been reduced to a pile of glowing embers and smoking rubble. The city's most important church was no more.

Getting up, I stumbled down to the river, and after persuading a sailor to sell me some meat, bread, and a flask of ale, I hurried back towards the fire. A large group of men were doing their best to create new firebreaks between the houses that were still standing, while others continued trying to extinguish the ever hungry flames.

"Here, Your Majesty, take this pole," I heard someone shout.

"Aye, and give this one to the prince. It's longer than the one he's using now."

Your Majesty? The prince? What was happening here? Then I saw them. The king, King Charles the Second, and his brother, James, the Duke of York, were helping to pull down houses, trying to prevent this gigantic blaze from destroying their beloved city. Later, I discovered that in addition to helping fight the fire, the king had ordered food to be sent to the crowds of homeless victims, who were now sleeping out in the open in Moorfield, north of the city.

The fire burned for four days, during which time I tried my best to play my part as a fireman. In addition to the destruction of St. Paul's, thirteen thousand houses, nearly ninety churches and many public buildings were destroyed. Most of the city's population were rendered homeless and, at the height of the fire, the orange sky over the blazing city could be seen from over forty miles away.

As I walked amongst the camps of displaced homeowners, I heard several rumours saying that it was the Catholics or the Jews who had started the fire. The Jews had only recently been allowed to return to England from the Netherlands, and given that we were currently at war with the Dutch, they were the obvious scapegoats.

"No, no," I heard one old greybeard say. "It wasn't the Jews. It was the Good Lord. D'you remember those stories from the Bible about God punishing the wicked by sending down fire and brimstone? Well, that's what happened."

I looked quizzically at his wrinkled face with its white wisps of beard.

"You don't believe me?" he asked. "Think about it. Last year, He sent the plague, just like the plague He sent the ancient Egyptians in the Book of Exodus. But our godless king and his court didn't take heed, so now He's sent this fire. Perhaps now His Majesty will put aside his whores and his immoral court. You'll see if I'm right or not."

I thanked him, and was about to turn away, when he called me back.

"Listen, young man," he said, showing his rotting yellow teeth. "How well do you know your scriptures?"

I shrugged.

"It's all written in the Book of Revelations," he began. "Chapter thirteen, verse eighteen. Just listen carefully to what it says. '*Let him that hath understanding count the number of the beast: for it is the number of a man; and his number is six hundred, three score and six*'."

"So?"

"So, don't you see?" he asked, as though I was his foolish pupil. "That number: six hundred, three

[218]

score and six. It's this year!"

"What d'you mean? It's 1666."

"Exactly," he almost shouted. "And *that* is proof that the Good Lord brought this Great Fire, as well as last year's plague. Just think on it, young man. It's all written down in the Good Book."

I promised him that I would think about it and hurriedly left before he could tell me any more about why London had suffered these two terrible tragedies.

After that I remained in London for three quiet months, lying low in my newly rented room, and making occasional visits to the Green Tree, the local tavern. There, one of the regulars, a Scotsman called Jamie McDonald, with whom I had become friendly, told me about several small rebellions that had broken out near Glasgow.

"Aye," he said, his eyes glistening. "They're against the government and against the king as well. I canna tell you who's leading them but I've heard that they're certainly making a lot of bother for the king's men up there."

This news was music to my ears, and two days later, I left London for Scotland, hoping that I would arrive in time to take part, and perhaps even play a leading role in one or more of these uprisings.

This latest rebellion I learned had started in an unexpected way. A group of the king's soldiers in Dalry, a small town between Glasgow and the south-west coast, had started bullying an old man about not paying his fines. As he was trying to fend off his attackers, four local townsmen attacked the soldiers, shot one of them in the stomach and taken the old man away with them.

The Scottish uprising had grown from there, and not long after I showed up, two hundred of us rode south to Dumfries, on a mission to capture and imprison Sir James Turner, the local military commander. When we finally managed to catch the bastard, he was still wearing his nightgown.

"No, no, please! Allow me to dress myself!" he pleaded.

"You'll go with your men as you are," one of our men jeered. "Let them see how useless their commander really is."

From Dumfries, the word spread over the southern hills of Scotland like a fog, and soon, two thousand others had joined us. To my disgust, they still insisted that they were loyal to the king and that they were only rebelling because they could not accept his Church in Scotland.

"We want our Presbyterian rule back," they demanded. "And aye, we want all our sacked ministers to be returned to their kirks."

Of course, the king's officers in Scotland refused to stand for this and decided to put down this insurrection before it could get out of hand. On the twenty eighth of November 1666, the two sides met at Rullion Green in the Pentland Hills, south-west of Edinburgh, ready to do battle.

"Where are all our men?" I asked one of our

officers as I surveyed our ranks. "There can't be two thousand here. I doubt we've got even one thousand."

"The rest must have deserted," he replied.

"Dastardly cowards!" I spat. "Won't they fight for their religion?"

The officer shrugged. What else could he say?

"At least we have a good defensive position," I said as I looked out over the rough open land below us. "We should be able to put up a good fight here. They'll have to charge us uphill. If we're lucky, they'll have no energy left by the time they reach us."

Soon after this I saw my prediction come true. The king's men, under the command of Lieutenant General Dalziel, charged up the hill where we had made our stand. Few of them made it, and those that did were quickly shot or bayonetted. The others rapidly retreated. Sometime later, Dalziel ordered another attack, but this came to a similarly swift end as we were able to drive them back.

My only concern now was that Dalziel might order a third attack. The last two attacks had cost us several men which were critical to our cause and we could not afford to lose any more. As I watched the enemy regroup at the base of the hill, my stomach sank.

He must have given his men a truly encouraging talk, for they charged up that hill like young lions, their eyes burning with determination. We desperately tried to fight them off as we defended our hilltop advantage, but the overwhelming disparity in our numbers and their better training proved to be too much for us. I saw dozens of our men fall, and in the descending gloom of the late November twilight, I saw their broken and wounded bodies lying in the rough grass all over the place. I easily counted off at least fifty of our men and saw most of the others flee in the oncoming darkness.

As I cast aside my military cloak, I noticed that my old fighting friend, Andrew McCormack, was lying there among the dead. He had plotted with me to capture Dublin Castle and assassinate the Duke of Ormonde, all those years ago. I made a quick sign of the cross over his bloody remains and, grabbing his pouch full of coins and his Bible, I disappeared into the darkness. Fortunately, I was able to escape. Many were not so lucky. The following day, disguised as John Hogan, a merchant from York, I heard that Dalziel's men had captured one hundred and twenty of our Scottish Presbyterians.

"Och aye," an old man sitting by the wayside told me. "And tha's not the half of it! Another five hundred of the poor bastards were killed. Aye, anyone who managed to escape that night was bloody lucky, that's all I can say. Bloody lucky."

A few days later, I heard tell that Dalziel had decided to make an example of the 'rebels' as he called them. Fifteen of my men were hung, drawn, and quartered in the middle of the town square; two of them had only just turned eighteen. What had happened to them truly shattered me and I decided that

[222]

the time had come for me to return south. The smell of defeat was everywhere and every person I spoke to always gave the same answer.

"Aye, we lost this fight, but there'll be another one yet. You mark my words. That you can count on."

"When?" I would ask.

"Don't know, but it'll be. You canna keep us Scots down forever."

Then they would shrug, shake their heads, and continue with their drinking.

Chapter 18
Rescuing Captain Mason

I returned to London in time to discover that my friend and fellow conspirator, Captain John Mason, was now rotting in a cell in Newgate prison, and was soon to be taken to York to stand trial. He had been rounded up with several others by the king's spymaster, Sir Joseph Williamson, and had been charged with treason for his part in the failed northern rebellion. When my old friends Captain John Lockyer, a member of the Fifth Monarchists, and Timothy Butler, a past quartermaster, told me what was due to happen, my immediate reaction was that we could not let Captain Mason hang.

"What are you going to do about it?" Lockyer asked when the three of us met in my room the evening I returned to the capital.

"What do you mean 'What are *you* going to do about it'?" I replied. "It's what *we* are going to do."

"Which is?"

"Rescue him, somehow," I answered. "Do you know anything about their plans to transport Mason to York?"

Lockyer nodded. "After crossing his palm with some silver, I learned from one of the guards at Newgate that they are taking him up there next week, together with William Leving."

"The government agent?" I asked.

Lockyer nodded again. "Aye. They want to use Leving as a prosecution witness, to give evidence against Mason. Leving will do anything to make some money. He claimed that the government hadn't paid him enough for his services, so he became a highwayman. Unfortunately for him, he wasn't a very good one, so naturally, when he was offered the chance to make some more money at York, he agreed."

"And did your friendly guard tell you anything else?" I asked Lockyer.

"Aye. He said that the captain and Leving will be escorted to York via the Great North Road. A party of about eight soldiers will be guarding them under the command of an officer called William Darcy—"

"He's no officer," Butler interrupted. "He's a mere corporal, but he's an ambitious bastard. I don't know why they've given him this job, but I'm sure that he'll do everything and anything to make sure his prisoners arrive in one piece."

I grinned. "Well, we are just going to have to make sure they don't, arrive that is." I poured three glasses of red wine and handed one to each of them. "I would like to propose a toast."

"What for?" Butler asked.

"We are going to rescue Captain Mason," I replied. "That's what friends are for, aren't they? To help out when necessary."

We raised our glasses in unison, and swore that we would do our best to rescue our old friend.

The remainder of the evening was spent talking about horses, how and where to best ambush Darcy and his men and where we would hide Mason once we had freed him.

"What about Leving?" Lockyer asked.

"We'll shoot him," I immediately replied. "He's a rat and doesn't deserve to live."

Neither Lockyer nor Butler protested.

The week following our discussion, we took turns noting the movement of prisoners in and out of Newgate, all of whom were always guarded by half a dozen soldiers or more. Our vigil was finally rewarded when, after several days, I saw a party of red-coated soldiers and two men in brown shabby jackets canter out of the prison gates. One of them was Captain Mason. Disguised as a poor man, no one paid me any heed as I loitered around the prison entrance, pretending to beg. My horse was tied to a tree, around the corner from the prison.

As soon as I saw them leave, I shuffled over to

my horse, so as not to draw attention to myself, threw my stained jacket into my saddlebag and galloped off to meet Lockyer and Butler. In no time at all the three of us had sighted our target and began following Corporal Darcy's armed escort as they travelled north.

To prevent our quarry from becoming suspicious, we changed our pattern of travel, sometimes riding as a threesome, sometimes riding as a pair and a single horseman. To make our deception even more convincing, I made sure that we wore different coloured riding coats at different times of day so that they did not realise they were being followed by the same riders all the time. I also counted on the fact that it was not unknown for travellers heading north up the Great North Road to do so in groups. After all, it was a wise precaution, given the ever-present threat of highwaymen and other nasty characters. At night, we would sleep in rotation at the same roadside tavern that our quarry used, one of us always keeping a watchful eye on Mason and company.

I assumed that Corporal Darcy had been informed about Mason's successful escape from the king's guards in the past, as I noticed that his horse was tied by a rope to one of the soldier's horses, meaning that Mason could not try to escape.

On our fifth day out of London, as we were riding past Pontefract Castle, in Yorkshire, Lockyer brought his horse alongside mine.

"Tom, we should carry out our plan soon. We

are but twenty miles from York, and once there, it will be impossible to rescue the captain."

"I know. We should attempt to free him just before sunset. That way, it will be dark when we make our escape, making it harder for them to give chase. We just have to hope that they stop at an isolated tavern on the way. The last thing we want is for Darcy's soldiers calling for reinforcements."

Our luck was in. Late that afternoon, Darcy decided to take a break in their journey. They stopped at a small tavern and all of his men, including Mason and Leving, went inside, leaving one soldier outside to look after their horses. When they left an hour later, Darcy, for some reason unknown to me, decided to split his men into two groups. He and four others would take Mason and Leving with them, leaving the others to follow on soon after.

We immediately set off to attack the second group, and succeeded in dismounting and injuring two of them. However, the third man managed to escape, and charged ahead to catch up with Darcy's prison party.

"What are we going to do now?" Butler asked.

I stopped to think for a moment and then looked around at the surrounding flat countryside.

"Let's get ahead of Darcy and his men, and finish them off before they reach York."

Galloping fast along little-used side lanes and tracks, we soon found ourselves ahead of Darcy's men. Just as they were coming around a narrow lane, between Wentbridge and Darrington, they found themselves facing me, alone on my horse. Lockyer and Butler were waiting behind the bushes ready to ambush Darcy's group.

Holding my pistol in one hand and my sword in the other, I shouted, "Darcy, hand over your prisoner, or you are all dead men."

"Get out of our way," Darcy shouted back. "We are on the king's business."

As he said this, I caught Mason's eye and saw him grin.

"Hand Captain Mason over," I shouted again. "I don't want to kill any of you, but I will if I have to."

Hearing this, Darcy pulled out his sword and made ready to attack me. That was all the signal that Lockyer and Butler needed. They jumped out of the wayside bushes, fired their pistols and charged Darcy's men from the rear. The guards were completely taken by surprise. As I charged in from the front, I saw that a couple of Darcy's men had already fallen off their horses and were writhing on the ground.

In the sudden surge forward I made as I charged, the girth of my saddle, which had not been tightened properly, suddenly loosened itself and I fell off my horse. Seeing this, two of Darcy's men rushed towards me, aiming to cut me down, but being an experienced soldier, I was on my feet within seconds. Brandishing my longsword, I very quickly made them retreat. I tried to mount my horse again, but the loose saddle slipped once more and I found myself standing between two of Darcy's men. One of them was pointing his pistol at me, the other was holding a sword.

Lunging forwards, I swung my sword in a wide arc and knocked the pistol out of the first guard's hand. I must have cut him badly, for he grabbed his bloody right hand with his left and screamed in agony as he rolled over in the mud. His fellow soldier ignored his plight and tried to run me through with his sword. However, Mason, who had cut himself free, flung himself off of his horse and jumped onto my would-be killer, grabbed his sword and stabbed him in the chest. The wounded guard fell into a muddy puddle, groaned as his hands clutched the front of his bloodstained jacket.

"Tom! Behind you!"

I whirled around to find the last remaining guard swinging his sword above his head, ready to cut me down. I jabbed my own sword upwards, catching him between the legs. He collapsed on the spot like a newly felled tree, yelling in agony and cupping his crotch. I kicked his blade aside and rammed my own sword through his stomach.

Free from immediate danger, or so I thought, I grabbed hold of the saddle of one of the guard's horses and hoisted myself up, turning the horse about to face my companions. Before I could see what was now happening, I was knocked backwards. I felt a stinging blow between my eyes and blood began to flow down my face.

I shook my head, trying to focus my eyes. "What happened?"

"That bastard threw his pistol at you," Mason replied, pointing to one of Darcy's men lying still on the ground.

Wiping the blood out of my eyes with my cravat, I rode over to where the fallen man lay. Just as I was about to deal with him, Mason rode up behind me.

"Spare him, Tom. He was the only one of them who showed me any kindness."

Hearing that, and seeing me move my sword away from his stomach, the guard scrambled up, looked at Mason for a moment and scurried away. No doubt he was thanking his former prisoner for saving his life.

Mason glanced down at my sword hand. "Tom, you're cut badly. And your other hand as well. Doesn't it hurt?"

I looked down at my lacerated hands. I had been so preoccupied with the rescue mission that my mind had blocked out the pain, but now that the danger was over, they hurt like the devil. I stuck my hand into the saddle bag of the soldier's horse and found a piece of soft cloth. Ripping it in two, I bound my wounded hands and looked around.

"Mason, where's the other prisoner? I can't see him."

"Who? Leving? He fled as soon as the fighting started. I saw him racing over towards that old farmhouse over there." Mason pointed to a tumbledown building to the south. "I suppose Darcy will send a couple of his men to bring him back. He needs to turn up at York with at least one of his prisoners, for his own sake. As for me, I'll be off now. I'll thank you properly when I see you in London."

That left me with Lockyer and Butler.

"I think it's time we made ourselves scarce as well," Lockyer said, wiping the blood off his sword and thrusting it back into his scabbard. "I don't fancy still being here when Darcy has finished seeing to his wounded men."

Butler nodded in agreement. "Come, Tom. We've done what we set out to do, so let's get moving. It'll be night soon and Darcy won't have much chance of finding us in the dark."

With a quick backward glance, to see Darcy leaning over one of his men quite a distance away, the three of us followed Mason and set off for the south at a fast gallop.

Our first stop was in a small woodland clearing, where we cleaned ourselves up and changed our coats and jackets.

"I don't want to be recognised in this one," Butler said, as I washed my bloody hands and face in a small stream.

"Remember," I said, as we cantered south. "We are three friends from York who are on our way to a friend's wedding in Chesterfield. I'll be Colonel Hogan, and you two will be men who served with me

[232]

in the army."

"Which side?"

"That'll depend on who we are speaking to," I grinned.

We continued our way south for another two hours, spending the night in a miserable tavern near Rotherham. We left early the next morning, after persuading the tavern-keeper's wife to give us some bread, cheese, and apples instead of breakfast. An hour after we set off, I suggested we split up.

"It will be safer that way," I said. "If Darcy sets up a hue-and-cry looking for three men, we're more likely to be left alone if we are two and one, not three."

After a brief discussion, we decided that I would go alone and that we would all meet at the Old Oak Tree inn at Shoreditch, the following Wednesday evening. However, my journey south took longer than I had anticipated. Despite my casual remarks to my friends about the wounds I had sustained rescuing Captain Mason, the continuous jogging up and down on a horse did not help the healing process. By the time I reached Norton, in south Yorkshire, I was feeling very weak.

Fortunately, my old army friend, Captain Robert Armstrong, lived in the next village. He had been an army surgeon in the past and had served with me in the south-west. I was sure that he would know how to tend to my wounds. While I was there, I learned from Armstrong's grapevine that Leving had decided not to escape in the end, but had surrendered himself back to Corporal Darcy.

"He had to really," Armstrong said to me that evening as we were discussing my rescue mission. "He was a government informer. He knew that running away again would only result in him being hanged."

"True," I said. "But now he can disclose all sorts of details about me, Lockyer and Butler."

Armstrong nodded solemnly. "I didn't want to tell you earlier, Tom, especially when you were so weak, but now that you've recovered, you need to read this."

He handed me a news sheet. Written on the front page, under the crest of King Charles the Second, was a long proclamation.

By the King.

A Proclamation for the Discovery and Apprehension of John Lockyer, Timothy Butler, Thomas Blood, commonly called Captain Blood, John Mason, and others.

Charles R.

The closely printed page went on to say...

...we have been informed that John Lockyer, Timothy Butler, and Captain Blood, with several other persons, did lately and in a most riotous and rebellious manner, at Darrington near Wentbridge, in the county of York, violently set upon and assault the guard entrusted with the care of conducting one John Mason,

a prisoner for treason, from our Tower of London to our city of York, in order to conduct his trial there. Having killed and desperately wounded several of the said guard...

...and that as a result...

...we do hereby further declare that one hundred pounds sterling shall be given and paid by us to any person or persons, as recompense for their service, who shall apprehend and bring in the said Lockyer, Butler, Blood, and Mason, or any of their accomplices in the said rescue.

"Hmm, so that means that now I'm an outlaw and that there's two hundred pounds on my head," I said to Armstrong. "That's one hundred more than the last time," I said with some sort of pride.

"Aye. As soon as you can, you should start moving south. It's not that I object to looking after you here," he added. "But it isn't a good idea to stay here in the village. Anyone new here sticks out, and there'll always be someone who wants to make a lot of money blabbing to the authorities."

I left early the next morning, arriving in London by the end of the week. After making some cautious enquiries I found out that my wife had made two major changes in her life: she had changed her name to Mary Weston and that she had moved from Ireland to the neighbourhood of Shoreditch in London.

Her new residence was over an apothecary's shop near one of the main roads leading north out of London.

It was not long before I was reunited with her and my children. I was impressed to see how much my eldest son, Thomas, had matured while I was away. He told me that he was now apprenticed to an apothecary in Southwark and that his ambition was to set up his own apothecary one day. The path of the Blood family had changed so much within my lifetime. I wondered what other changes the coming years might bring.

Chapter 19
Ambushing the Duke of Ormonde

Having seen that my wife and children were happily settled down in Shoreditch, I decided to leave London again.

"Why?" Maria asked late one night, after an exhausting session of love-making.

"Because, my dear, I am beginning to feel the tightening of His Majesty's noose around my neck."

"What do you mean?"

"I mean that people are beginning to notice my presence. I am sure some swarthy fellow was following me when I was walking down the High Street this morning when I went out to buy some meat pies."

"Did you see him again later?"

"Yes. When I left the shop he was standing on

the other side of the street pretending to read a news sheet."

"How do you know he was pretending, Tom? Perhaps he really was."

"He was holding it upside-down."

"Has this sort of thing happened before?"

"I think so, my dear. I had a strong feeling that someone was following me when I was in the market yesterday. Every time I looked behind me, he was there. The same swarthy looking fellow, in a long brown coat."

"Perhaps it was merely a coincidence."

I shook my head. "No, Maria. That would be too much of a coincidence."

"So, where will you go this time? Back up north? Back to Ireland?"

"No, to neither of those places. I'm going to Romford, actually."

"Romford? In Essex?"

"Yes. One of the sergeants who served with me in the army lives there and I've got word that he would like to see me."

"But won't you stick out there, like you would have done if you'd stayed up there in Norton?"

"Perhaps. But if life becomes too hot there, I can always come back here. After all, Romford is less than twenty miles away."

"What will you do there?"

"Fear not, my love. I'll figure something out."

And I did. After two weeks in Romford, I had already settled into my new character. Taking a break from disguising myself as a man of the cloth, I had decided to become Doctor Ayliff, or if necessary, Doctor Allen. I would use the medical knowledge I had acquired during my years in the army to tend to the sick and injured of Essex. To my surprise, I was successful, and most of the people I treated did indeed recover under my allegedly medical hands. My only concerns during this period of my life were that one of my patients might die or that one of my former army acquaintances would appear and divulge my secret. Fortunately, the latter worry was the only one that came to pass and it happened only once. This was when a local pig farmer came to see me about treatment for a nasty gash on his right leg.

"Doctor Ayliff you said your name was?" he began.

I nodded as I wrapped a bandage around his leg.

"That's strange," he said looking at me very intensely. "You look exactly like this officer who I knew in the army. Fought with him at the Battle of Naseby. Good man he was, but he disappeared soon after the battle and I never saw him again."

I shrugged. "Well, I think I have a common enough sort of face," I laughed. "And as for the army, I was wounded soon after the king declared war on

Parliament, so that was the end of my military career."

"Where did you serve?" he persisted.

"In Cornwall, but only for a couple of months."

"And you don't have a twin brother or anything like that?"

I shook my head, quickly finished his treatment, and told him that I had to leave immediately to treat a sick widow near Hornchurch. I left him by my front door, scratching his head, muttering that he was sure he had seen me before.

Despite taking on a caregiving role in society, my determination to have revenge on the Duke of Ormonde remained strong. Twenty years had passed since he had confiscated my lands, but I could never forgive him for depriving me of a large income and the possibility of leaving my family with a healthy legacy.

By now, it was the winter of 1670, and the duke was sixty years old; a married man with seven children. He was His Majesty's Lord High Steward, as well as the Chancellor of the University of Oxford. But none of that concerned me. All I wanted was revenge and, if possible, to recover some or all of my lost estates and the money that went with them.

One evening, during one of my visits to London from Romford, I was having a drink with my oldest son, Thomas, at the Bull Head tavern in Charing Cross. Just as I was about to order us two meat pies, six tall, dishevelled men burst into the tavern and demanded some drink. They were all panting heavily.

"Father, d'you know who those men are?"

Thomas murmured.

"No, who are they?"

"They're the Duke of Ormonde's men. They run alongside his carriage as bodyguards and shout 'Make way for the Duke of Ormonde' and all that."

"Why do they run alongside? Doesn't he allow them to ride on the front or the back where bodyguards usually ride?"

"No, father. The duke has put iron bars on the back of his carriage so that they can't ride there. The only one who's allowed up front is his driver. Everyone else who's guarding him has to run alongside."

"So that's why they're so out of breath," I said. "Poor bastards, having to run like that just to keep that accursed duke alive. All I can say is that he's lucky that I'm not one of his men. I'd never stand to be treated like that."

Thomas nodded in agreement. "You know, they come here most nights after they've taken him to his mansion."

"Most nights?"

Thomas nodded again. "You can tell the time by them. They come in at the same time every night, exhausted and thirsty after all that running."

An idea began burning in my head. "Listen, Tom. Be here on Thursday night at the same time as now. I may have something to tell you about the duke and his carriage."

"What are you going to do?"

[241]

I put my finger to my lips. "I'm not sure yet, son, but I'll tell you when we next meet."

With that, we parted, the ideas in my head whirling as I planned out my next meeting with James Butler, the Duke of Ormonde, one of His Majesty's most important officers and servants.

The next day I met with my old friend, Lieutenant Colonel William Moore, two past Fifth Monarchists, Captain Richard Halliwell, Bill Smith, and another friend from the past, Master Simons.

"What's the problem, Thomas?" Moore asked, as he helped himself to a plate of pasties. "What are you cooking now?"

"Aye," Halliwell winked as he played with his long black moustache. "You wouldn't have asked us here just to ply us with tankards of ale for nothing. I know you."

"Mc too," Smith said.

Master Simons nodded.

"All right, my merry men," I grinned. "You are right. I have a new plan, a new treat in store for the Duke of Ormonde."

"Again?" Moore asked. "Wasn't that fiasco at Dublin Castle enough?"

"No, it wasn't. And besides, this time, it won't be a fiasco. It's going to be well planned and it's going to *work*!"

"Alright, Tom," Moore said, looking at the others. "We're with you. What's your plan this time?"

I looked around carefully, made sure that no

one was within listening range and told my friends to come and sit closer to the table. I pushed the tankards and the plate of pasties aside and placed a small sketch map in front of them

"That's not far from here," Simons said. "I can see Piccadilly and St. James's Street. Tom, what's that square with a cross in it at the end of St. James Street?"

"That's the duke's house," I replied.

"What, that big one with the black iron gates and the porters' lodge?"

"The very same."

"Are we going to break in?" Smith asked eagerly.

I shook my head. "No. We're going to kidnap the duke while he's on his way there."

There was a moment's silence as they absorbed this idea.

"What are we going to do with him after we've kidnapped him?" Moore asked. He was always the first off the mark. "Are we going to kill him? Ransom him? Make him return your land to you? What?"

"Yes, William. We are going to kill him," I replied quietly. "But not in his house. We're going to grab that bastard while he's riding along St. James's Street in his fine carriage and take him to the Tyburn Tree and string him up there. Right there, in front of everyone. That way they'll know that justice has been served."

"But he could be riding down St James' at any time. How will we know when to be ready?" Moore, as sharp as ever, asked.

"My son, Tom, has unearthed that precise information. He will join us tomorrow and we will go over all the details with him. Are we all agreed?"

My companions all nodded, and after warning them not to whisper a word of it to anyone – 'not even to your wives and wenches' – we went our separate ways.

A similar scene was played out at the Bull Head tavern the following night, but this time with Tom joining our motley crew. After ordering a round of ale and meat pies, I introduced him to everyone present, and Tom told my fellow conspirators what he knew about the duke's regular carriage rides along St James's Street. He also added that he thought we might have problems dealing with the guards who ran alongside the carriage.

"Ah, not if we grab the duke towards the end of his ride," I said, looking around to check that no one could overhear us. "According to what you told me, Tom, those guards will be exhausted by then, and won't be able to put up much of a fight."

"Aye, I'm sure of that," Simons grinned. "Especially since that mean bastard of a duke probably pays them very little. Why should they risk their lives for him?"

After a few more choice remarks about the duke, mainly relating to his parentage and his stinginess, we decided that our attack would take place the following Tuesday at seven o'clock in the evening.

We then went over the details such as who was to wait where and which weapons we were going to use.

"And don't forget, father, I am in this as well as you," my son said. "I've heard for so long how much you hate this man and now I want to help you get rid of him once and for all."

I clapped him on the back, and after another round of drinks, we all left the tavern.

*

The weather on that Tuesday evening was typical of a London winter: cold, damp, and with a light wind blowing in from the west. When we met, I made sure that my men were all wrapped up warmly in thick jackets, riding coats, and wide-brimmed hats. Apart from protecting us from the elements, our voluminous clothes would also hide our swords, pistols, and cudgels.

Standing at the end of St James's Street, we took our pre-arranged positions and waited for the duke's carriage to appear. I was a little concerned that the people in the street might grow suspicious of us, but in fact, no one showed any interest. To them, we were simply a few friends, chatting and taking in the evening air. My son, who knew Ormonde's route better than any of us, was waiting a quarter of a mile down the street. His job was to race up the road and warn us of the duke's approach.

As I stood waiting behind a massive plane tree,

by the side of the road, I kept saying to myself, 'All right, Ormonde, you miserable bastard, this time you're going to pay for what you've done. Seven or more years may have passed, but you're not going to get away with it this time.' That train of thought was accompanied by a graphic image of James Butler, the Duke of Ormonde, swinging from the Tyburn Tree, his neck strangled by a knotted rope. I smiled to myself, envisaging his portly form swaying in the wind, his legs kicking helplessly as his life was slowly throttled out of his loathsome body.

I was dragged out of my reverie by the sight of my son, running up the street towards us. I raised my hand as arranged, knowing that my men would take out their swords and cudgels in response to my signal. Seconds later, the duke's carriage, pulled by four horses, came into view. I had been correct in my assumption; his guards were clearly exhausted. Two of them were clutching their chests, and one looked completely out of breath. I felt pleased with myself. Everything was going to plan. No more fiascos like the one at Dublin Castle.

"*Make way for the Duke of Ormonde!*" the tallest guard, who was carrying a flaming torch, shouted, as the carriage drew close to where we were hiding. "*Make way for the Duke of Ormonde!*"

Just then, Moore, now sitting on his horse, rode up straight in front of the carriage and raised his right arm. "Stop!" he shouted. "Stop right here!"

The coachman pulled on the reins. "What's the

matter? Why should I stop?"

Moore rode towards the carriage and looked up at the coachman, high up on his seat. "Do not proceed any further," Moore said. "There is a dead man lying just up there in the street, and I'm sure that you don't wish to drive over his body, do you?"

As the coachman was pondering what to do, Simons and Smith, rode up to the side of the carriage, poked their pistols through its windows and pointed them at the duke.

"Don't shoot! Don't shoot!" he pleaded. "I've got a wife and four children at home. Don't shoot, please!"

I could see my son and Halliwell on their horses, chasing the duke's guards away. They dropped their torches as they ran off, quickly disappearing amongst the houses and trees in the evening gloom. I smiled to myself. So far, everything was going to plan.

Riding up to the side of the carriage, I yanked open the door. The duke was lying on the floor, holding his hands over his bald head. His long, curly periwig had fallen off and was lying there next to him. My immediate thought as I prodded him with the tip of my sword was that he didn't look so proud and aristocratic now.

"Get out of your carriage!" I commanded.

"I...I—"

"Get out!" I shouted, as I poked him in the belly with my sword. "You're a repulsive worm and you deserve to die. Now get out!"

"But I—"

"I said, get out!"

"I'll give you forty guineas," Ormonde pleaded. "Forty guineas and a thousand pounds in jewellery. Just let me go."

"I don't want your money or your jewellery," I said. "I just want you dead. I want you to pay for what you did to me all those years ago. Now stop jabbering and get out!"

"Captain Blood?" he gasped as he realised who I was. "Please, let me give you—"

"Nothing you give me will change anything," I snarled, pointing my pistol at his head.

Seeing that he had no choice, he squirmed his way out of the carriage, and as soon as he was out, lying on the street, my son picked him up. With the help of Moore, we hoisted him onto the back of Tom's horse. The duke looked around helplessly, hoping that someone would appear out of the murky evening light to save him. His luck was out. Tom quickly climbed up onto the saddle in front of him and Moore tied them together with a short piece of thin rope.

I galloped ahead of them, down St. James Street and Piccadilly, setting off to check that the noose was still hanging off the gibbet of the infamous Tyburn Tree. Suddenly, I heard shouting coming from behind me, and I looked back to see that the coachman had taken the opportunity to ride away with the carriage. I heard him shout 'Go! Go!' to his horses as he whipped them and galloped off in the direction of nearby Clarendon House, the duke's London home.

Deciding that this did not interfere with my plans, I continued my race to the fatal spot where the duke would meet his Maker. Checking that the noose was ready, I turned back to see how matters were progressing. My son and his 'passenger', together with the others, were catching up with me, the sound of the duke's cries and the beating of horses hooves muffled by the mist. I smiled, gripped the reins and dug my spurs in to my horse's sides.

Suddenly I heard some shouting. "He's free! He's free!"

Immediately, I pulled my horse to a stop and turned around. The duke had somehow managed to wriggle out of the bonds that had bound him to Tom. As I galloped towards them I heard the sharp crack of a pistol shot and saw that the duke had knocked Tom's pistol out of his hand.

Just as I was about to charge forward, Ormonde forced his foot under my son's and somehow lifted him up out of the saddle. The two of them fell, twisting in the air and falling to the ground from the moving horse. One moment Tom was on top, the next, the portly duke was sitting astride my son. Tom was lying on his back, the duke keeping him pinned down as he leaned forward to grab my son's sword for himself.

As I saw the duke smiling the smug smile of a victor, my son gave him a push and pulled himself out from under the man. Tom ran for his horse, leapt into the saddle and galloped away. As the duke stood up,

Moore and the others fired their pistols at him and galloped off after my son. Their shots must have missed, for as I galloped after my men, I saw my enemy standing there, brushing himself off and shouting 'Kill them!' to a group of figures who had appeared out of the shadows.

Later, I learned that one of those figures had been Thomas Clarke, one of Ormonde's chief servants. Fortunately for his master, he had been in the vicinity when the fracas had begun and had now come to help his master.

As for us, we galloped as fast as we could towards Westminster and crossed the Thames on the ferry. From there, we turned east, raced along the south bank and then headed off in the direction of London Bridge. Once there, we made for the nearest tavern, where we decided it would be best if we separated and made our own ways home. For my part, I fell into bed in a small inn that night: I was filthy, exhausted and, above all, extremely disappointed. Once again, the Duke of Ormonde had escaped. Worse than that, he knew who had set upon him and I knew it would not be long before the hue and cry would begin.

The next day, disguised as a priest, I walked along the south bank of the Thames and bought a newssheet. In thick, black headlines, it informed the literate members of the public that the king was offering a reward of one thousand pounds...

...to any who shall discover one or more of the six

persons who…forced the Duke of Ormonde out of his coach…set him behind one of them on horseback, with intent to carry him to some obscure place out of town, where they might, with more privacy, have executed their villainous and bloody conspiracy.

Not only had the king been informed almost instantly of our attack on the Duke, but he also appeared to have a suspiciously detailed knowledge of what had transpired. The news sheet continued…

…The Duke of Ormonde is now languishing under his wounds at his lodgings at Clarendon House, and is prepared to give another one hundred pounds in addition to the king's prize to any who could but tell who owned the horse and pistol which the conspirators left behind them.

The following evening, I met my son in a wooded area east of the city. Tom asked me what the chances were of anyone being able to identify us.

"The duke knew it was me who ordered him out of his carriage," I replied. "But I'm not sure he recognised anyone else. Remember, I told you not to use names, so hopefully, the king's men will be groping in the dark."

Despite the duke knowing full well who had attacked him, the description of me in the *London Gazette* was amusingly inaccurate.

A man of down look, lean-faced, and full of pock-holes, with a stuff coat, wearing a worsted camlet cloak and a brown, short periwig, inclining to red. About thirty-six years old.

Tom smiled for a second. "Well, father, thank the Lord that this is not an honest description. You are much older than thirty-six and you usually wear a black or white wig. Besides, you spend most of your time these days dressed as a priest."

"Let's hope that keeps me out of the king's hands," I said, as I quickly read how the authorities had described my son. "Here, they call you Thomas Hunt," I said, reading the bottom of the page. "This is who they are also looking for:

A tall and well-proportioned man, of a ruddy complexion, about thirty-three or thirty-four years of age, wearing a flaxen periwig of a large curl. But sometimes, of late, a black one. His clothes black and sometimes wearing a black worsted camlet coat, long, and has one leg a little crooked or bowed.

"Ah, that's from when I fell of my horse years ago," Tom recalled. "But I'm sure that there are lots of men in London with a leg like mine. But see here, father, look how they have described your friend, Richard." He pointed to the following paragraph.

Richard Halliwell, a tobacco cutter. A middle

sized man, plump faced, with small pock holes, of a demure countenance, wearing a short, brown periwig and sand-coloured clothes, about forty years of age.

"You know what this means, son," I said. "It means we all have to lie low and avoid places where the king's men might expect us to go. I will get the word out to the rest of the men. Tom, if they catch any of us, it's…" I drew my finger across my throat.

"It will be us, not the duke, swinging at Tyburn," Tom said.

Soon after this, we parted, hoping fervently that the search would peter out as various other matters arose and distracted the king's attention away from us.

Chapter 20
The Duke of Buckingham

My hopes were short-lived. A few days later, I learned that one of the king's closest advisors, Sir Henry Bennet, was employing all his officers and informers to find out what he could about us. My son's lodgings off Bishopsgate Street were searched, and his neighbours were questioned about what they knew of his activities. Later, Tom reported to me that he had been described as 'a lusty, proper young man, full-faced, about twenty-one years of age.'

"And father," he grinned. "They said they knew nothing much about me, but had been told that you were a desperate man, still living in London."

"Are you sure that's all the authorities have on us, Tom? There's nothing more?"

He shook his head. "No, father, there is more.

The king's men, those working with Sir Henry Bennet and Sir Joseph Williamson, also questioned the duke's servants, you know, his coachman and his footman and his porter."

"And did any of them say anything helpful?" I was very impressed by how much information my son had acquired about the king's investigation.

"No, father, but they went to see mother at her house in Shoreditch. But when they arrived, she wasn't there."

"Where was she?"

"She had moved to the house of a schoolmaster," Tom replied. "A rented place, owned by a Master Jonathan Daveys in Mortlake, south of the river."

"And did they find her there?"

Tom nodded.

"What did she tell them, anything useful?"

My son grinned. "No, father. Nothing."

Now it was my turn to look pleased. I had always been concerned that Maria would not stand up well to an interrogation by the king's officers. I knew that both Bennet and Williamson were reputed to be very persistent, and reportedly had sometimes used violence when they wanted to 'persuade' their victims to divulge the truth. Of course, they would not get their own hands dirty doing so; they would leave that part of the interrogation to their assistants. In addition, I did not know how gentle – or otherwise – they would be if they had reason to question a woman. I knew that my wife was spirited, but I did not know how long she would last against some tough men determined to carry out His Majesty's business.

"Father," Tom continued. "When they came to Master Daveys' house, they decided to search it for any other evidence that you were involved. You know, weapons and messages. Things like that."

"Did they find anything?"

Tom nodded. "They found a message signed 'TA', which they assumed stood for 'Tom Allen', a name you've used in the past."

This last piece of information worried me. I did not remember writing a message; I sincerely hoped I had not given anyone away.

"What did this message say? Did it give away any secrets?"

Tom shook his head. "I don't think so. All I was told by one of Master Daveys' servants was that you wished to meet someone – no name was mentioned – at your lodgings on a Friday morning, and that they should bring a cloak with them. The servant told me that the message was signed 'Your friend, TA'."

"Hmm, that 'TA' could have referred to either of us," I said. "But there's nothing damning in that message, so I'm not too worried. Now, how about we go to the tavern at the end of the street and have something to eat? I could happily fill my stomach with a meat pie and a tankard of ale."

Ten minutes later, now dressed in our black

cloaks, and with our hats pulled down well over our heads, we were sitting in a dark corner of the Black Bull. Once we had eaten our first pie each and were well into our second, Tom asked me what I knew about George Villiers, the Duke of Buckingham.

"What do you want to know, Tom?"

"Well, I've heard his name mentioned several times, and I've also heard that he hates the Duke of Ormonde as much as you do. And yes, Halliwell or one of the others said that it was Buckingham's idea to attack Ormonde when we did."

I looked around carefully. There were only two other people in the tavern – a young man and a woman – and they were sitting at the far end, near a window. She was a pretty red-head and her bodice was not laced modestly. He was concentrating his gaze on the gorgeous expanse of female softness she was exposing above her loose clothing. I thought it safe to assume that he was more interested in his companion's seductive assets than he was in trying to overhear what we, two soberly dressed gentlemen sitting at the far end of the room, were talking about.

"No, Tom. It wasn't Buckingham's idea to attack the Duke of Ormonde when we did. It was mine. But when I told him what I was planning to do, he didn't try and persuade me not to. You see, he can't stand Ormonde and—"

"Why?"

"Why? Many reasons, though mainly due to a failed marriage settlement, so I've been told. Six years

[257]

ago, there was due to be a marriage between the two families, that is, Buckingham's and Ormonde's, but in the end, the whole thing came to naught."

"Why? What happened?"

I shrugged. "I don't know the details, Tom. All I know is that Buckingham lost a great deal of money, and like me, he's never forgiven Ormonde since. In addition, and probably as a result of this feud, Buckingham used his influence with the king to have the duke recalled as the Lord Lieutenant of Ireland. That really hurt him and—"

"Is that why I heard that Ormonde's son, the Earl of Ossory, is said to have hired two assassins to murder Buckingham?"

"Tom, where did you hear that?"

My son shrugged. "I can't recall precisely, but if I remember rightly, I overheard two men talking about it in a tavern in the city last week."

"Well, what you heard was true," I said. "The Earl of Ossory employed two men to get rid of Buckingham, but soon after he hired them, they were poisoned. And, just before they died, they confessed to the plot, though of course, that didn't help them."

"Where does His Majesty stand in all this? Who does he prefer? Buckingham or Ormonde?"

I shrugged. "I'm not sure, Tom. You see, in the past, that is, over the past twenty years or so, the king's attitude towards Buckingham has changed several times. And in an extreme way as well. You see, during the Civil War, Buckingham fought for the king;

indeed, he fought with his nephew, Prince Rupert, at the Battle of Lichford Close. And not only that, but he also fought for the king at the Battle of Worcester, back in 1650—"

"Which the king lost."

"True. Then, when the king went into exile, Buckingham did the same. However, he went to Rotterdam, not France. Soon after that, they fell out."

"How? Why?"

"First of all, apart from having some disagreements with the king about money, Buckingham also had a major argument with His Majesty over how the Church should be treated. And if that wasn't enough, Buckingham started courting the king's widowed sister—"

"Mary? The Princess of Orange?"

I nodded. "The king was furious with Buckingham about that. But that's not all. Buckingham returned before the Restoration, and Cromwell had him arrested because he thought Buckingham was plotting against him. However, Buckingham managed to escape but he was soon recaptured and Cromwell then threw him into the Tower."

"How long was he there for?"

"Not long. He was freed after he promised not to assist Cromwell's enemies—"

"The Royalists?"

"Yes. In fact, in the end, Buckingham was one of the lords who met with the king after Cromwell's death at Dover, you know, when he returned here from his exile. But then, Buckingham lost favour once again, when he made advances to the king's other sister, Princess Henrietta. He was escorting her to Paris to marry the Duke of Orleans, but when Charles found out, he had Buckingham brought back to England immediately, probably because he didn't trust him."

"And was that the end of the duke's career?"

"No, Tom," I replied. "The king was in a lenient mood, and Buckingham had his confiscated property returned to him. Not only that, but he was admitted to the Privy Council. However, the Chancellor, the Earl of Clarendon, was against Buckingham, and then Ormonde's son, Ossary, challenged Buckingham to a duel."

"What was the result of that?"

"There wasn't a result. Buckingham refused to take part and Ossary was sent to the Tower."

Tom raised his eyebrows. "*That* must have pleased the Duke of Ormonde."

I nodded grimly. "He was furious. Soon after that, Buckingham came to blows with the Marquis of Dorchester in the House of Lords. He pulled the marquis' wig off and both of them were sent to the Tower to cool things down for a while. After a few weeks, and a promise that they wouldn't do anything like it again, they were released. Then, to continue this saga, in revenge, Buckingham claimed a title that was held by the Marquis' son-in-law. By this point, the king had run out of patience with Buckingham, so he dismissed him from all his offices and sent him to the

Tower again."

"The marquis and the Earl of Clarendon must have been delighted."

"I'm sure they were, Tom, but then the wheels turned again. Buckingham was released, prosecuted Clarendon for something or other and then he took over Clarendon's offices and duties. And then, just to annoy Clarendon and Ormonde even more, Buckingham became the Chancellor of the University of Cambridge."

"But, father, how does all this concern you?"

"Oh, that's simple. In Ormonde's eyes, anyone who is friendly in any way with Buckingham naturally becomes one of Ormonde's enemies."

"So that's why people are saying that Buckingham helped you when we attacked Ormonde in St. James's Street?"

I nodded. "Yes, Tom, but he didn't really help us; he merely supported us."

"If you decided to do anything against the Duke of Ormonde again, do you think Buckingham might support or help you?"

"I suppose so, but what I *really* want to do is something that will really annoy His Majesty."

"You mean, annoy him by doing something serious against the Duke of Ormonde again, or perhaps the Earl of Clarendon?"

"No, no, Tom, something personal. I might even ask one of the king's mistresses to help me."

"Which one? He has quite a few."

"I was thinking about Barbara Palmer, the Duchess of Cleveland."

"The attractive red-headed one?"

I nodded. "I think so. I've heard she cannot stand the Duke of Ormonde, and it's said that she loves to meddle in court politics. It makes her feel important."

"But is that wise, father? She's also known to blow hot and cold. I'm not sure how reliable she would be as an accomplice."

"Maybe you're right but I'm still thinking about this. Have no fear," I said, placing a hand on his shoulder. "Once I've started on my plan, you'll be the first to know. Now," I said, finishing off my tankard of ale, "you can escort me back to my lodgings and then go back to yours."

Leaving some coins on the table, we left the tavern, as the wheels in my head continued turning and plotting. I refused to give up. One way or another, I *would* have my revenge on the Duke of Ormonde as well as do something that would annoy His Majesty, King Charles the Second.

Chapter 21
Stealing the Crown Jewels (1)

Shortly after my conversation with Tom, disguised as an ordinary citizen and not looking anything like the description the king had published of me, I, together with my son, Tom, attended a service in Westminster Abbey. The king, sitting upon his throne in all his sartorial glory, was there to play a key role.

In addition to his crown and regular white suit, consisting of a silk shirt, breeches, and hose, he wore a long ermine-trimmed red cloak, and his gold chain of office. He was holding his sceptre in his right hand and a bejewelled golden orb with a cross in his left. I must admit, he looked very impressive, especially as the sunlight pouring through the windows caught the diamonds, rubies, and emeralds in his crown, sceptre and orb. This caused them to gleam and sparkle, sending out darts of light in all directions.

However, what really caught my attention was the loving way he kept caressing the orb. It was as if it were his pet cat. His long fingers were continually stroking it and it was not difficult to see that he was very proud and pleased to be holding one of the ancient symbols of state in his hands. More than once, I saw him look down for a second as he ran his fingers over the jewelled orb, smiling as he did so. He seemed to see the orb as his own personal possession.

It was then, just as he stood up to address us, the assembled throng, that the idea of how to get back at him struck me. I would steal his Crown Jewels! The crown, the sceptre, and the orb. Everything! *That*, I decided, would hit home far more than merely killing one of his chief officers. The more I considered this idea, the more I liked it.

"What are you smiling about?" Tom whispered to me.

"Shh! I'll tell you later," I whispered back. "I've just had an idea. Don't worry, I'm sure you'll like it."

He did. When I told him that night, instead of warning me of the risks involved, he clapped me on the back in giddy excitement.

"Father, if this succeeds, you'll go down in history!"

"Aye, and if I don't," I replied. "I'll go down to Hell for treason."

"No, no," he grinned. "Don't say that. With

some careful organisation, we should succeed."

"We had better start planning then. First of all, who are we going to include? We can't have too many, mind you. This will definitely not be a case of the more the merrier."

My son scratched his head for a minute, looked down, and then looked at me. "Well, for starters, there's you and me. Then I think we should ask your friend, William Moore. I'm sure he'll agree, and he's a good man to have around for such a bold action as this. He didn't even panic when our attack on Ormonde went wrong."

"Agreed, Moore is a good choice. I think five or six should be the most we'll need."

"How about Captain Richard Halliwell? He also did well when we ambushed the Duke."

"Good point…in that case, we should also ask Captain Perrot—"

"Captain Perrot? I've never heard you speak of him before. Who is he?"

"Captain Robert Perrot is one of the men I met when I was involved with the Fifth Monarchists," I explained. "He was once a lieutenant in Cromwell's Army, but now he works as a silk-dyer on Thames Street. And while we're talking about Fifth Monarchist men, I think I should speak to Bill Smith. He was one of the men who was with us when we tried to grab the Duke of Ormonde."

"So that makes six of us," Tom said, counting off the names on a piece of paper. "You, me, Moore,

Perrot, Smith and Halliwell."

"That should be enough," I smiled in expectation of my forthcoming attack on the king. "Now all we have to do is round them up and meet somewhere to inform them of our plan."

"Where? It'll have to be somewhere secret."

I snapped my fingers. "I know just the place. It's a small, rather obscure tavern in Romford. Actually, it's near Becontree. It's the sort of place where no-one will think anything if the six of us have a meeting there. I'll tell the owner that we're just a group of old army friends, meeting to chat about old times. He won't ask any questions. He'll be more than happy to have the extra trade. In fact, I don't know how he stays in business. Whenever I've stopped there, there's only been the odd farmer or labourer having a drink and a pie."

"When should we have this meeting?"

"How about two weeks from tonight? That will give me time to speak to everyone, and for them to make their own plans."

"Sounds fair enough to me," Tom said, his eyes sparkling at the thought of what we were planning to do. "Just think about how much the Crown Jewels must be worth. Of course, we won't be able to sell them as they are, but I'm sure the individual diamonds, rubies, and other stones will be worth a fortune."

I nodded and grinned at my son's enthusiasm. He reminded me of myself when I was his age. Fast, keen and burning to carry out any risky venture that came along. "Remember, Tom, we're not only doing this for the money. We're doing it to get back at the king, for all he's done to me."

"For confiscating your land back in Ireland?"

"Exactly. As you know, I've never really gotten over that. Now, we had best get going. We'll meet in Becontree next week. When you get there, ask for the Heath Inn. Everyone there knows it. It's near the church, just behind the graveyard."

With that, we quickly hugged each other and left the tavern to go our separate ways. As I walked towards my lodgings, I prayed that I would be able to recruit my friends into this venture. I knew it would be a chancy undertaking, but if it worked, it would be well worth it. I spent the rest of the evening drawing up plans, all the while imagining the look on the king's face when he was informed that his beloved Crown Jewels had disappeared.

*

My plans for the meeting were fulfilled. Two weeks later, on a Monday evening, I met with Tom and my four chosen friends at the Heath Inn, Becontree. I had arrived early, and asked the owner, who himself was an old soldier, if he could give us a room to ourselves where we would not be disturbed. A few shillings, and the promise of selling more food and drink than he normally did on a Monday evening, was enough for him to grant my wishes.

[267]

Tom, as expected, arrived first. Ten minutes later, Captain Robert Perrot and Bill Smith, both past members of the Fifth Monarchists group, arrived together. They had spent their journey from London reliving their past as active members of the organisation and discussing why it had failed to make a greater impact on English society. Just as we were ordering our ale and meat pies, and wondering whether the other two would arrive, Lieutenant-Colonel William Moore and Captain Richard Halliwell entered the tavern.

Naturally, everyone was pleased to meet up again, and the first half-hour of our meeting was spent exchanging news as well as asking and answering questions which all seemed to begin with 'Have you heard about…?' or 'Do you know what happened to…?' The only one who did not join in was Tom, who had neither fought in the army nor had been a member of the Fifth Monarchists.

When I felt that the tempo of this nostalgia was beginning to slow down, I tapped on the side of my tankard with a knife and called the meeting to order.

"Gentlemen," I began. "I have not gathered you here today just to reminisce about your brave exploits of the past. Indeed, the purpose of this meeting is to discuss a possible future venture that will hopefully gain us a fortune but no fame."

"How much of a fortune?" Moore asked.

I shrugged. "I don't know exactly how much, but I would say that we are talking about thousands of pounds."

"For each of us?" Perrot asked.

"Possibly," I replied. "But I'll have to figure that out later."

"And how exactly are we going to get our hands on this fortune?" Halliwell asked.

"If you'll allow me to explain, gentlemen, I have asked you here, to this out-of-the-way tavern in Becontree, because…" I paused for effect, giving their curiosity a chance to pique. Everyone's eyes were fixed on mine, their faces eager, all expect for my son, who sat there quietly, smiling to himself. I leaned forward into the centre of the table. "…we are going to steal the Crown Jewels."

There was silence for a moment, before everyone spoke at once.

"*The Crown Jewels*?"

"The ones in the Tower?"

"The ones belonging to the king?"

"When? How?"

"What? All of us?"

I leaned back and held up my hand for attention. "Gentlemen, if you are patient, I will tell you all about my plan. But, but before I do so, I will ask our friendly innkeeper to bring us some more pies and drink. And, in celebration of our future wealth—"

"We hope," Moore added.

"I propose that we sup wine instead of ale. Are there any objections?"

As I had expected, there were none, so I sent

Tom downstairs to order a fresh round of beef pies and three bottles of claret and Rhenish. I knew that both these wines tasted well, but weren't too strong to dull our senses. A few minutes later, the landlord, Master Josiah Hawkins, accompanied by his comely young daughter, came up to our room, bearing trays of food and drink. I asked them to stay for a few minutes while we all exchanged stories and memories of our days in the army, and soon after, he and his daughter left. This way, if he was ever asked about us, he could honestly say that we had indeed wined and dined at his establishment for the purpose of enjoying a nostalgic evening together.

I tapped my tankard again with my knife and called for silence. Now, all I could hear were the sounds of five contented men eating beef and vegetable pies, washed down by good wine.

"Gentlemen," I began. "Now that I have your attention, I will inform you of my plan that will not only make us rich, but will also cause His Majesty a certain degree of ridicule and embarrassment."

"Hear! Hear!" cried Moore and my son together, raising their glasses.

Holding up my hand, I continued. "Last week, I paid an exploratory visit to the Tower, dressed as a parson and accompanied by a young lady, an actress named Jenny, who posed as my wife. It did not take me long to find out where the jewels are stored. They are on public display and anyone who pays a small entrance fee may see them."

[270]

"Where are they?" Perrot asked.

"They are kept in the Martin Tower, that is, the furthest right hand tower at the back, assuming you are facing the Tower from the river."

"Is this Martin Tower inside the Tower or part of the Tower's outer walls?" Smith asked.

"It's an outer tower, between the Brick and Constable Towers."

"So, perhaps we could enter it from the outside," he suggested. "Without having to go through the main building at all."

I shook my head. "No, no. I thought about that but saw that it will be easier to enter the Martin Tower through the central courtyard. As I said, we will have free access to the jewels because they are on public display in the Jewel House. It seems that His Majesty is so proud of them that he wants everyone to see them. He sees them as a symbol of his reign."

"And did you see them?" Halliwell stopped eating long enough to ask.

"Yes, I did. As I said, I was dressed up as a parson and took this young actress with me as my wife. We paid the admission charge and then the Keeper of the Crown Jewels, an old man called Edwards, took us to where they are being displayed."

"How are they stored?" Perrot asked.

"They are—"

"What exactly is on display?" Moore interrupted, before I could reply.

"To answer Robert's question, they are kept in

a large iron cage in the Jewel House. They consist of the king's crown, the orb, and His Majesty's sceptre. There are also some less important but still valuable items as well. Jewelled swords and the like."

"So, what happened while you were there?" Moore asked. "Knowing you, I'm sure this wasn't just a casual visit."

"You're right, it wasn't. As we, that is, my actress wife and I, were standing there with the Keeper, looking at the jewels, my 'wife' suddenly collapsed in front of the cage which contained the jewels, after a subtle signal from me. I feigned panic and asked for a glass of wine to revive her. Master Edwards ran upstairs to his apartment to fetch one and—"

"And you picked the lock," Halliwell grinned.

"No, no, my plan was better than that. The Keeper returned with the wine and suggested that, once my wife had recovered from her fainting episode, we should both come up to his chambers and rest there for a little while. Naturally, I agreed, so we accompanied the good man upstairs to meet his wife in their rooms at the top of the Martin Tower."

"Then what happened?" the ever-impatient Perrot asked.

I grinned. "Nothing dramatic. Mistress Edwards took my supposed wife to a side room where she lay down to recover from the 'qualm on her stomach', as she called it. In the meantime, I chatted with the Keeper and his wife, and when my 'wife' recovered, we profusely thanked them for their help and left."

"So, you left without the jewels?" Smith asked, sounding somewhat disappointed.

"Yes, I did, but I came away with something else." I tapped the side of my nose. "Knowledge, gentlemen, knowledge."

"What knowledge?" Perrot asked.

"The exact location of the Jewels in the Martin Tower," I counted off on my fingers. "The knowledge about who is guarding them – a doddery old man who, incidentally is of no threat to us given that he is seventy-seven years of age. I also learned that he keeps a couple of pistols in a box next to the cage holding the jewels."

"Doesn't he walk around armed?" my son asked.

"No, Tom, he says they are too heavy for him to carry around on him all the time"

"Is this box locked? Does he have a key?" Halliwell asked.

"No, the box is unlocked. I discovered that when he went upstairs to fetch the wine for my 'wife'. He keeps them loaded as well."

"So, is that the end of the story?" Perrot asked.

"Yes, and no. You see, after my actress-wife recovered, we left, but not before the Keeper and his wife invited us to return the following day for a meal."

"Which you accepted?"

"Aye, and I must add, she wasn't a bad cook

either. I have been to see them a couple of times since then and to strengthen this new friendship, I took several pairs of finely embroidered gloves as a present for Mistress Edwards."

"All right, so now that you are best friends with the Keeper and his wife, how are you going to steal the jewels?" Smith asked.

"Well, since I am now a familiar sight at the Tower, none of the guards asks me what I am doing there. In addition," I grinned. "I have learned where all the various buildings and passageways are."

"More knowledge," my son grinned.

"Exactly," I continued. "I have since met the Keeper's daughter, a young lady called Elizabeth. Her parents are most worried about her because she is thirty years old and not yet married."

"What does this have to do with your plans?" Halliwell asked.

"Don't you see? I was there disguised as a parson and they decided to seek my help with their predicament. They are old, and worried about what will happen to their unwed daughter once they have departed this world."

"So, father, are you now going into the matchmaking business?" my son smiled.

"No, not exactly, but I thought that this situation might help our cause. I told them I had a nephew, a nice young man, who was looking for a suitable wife. I informed them that he was my ward and that he had a yearly income of between two and three hundred pounds. I knew that this would certainly be a tempting enough sum for an unmarried lady, especially one who has ageing parents."

"And what did they say to this proposition?" Perrot asked, finishing off his glass of Rhenish.

"They were delighted," I grinned. "They told me to bring my nephew with me next time I came to dinner, so that we could all see whether he and the fair Mistress Elizabeth Edwards found favour in each other's eyes."

"And?" Tom, Halliwell and Moore asked.

"And," I repeated. "That is the next stage." I turned to Tom. "Son, you are about to become betrothed to a pleasant young lady, by way of which you will open the doors of the Tower of London to the rest of us."

"Father!" Tom gasped. "This you didn't tell me!"

"Well, I'm telling you now."

"I don't know whether to be pleased or not. I hadn't realised that I was going to become engaged," Tom said. "Tell me, father, honestly this time, is she really a pleasant-looking lass, or are you telling me another of your Irish yarns again?"

"No, son, she really is pleasant enough. Pretty eyes and face and a good figure to match," I replied. "You'll see her when we go to the Tower tomorrow, and then you'll be able to make up your mind for yourself. In the meanwhile, we'll all meet here again next Monday evening. Is that agreed?"

[275]

It was and then I saw Perrot nudge Halliwell.

"Young Tom is a lucky bugger," he grinned. "Not only is he going to get himself some money, he's going to get himself a wench as well. This really *is* going to be some caper: money, jewels and a wench thrown in for good measure."

Chapter 22
Stealing the Crown Jewels (2)

We all met again a few days later as planned and Master Josiah was more than happy to let us use the room upstairs as before. We were the best business he had had for a long time. It was late evening when we arrived, and as the room was dark, I sent Tom to ask the landlord for some candles and a lighted taper. Tom returned a few minutes later with everything together with the landlord who was delighted if not a little confused, to see us all again so soon.

"I forgot that you said you'd be coming back here," he said. "You really must have a lot to talk about."

I smiled at him. "Oh, yes, we certainly have. As I told you last week, it's years since we six last saw one another and we have much to talk about. I'm sure you know what it's like when old army friends get together. The passage of time has no meaning," I told him wistfully.

The innkeeper nodded and smiled, before taking our order and leaving promptly. Shortly afterwards, his daughter, whose name we learned later was Alice, reappeared, carrying a tray loaded with bottles of wine and honey cakes. As she bent over to place it on the table, Halliwell stroked her behind. I assumed this was not the first time a man had behaved in this way towards her, for she smirked in response. Standing upright, she placed her upward facing palm in front of Halliwell, her eyebrows raised quizzically. He begrudgingly handed her some coins, as payment for the drinks, and she smiled brightly, taking the money and leaving the room.

"Now," I said. "Where were we?"

"In the Tower, playing matchmaker," my son smiled.

"Ah yes, now we enter the next chapter of the story. Two days ago, I returned to the Tower with my actress-wife, Jenny, together with young Tom here. We had a very pleasant meal with the Edwards family and Tom enjoyed himself telling tall stories to Elizabeth—"

"They weren't *all* tall," Tom protested. "Let's just say I have inherited your Irish way of decorating the truth."

I grinned, before continuing. "After the meal was over, I asked Master Edwards if he would take my son and show him the Crown Jewels, telling him that Tom had heard me describe them so fulsomely that he was eager to see them for himself. Naturally, our host was delighted, and so, leaving the ladies upstairs to gossip, we went down to the Jewel House. It was while we were there that another idea came to my head—"

"That you could try and take Edwards' money as well!" Perrot exclaimed.

"No, something better than that. I decided to ask Edwards if I could buy the brace of pistols he kept near the jewels."

"Why?" Smith asked. "You don't want to shoot him, do you?"

"No, certainly not, but by buying the pistols, I have removed his means of defending himself when we go in and steal the jewels."

"That's brilliant!" Smith guffawed, pounding the table.

"Considering what I offered him, he could hardly refuse my request. Soon after, we went back upstairs to join the ladies—"

"That's right," Tom interrupted. "When we returned to the ladies, they said that they'd had such a good time gossiping that we should have another meal together, so the following day, we returned to the Tower."

"Apart from the meals and the chit-chat," I continued, "the best part about this whole thing is that now, when Tom, my so-called wife, and I turn up at the Tower, none of the guards say anything, because they are so used to seeing us there."

"So, what happened at your meal yesterday?" Moore asked. "Did young Tom here propose to the delectable Mistress Elizabeth?"

Tom blushed.

"No, gentlemen, something more than that, and this is where you are going to play your part. I told Master Edwards that I had a few friends who would like to see the jewels—"

"Like to steal them, you mean," Moore grinned.

I grinned back and nodded. "Aye, but I told him that these friends would only be able to come and see them early in the morning, next Tuesday. At seven o'clock to be precise. I told Edwards that my friends were businessmen, and that they were planning to leave for the north, for Newcastle, later that day. Naturally, I said, he would be well-paid for being so helpful."

The others nodded in approval of my detailed planning.

"Will the sun be up by then?" Perrot asked.

I nodded. "I'd already thought of that. The sun comes up at around six o'clock."

"Why are we going to meet so early then?"

"Because, at that time, there will be hardly anyone about in the Tower, so we should be able to make our escape swiftly and easily."

The others nodded in agreement, and seeing that there were no more objections, I bent down and took a map of the Tower out of my pouch. Moving the two brass candlesticks aside, I spread it out on the table and showed my fellow conspirators where the Martin Tower was in relation to the rest of that mighty fortress. I showed them that we would enter by the Wakefield Tower which faced the river, cross the open area surrounding the central White Tower and then head for the Martin Tower to the far right.

"Are all of us going to be there?" Perrot asked. "I mean, aren't one or two of us going to remain by the entrance with the horses ready to get away afterwards?"

I nodded. "I was just coming to that." I turned to face Smith. "I suggest that you remain behind with the horses."

"Why me? I don't want to miss out on all the excitement," he protested.

"With your leg the way it is, I think it would be best if you wait outside. If we have to do any running, you'll most likely be caught. Don't you agree?"

Seeing that he didn't really have much choice, Smith nodded.

I smiled and patted him on the back. "But don't worry, my friend. When the time comes, you'll get as much money as the rest of us." I drained the last of my wine before continuing. "Now, let's decide what weapons we're going to take with us, and remember, we won't be allowed into the Tower wearing our swords."

"In that case," Moore began. "I suggest that we

each carry a dagger and a pistol, hidden in our jackets—"

"We should all be carrying swordsticks as well. Like rich gentlemen," Halliwell added.

"Good idea," I said. "We should also take a wooden mallet or two with us, in case we need break anything up to make it fit inside our pockets—"

"And in case we need to knock anyone out," Moore grinned.

I nodded, reminding them all that we should meet at the riverside entrance to the Tower at a few minutes before seven, on May the ninth.

"And don't you be late this time," I said, looking at my son.

"Fear not, father," he grinned. "For a caper worth thousands of pounds, I shan't even go to sleep the night before."

With that, I broke up the meeting, and we all left with smiles on our faces, thinking of future riches and what pleasures we might spend our money on.

*

May the ninth dawned grey and dry, and I shivered a little as I left my lodgings to collect my horse from the stables. In the calm of early morning, I wondered what the day would bring. Would my plan succeed, or not? Would I end up rich, or would I soon find myself in prison? Would I, or anyone else, be hurt during this attempted robbery?

I reached the stables, paid the stable-boy for hay and the usual services, saddled up and set out for the Tower. I arrived just before seven, and saw that Tom was already there. When he saw me, he immediately broke into a wide grin.

"Forgive me, father," he said in a contrite voice. "For I have sinned. Last night I was with Mistress Lucy and we—"

"Enough, Tom," I said, holding up my hand. "You've seen me dressed as a parson before."

"I know that, father, but every time I see you like this, I cannot help but think that you are the last man on God's earth who would suit such a role."

I laughed softly. The boy was right; it was rather ironic. "Have you been here long?"

"About five minutes."

"Have you noticed anything unusual? More guards about? Anything like that?"

He shook his head and then pointed. "Look, father, there's Perrot and Moore."

I waved to them to join us and, two minutes later, Halliwell and Smith trotted over. Our number was complete.

After we had greeted each other, I checked that everyone was armed. We handed the reins of our horses to Smith who, with a resigned expression on his sallow face and still complaining about being left out, took the horses off behind some trees and prepared himself for a long wait.

"Now you, Tom, as my nephew, stay close to

me. And you three…" I pointed to the others. "Remember that you are my friends from the army, who want to see the jewels. Play your parts, but only when I give you the signal. Is that clear?"

The three of them nodded.

"And remember, don't silence the old boy before he opens the Jewel House. I'll give you the signal. Will, when we enter the Jewel House, you remain outside on guard, keeping your eyes and ears open."

"What for?"

I shrugged. "I don't know…in case there are any surprises. Maybe a guard will happen to come along. Who knows?"

He nodded in agreement and we entered the Tower. I gave a cheery wave to a fat guard who I'd chatted with on my previous exploratory trips.

"Hello, George," I said, thrusting out my hand to shake his. "How are you? How's the wife and your little girl?"

"They're well, thank you," he smiled. "But who are these men with you?"

I nudged Tom forward. "This is my nephew, you remember. The lad who's interested in Keeper Edwards' daughter. And these other three are my friends from my old army days before I became a priest. They want to see the Crown Jewels. Master Edwards told me that I could bring them with me one day and that he would show them to my friends."

George scratched his head. "Oh, well, if old

Edwards said that was alright, then there's no problem, is there? I'll see you all later, I suppose."

I nodded, and we all set out for the Martin Tower.

"If it all goes as smoothly as that, father," Tom said quietly. "Then we're all going to be rich men tonight."

I smiled at the thought, and we entered through the dark doorway of the Martin Tower and started to climb the equally dark, circular staircase. I could feel the damp as my hand slid along the wall. Even though I had climbed up those steps several times recently, the Tower still gave me the shivers. It seemed that I was not the only one.

"I'm glad I don't live or work here," I heard Halliwell whisper to Perrot. "This place gives me the creeps. Just thinking about all those people, like Anne Boleyn and Sir Thomas More who had their heads chopped off here. Ugh!"

"Well, think about the money we're going to get instead," Perrot whispered back. "That'll stop your shivers."

I turned around to face them and put my finger to my lips. "Enough talking. One more floor and we'll be at the Keeper's apartment."

Once we reached the top, I made everyone stop and make sure that their weapons were well concealed. Then I knocked on the heavy wooden door. After a moment it creaked open and Master Edwards' wrinkled face appeared. With a smile, he beckoned us into his apartment.

"An Englishman's home is his castle," he smiled. "And look at my castle. The most frightening one in the country. Certainly not a place for thieves, robbers, or treasonous souls."

I smiled back and introduced him to my friends.

"Oh, yes, I remember. Just let me tell the wife I'm going downstairs. And give me a moment to fetch my coat. It's a bit too damp down there for an old fellow like me."

I heard him tell his wife that 'the nice priest, the one with the nephew who's interested in our Elizabeth, is here together with some of his friends who want to see the jewels'. He finished off by saying that he'd be back within half-an-hour at the most.

As he stepped out onto the landing with a lantern, I asked him to lead the way to the Jewel House. The others wished him a polite good morning, but didn't say anything more. No doubt my friends were thinking about what they were going to do in a few minutes' time.

When we reached the bottom of the staircase, Edwards took hold of a candle from a nearby sconce on the wall, lit it and handed it to Halliwell as we followed him to the Jewel House. The old man then took out a heavy black iron key, unlocked the door and ushered us inside the dark room. At the same time, I signalled to Tom to stand by the door as a look-out.

He nodded and remained outside.

Once we were all inside the Jewel House, Edwards turned around to lock the door behind him.

"What's with your friend?" he asked. "Doesn't he—"

He never finished his sentence as I threw my heavy cloak over him. At the same time, Perrot stuffed a wooden plug with an air-hole into his mouth. Naturally, the old man started to make all sorts of panicky sounds and I was scared that he might alert some nearby guards.

"Shut up, old man!" I hissed, but he kept waving his arms about and trying to shout for help. "Listen," I hissed at him. "If you stop this noise, nothing will happen to you. Do you understand?"

He did not reply but kept trying to call for help.

"Tie up his hands," I said to Halliwell, who promptly took a length of thick twine from his pouch and bound the poor man's hands behind his back. However, this did not stop the Keeper from trying to call for help.

Now feeling thoroughly exasperated with him, I asked him again, "Are you going to shut up, or no?"

His answer was to continue with his cries for help, so I hit him on the head with my mallet and he slid to the ground, silent at last. I wrenched the keys out of his hand and gave them to Perrot.

"Quick, grab the orb and sceptre and that crown on the left," I said to the others. "And stuff them into your bags."

"What about this other crown?" Halliwell

asked, pointing to the St. Edward's Crown.

"No, leave it," I said. "That one's too heavy. We'll just take the State Crown instead. It's much lighter."

I looked down at the candle's dancing shadows on the wall and saw that Edwards had not been knocked out completely. He lay there, writhing on the ground, and had started groaning horribly.

I bent down to him as Perrot, Halliwell and Moore were stuffing the Crown Jewels into their pouches. "Listen again, old man. If you don't stop this noise now, I'm going to have to kill you. Do you understand?"

He didn't say anything, so I pulled my cloak off of his head and showed him my dagger. I could see his eyes concentrating on the pointed end as I moved it closer to his throat. He remained silent and I pulled my cloak back over his head.

"Tom," I heard Perrot say to me. "I can't get this crown into my pouch. It's too big."

"So hit it with your mallet and push it in," I replied and turned my attention back to Edwards who was still groaning. After another warning, which did not frighten him into silence, I hit him again on the head with my mallet. The old man now lay there, sprawled out in the half-lit gloom of the corner. For a moment, I thought that I had killed him, but then I saw his chest slowly rise and fall.

"How are you doing?" I asked urgently.

"The sceptre thing is in my bag," Moore

replied. "I bent it over so it would fit inside."

"And I bashed the orb a bit to get it into mine," Halliwell added.

"What have you done with the crown?" I asked Perrot. "Did you get it inside your pouch?"

In the half-light, I could see him nod his head. "Aye, but I had to hit it a bit also. Here, take a look."

I looked inside his pouch and saw that the sides had been dented, the ermine ring at the bottom was torn, and that the jewelled cross on the top had been bent over to one side.

"Did you have to be so violent with it?" I asked.

"Sorry, Tom, but I had no choice. I couldn't get it into my pouch any other way. But fear not," he added, pulling out two large diamonds and a sapphire, "I didn't lose any of the jewels. We'll still have these to sell and I'm sure they'll be worth a fortune."

Just as he was saying this, Edwards started groaning again. Halliwell looked at the old man, then at me, before ramming his dagger into the old man's stomach. That stopped his groaning. I looked to see if he was bleeding, but in the darkness I couldn't see any blood on the floor. Neither could I see whether he was breathing or not. I put my hand to his face. It felt cold and clammy. I could not tell whether he was still alive or not.

"Quick," I said, taking the crown from Perrot and hiding it under my robes. "Let's go. Remember, once we are outside, walk to the entrance like nothing happened."

The others nodded. Then just as we were about to leave, I heard some shouting and scuffling in the outside passageway which led to the entrance of Martin Tower. I felt for my dagger with my right hand as I wrapped my left around the crown hidden within my robe.

"What is it " Tom Perrot. "It sounds like there's someone outside…"

I nodded and carefully stuck my head out of the Jewel House to see Moore hurrying towards me.

"Quick, Tom! We must get out of here. Old Edwards' son has just arrived and asked me what I was doing here."

"Where is he now?" I asked.

"He's just gone upstairs but he said that he'll be back down in a minute."

We quickly made for the entrance to the Martin Tower, but just as I was thinking we had got away with it, Edwards, who must have been pretending to be dead or unconscious, started shouting *'Treason! Murder! Treason! Murder!'* He may have been weak, but his cries echoed around the Jewel House from the base of that dark stairwell.

As we stood, hidden in the shadows of the stairwell, I saw Elizabeth, Edwards' daughter, rush down the stairs to the Jewel House. I assumed she had found her father, lying dead on the ground, for she soon began to scream.

"Treason! Treason! They've killed my father

and stolen the crown!"

Hoping that she would not leave her father's side for at least a few more minutes, I signalled to the others to follow me and we rushed out of the tower. All we had to do now was cross the open area surrounding the White Tower, leave by the main entrance and make for our horses outside.

Suddenly, an armed guard appeared from behind the Bloody Tower and shouted for me to stop.

"Stand to!"

Signalling the others to follow me, we ran towards the Tower's main entrance. I felt, as much as heard, a musket-ball whizz past my face and I turned and fired my pistol at the guard. I missed, but I saw him fall onto the cobblestones in shock. As I turned around to face my men, I saw that more armed soldiers now stood between us and the entrance by the Wakefield Tower. We ran as fast as we could, the shouts from behind of 'Stop or I will fire!' spurring us onwards. I looked back in time to see a guard raise his musket and fire at me. I aimed my other pistol at him and fired back. Again, I missed.

Now feeling somewhat breathless, I cursed and turned back to face the main entrance. My long robes, and the crown hidden within them, were slowing me down, and before I knew what was happening, the same guard who had fired at me seconds before leapt onto my back. I tried to throw him off, but to no avail. The pair of us were rolling around in the dust and gravel like dogs fighting over a scrap of meat. I felt the crown digging into my stomach and my muscles began to tire. Moments later, the guard was standing over me having yanked my pistol from my hands. He grabbed my pouch and the crown from beneath my robes and forced me to surrender. I was his prisoner.

He shouted for some of his men to surround me and I was prodded by their bayonets to stand up. As I did so, I muttered, "It was a gallant attempt but I failed."

"Look here," a soldier shouted. "The Crown Jewels." He and two other guards bent down to pick up the diamonds, sapphires, and rubies which had come loose and fallen out of my pouch. They were now lying in the dust, glinting in the morning sunlight.

Seeing this, the guard who had captured me ordered me to raise my hands as he poked his own into my pockets to see if I had any other jewels hidden inside.

"Ha! What are these?" he cried, as he fished two pearls, three emeralds and two rubies from my pockets. "Thought you'd get away with at least these few baubles, did you? Here, Ashley," he ordered one of his men. "Put these in the pouch with the others. This one's coming with us."

Having bound my hands behind my back, the guards took me to a small cell in the White Tower and threw me inside. I landed on some damp straw, their manhandling leaving me bruised and winded. They promptly locked the door and left, giving me time to come to terms with the gravity of what I had done.

Edwards and his daughter had been correct when they had shouted 'Treason!' As far as I could see, there was no way out of this one. The punishment for treason was death, either by the axe, or by being hung, drawn, and quartered. If I was to die, I hoped it would be by the axe. At least that way the pain would be short-lived. I did not think I would be able to bear being half-strangled, then cut down and disembowelled.

I lay there for some time, thinking about my probable grisly demise when a burst of light flooded my cell. The door opened and my son was flung into the cell and landed next to me on the straw.

"Father!"

"Tom! What happened? I thought you and the others managed to escape."

"I did, or rather, we did. Me and Richard."

"What happened to the others?"

He shrugged. "I don't know. I managed to escape from the soldiers and get out of the Tower. I grabbed my horse from Bill and then he, myself and Richard galloped off along the Tower Wharf."

"So why are you here now? What happened?"

"We became separated, and in my haste I ran my horse into an empty cart near St Botolph's Church. I fell off the saddle and hit my head on the damned cart. Then, just as I was trying to stand up, I felt someone pulling at me. It was a constable, and of all the ill luck, he recognised me from when we ambushed the Duke of Ormonde. He called to a few passers-by and they bound my arms and took me to find a magistrate. After a few questions, he wrote out some sort of warrant, and now, here I am. Lying on this stinking straw in the Tower with you."

"When did you last see Smith and Halliwell?"

Tom shrugged. "I can't remember exactly. All I remember is the sound of them galloping away as fast as they could."

"And Moore and Perrot? Do you know what happened to them?"

Tom shook his head. "No, father. All I know is that every bone in my body is killing me. Even this foul straw is a welcome bed."

"Go to sleep, son," I said, patting him on the shoulder. "Let me spend some time thinking about our next move. I've been in worse situations than this before. Fear not, we are both still alive and the most important thing is to never give up hope."

So there I was, at the end of the day, lying on a putrid bed of straw in a dark cell with my son next to me. I had entered the Tower that morning, planning to leave it as a rich man. Now, I would probably leave the Tower to be hanged and join the other unfortunates, such as Lady Jane Grey and Catherine Howard, who were now rotting away in the chapel of St. Peter Ad Vincula.

Chapter 23
Locked up in the Tower

Despite everything that had happened that day, I must have eventually fallen asleep, for I woke to the first light of dawn streaking in through the barred window high up on the wall of our cell. The first thing I saw and heard was my son. He was sitting in the corner, hunched up, moaning to himself.

"What's the matter, Tom? Is something hurting?"

"No, father," he said quietly. "It's just...all I can think about is being executed. You know, being hanged, drawn, and..."

"Hush, son. Don't think like that," I said, moving over to him and resting his curly head on my chest. "Fear not. It won't come to that."

He raised his head and looked straight into my

[295]

eyes. "How can you tell? Just think about what we did. We were caught stealing the Crown Jewels. No one is going to let us get away with that. You can be hanged for a lot less. Just think how—"

"Shh, Tom. Until that takes place, anything can happen. Don't you remember those stories I told you, about how I thought I was about to be killed when I was fighting at Marston Moor and Naseby? When I was—"

"Yes, father, but then you were outside fighting in the open. You were a soldier. You had a sword in your hand, and you weren't alone. You were surrounded by men who were on your side. Tell me," he sniffled. "Who's going to be on our side now? Especially after what we did to the Crown Jewels and old Edwards. Can you see anyone rushing to defend us now?"

"Fear not, son," I repeated as I ruffled his hair. "While we're alive and breathing, there's hope."

"Hope for what?" he asked sadly. "Do you think your friends will come rushing in here with drawn swords and save us? Father, we're in the Tower. The Tower of London. People who were far more important than we are...Anne Boleyn...Sir Walter Raleigh...they never left here alive, and they had rich and powerful friends who could easily have saved them. Once you're a traitor, no one will help you."

I had no answer for this. He was right. All I could do was try to convince him not to give up hope.

"Father, I'm only twenty years old. I haven't

seen the world or done anything yet with my life. At least you've been a soldier and fought for the king—"

"And against him," I couldn't help adding.

"Aye, but at least you *did* something. What have I done? I mean…"

My son's musings were suddenly interrupted by a heavy metallic scraping as the door of our cell was pulled open. An important looking official stood there, in the pale light, with an armed guard on either side of him.

"Stand up!" he commanded. "Both of you."

Despite the difficulties of standing on the soft, wet straw while our hands were bound behind our backs, we managed to do so. We found ourselves looking at a well-built man, wearing a military uniform of sorts. He was holding a rolled-up piece of paper.

"Do you two villains know who I am?" he asked. His voice was deep.

We shook our heads.

"I am Sir John Robinson," he said, thrusting out his chest. "I am His Majesty's Lieutenant of the Tower. I have been commanded by the authorities to transfer you to another cell which is better guarded, so let's be moving."

Five minutes later, Tom and I found ourselves in another small cell although this one at least had fresh straw on the floor. As soon as the lieutenant and his guards had left, we sank down onto it. I wondered if this move meant anything, apart from what Sir John had said. Where they really just making it harder for us to escape?

"I'm hungry, father," Tom said. "And thirsty. D'you think they're going to feed us?"

"Let's see," I replied. I stood up and kicked the door as noisily as I could.

A voice shouted back, "What do you want?"

From the promptness of the reply, I understood that there was at least one guard on the other side.

"Food and drink," I shouted back. "And now!"

"Wha' do you think this is? A tavern? You think you can order wha' you want and when you want?"

I did not answer, but five minutes later, two guards entered our cell. The skinny one was bearing a tray of food which he placed on the floor, while the stocky one glowered at us and looked as if he was ready to beat us if necessary.

"There you go. Your breakfas' supplied by 'is Majesty. An' if you 'ave any complaints, you can take 'em up with 'im. That is, of course, if he don' chop your 'eads off first."

They were about to leave when I called out, "Hey, how will we be able to eat if our hands are bound behind our backs?"

"Good question," the stocky guard replied. "I'll go an' find out."

He returned a few minutes later, again with the skinny younger guard.

"Here, Ned," he said. "Undo their shackles. An' you," he said, looking at us. "No tricks, neither.

Remember, I've got this." He shook his bayonet at us.

It was a great relief to be able to move our arms again and it did not take long to polish off 'breakfast', which was barely much more than a mouthful. It became even less so especially after I had scraped the green mould off the chunks of bread and cheese, and Tom had bitten off the bruised parts of the apples and spat them into the corner.

It was probably early afternoon when our two guards returned. After asking whether we had enjoyed "'is Majesty's special fare', the stocky guard picked up the tray and turned around to leave our cell. Just as he was about to open the door, he turned back.

"'ere," he began. "Did you know tha' you two are already famous? You're already in the news sheets. Look a' this poem Master Andrew Marvell wrote about you." He paused as he fished a folded news sheet from the pocket of his tunic and handed it to me. I read it aloud to Tom.

> *When darin' Blood his ren' to 'ave regained,*
> *Upon the Royal Diadem distrained,*
> *'e chose the cassock surcingle an' gown,*
> *The fittes' mask for those who rob the Crown.*
> *But 'is lay pity underneath prevailed,*
> *And while 'e saved the Keeper's life, 'e failed*
> *With the priest's vestments 'ad 'he but put*
> *Bishop's cruelty, the Crown was gone.*

"Good, isn't it?" the guard grinned. "Tha'
[299]

Marvell feller really knows 'ow to write, don' he? I wonder what 'e'll write when you two are swinging a' the end of a rope at Tyburn?"

And with that, the pair of them left, but not before they had bound our hands behind our backs again.

Fortunately, the next day, when the Lieutenant returned to ask us further questions, I managed to convince him to order the guards to remove the cords which bound our wrists. This at least made our stay in the Tower more comfortable, although it was impossible to forget for one moment that we were prisoners who, one day very soon, were going to be charged with treason.

On our third or fourth day, Sir John Robinson, accompanied by a judge whose name I have since forgotten, entered our cell.

"Stand up!" he commanded. "His Lordship and I have some serious questions to ask you."

We stood and faced His Majesty's two officials as they waited for the two guards to bring in chairs and a table for them to use. It was clear that they intended this to be a long interrogation.

Taking a seat, the Lieutenant began. "You are both called Thomas 'Tom' Blood, and you both reside in London, is that correct?"

We nodded as he scribbled this down.

"You," he said, looking at me. "You were born in Ireland in 1618."

I nodded.

"And you, the younger Thomas Blood, were born in 1651, correct?"

"Yes, sir," my son answered.

"Good," Sir John continued. "Now that we have that out of the way, let me ask you some questions about this dastardly robbery that you very nearly succeeded in getting away with." He looked down at his papers before continuing. "How many men were with you and what were their names?"

My son was about to speak, but with one look from me he stopped.

"You were about to say something?" the judge asked.

Tom shook his head. "No, no, sir. I'll let my father answer."

"So," he asked, looking straight at me. "Captain Blood, who were—"

"Colonel, sir, colonel."

The judge looked down at the page in front of him. "It says captain here, so captain you'll be. Now, who was involved in this wretched plot with you? What were they called?"

I stood there silently.

"Didn't you hear the judge's question?" Sir John asked.

"Yes, sir."

"So who was in this with you?"

More silence. In fact, the silence was so deep I could hear the birds twittering outside.

"Come, come, sir. This is not what I expected,"

Sir John said. "I'll ask you one more time. Who was involved in this robbery with you?"

I remained silent.

"Are you not going to enlighten us?" Sir John asked, looking first at me and then at the judge.

"No, sir," I replied. "I will answer only to the king himself, His Majesty, King Charles the Second."

This was greeted by a loud guffaw from Sir John and a sardonic laugh from the judge. My son said nothing, but I could see the look of surprise on his face.

"Excuse me, Captain Blood, but did I—"

"Colonel Blood, sir."

"*Colonel* Blood, did my ears deceive me, or did I just hear you say that you would only answer to the king himself?"

I nodded.

"I see," Sir John said, and I could see, even in that gloomy cell, that he did not look very pleased with how this interrogation was proceeding. "Is that your final answer?"

"Yes, sir. That is my final answer."

Sir John stood up and indicated that the judge should step out into the corridor with him.

Once they had left the room, the stocky guard locked the door, muttering, "Well, I never. I never heard anyone talk to the guv'nor like tha' before."

"What are you doing, father?" Tom asked. "You'll have us hanged even quicker."

"Fear not, son," I said, placing a finger to my

[302]

lips. "I have a plan."

"What is it? Since when have you been friends with the king?"

"I'm not, but be patient. Remember, Tom, as long as we're alive, there's hope. Quiet now, they're coming back."

The Lieutenant and the judge opened the door and stepped into the cell. Looking beyond them, I could see that it was sunny outside. A vision of the past, of living in the green Irish countryside flashed through my mind.

Sir John sat down and asked, "Well, Blood, have you anything to say about your fellow thieves?"

"No, sir."

"Very well, I shall leave you to think on it. But don't think that you have won. The judge and I will return tomorrow and ask you the same questions again. However, in the meantime, please remember that you are in the Tower of London. We have a chamber or two here designed for the sole purpose of persuading obstinate characters like yourselves into divulging whatever we wish to learn. Is that understood?"

I nodded and so did Tom, even more vigorously. Without saying anything else, the two officials left the cell leaving the skinny guard to lock the door noisily with a large bunch of keys.

"Father, what was that about? They're going to hang us both for sure if you won't answer their questions."

"Shh, Tom. They might be standing behind the

door listening," I whispered. "Wait a few minutes and then I'll answer you."

Tom spent the next few minutes picking up bits of straw and fiddling with them. "So, father," he said at last. "What was all that about talking only to the king? You know that's not going to happen."

"I'm not sure, son. I've heard he's a strange man, interested in all manner of things in life, like plants and science. Perhaps he'll be interested in us."

Tom's face showed that he did not believe me. "Father, you're clutching at straws here." He bent down and grabbed a fistful of straw, which he thrust into my face, as if to demonstrate how ludicrous my plan was. "I cannot imagine the King of England being vaguely interested in two robbers, father and son, who tried to steal his Crown Jewels."

"Listen, Tom, I—"

"And not only that, father," Tom continued. "We also grievously injured the Keeper of his Jewel House, *and* we smashed up his crown and orb. We broke his royal sword as well."

I shook my head and sat down on one of the chairs the guards had left behind. "No, no, Tom, you are wrong. If we answer their questions immediately, we are done for. Once we give them all the answers, they'll hang us, just like that." I clicked my fingers to emphasise my point. "They'll have no more use for us then."

Tom did not look convinced.

I placed my hand on his shoulder. "Listen,

son," I smiled. "I've been in worse situations than this. Just have faith. We'll see what tomorrow brings."

The following day brought Sir John and a different official. Unlike the judge, this man was short, fat and poorly dressed. He wore an unkempt wig and leaned on a stick. His small piggy eyes constantly shot around our cell as if searching for something.

"Well, Captain Blood, have you thought any more about what I said yesterday?" Sir John began.

"Yes, sir," I replied, looking him straight in the eye. "My answer is the same as it was. I will speak only to His Majesty the King."

"And your son's answer?"

"He agrees with me," I said, and was pleased to see Tom nod his head.

"Hmm, do you see what I had to put up with yesterday, sir?" Sir John said, looking at his companion. "A pair of stubborn Irish donkeys."

The fat man nodded and poked me in the belly with his stick. "Is this your final answer? You will speak only to the king?"

"Yes, sir," I replied, dismissively pushing his stick aside.

"Well, we'll see about that," was his disgusted response. "Sir John, let us depart. I have more important things to do in life than waste my time on these two fools who wish to die a horrible death. Come."

With that, they promptly left our cell, but not before the guards had removed the chairs and table and tied our wrists behind our backs again.

As soon as the door slammed shut, Tom turned on me. "You see, father. See where you and your tricks have got us! Tied up again and Sir John and the others are surely against us. Even more so than before."

His outburst over, he spun around, moved into the corner, and turned his back on me. He refused to speak to me for the rest of the day, even when the guards brought in a plate of thin, stringy beef, some chunks of stale bread and some very weak ale. We ate in silence and I began to wonder if I had not gone too far. While I understood my own logic, I realised that I was taking on the king and his establishment. They could not be seen to be giving in to criminals like us. What would people say if the king or in fact, any of his officials, showed any weakness? Had I gone too far this time?

Only time would tell.

Chapter 24
Meeting the King

Our cell was cold and tense that night. Tom was sullen and silent for the most part, save for occasionally muttering that he was sure my behaviour would bring us to face to face with the Tyburn Tree.

"Father, don't you see? You're giving them no choice but to hang us…hang us and…" He stopped and shivered as he visualised the King's executioner cutting him down in order to cut out his guts while he was still breathing.

"But, Tom, listen—"

"No, father. I don't want to hear any more of your stories."

Like a small child, he clapped his hands over his ears and spun around to face the wall, which was so damp that much of it was covered in large clumps of spongy moss.

When I placed my hands on his shoulders to turn him around, he shook them off violently, remaining hunched up; drowning in his own macabre thoughts. Not long after that, as we lay there silently, wrapped up in our own grim visions of the future, exhaustion caught up with both of us and we drifted off to sleep.

The dawn did not bring any warmth or comfort. From the small, barred window, high above us, I could see that the sky was grey and overcast, and the thin stream of water tricking down the wall of our cell informed us that it was raining outside.

Trying to wake myself up, I shook my head like a dog that had just come out of the water and walked over to Tom.

"Good morning, son," I said. "Did you manage to sleep at all?"

"Yes," he mumbled. "But no thanks to you."

"I've been thinking about what I said to the Lieutenant and the other man yesterday. Perhaps I was a little too…" But before I had time to finish my sentence, we heard the sudden jangle of keys outside. We turned around to face the door. Sir John Robinson and the fat judge with his knobbly stick were standing there.

This time, they did not order the guards to bring chairs. They just stood there for a moment, dark grey silhouettes against the weak light before entering our cell. It was clear that this was going to be a short meeting.

"Captain Blood," Sir John began. "I don't know much about you apart from what Sir Joseph Williamson has told me. You know who he is, I suppose?"

"Yes, sir. He's one of the king's chief officers. A spymaster, I believe," I replied, wondering what this was all about.

Sir John nodded. "Correct. In any case, for reasons that I cannot fathom, you are to be taken to see His Majesty this morning. This is most unusual, but I am bound to follow orders, whatever they are. Do you understand?"

I nodded, and then asked, "Just me, sir, or is my son to accompany me?"

"His Majesty wishes to meet with both of you," the judge replied, with obvious distaste. "Like Sir John here, I cannot begin to understand why the king wishes to have anything to do with you, but there is no gainsaying him, is there?"

I looked at Tom. His face showed that he could not believe what we had just heard.

"Both of us, sir?" he asked. "We're both to be taken to speak to His Majesty?"

"Aye, in chains," Sir John added. "We don't want you running away or harming His Majesty, do we?"

Neither Tom nor I replied.

"Right," Sir John continued. "I'll have some breakfast sent down to you and someone will bring you some scented water for you to wash yourselves. I don't want it said that I don't look after my guests, do I?" He paused and held his hand to his nose. "At least you'll both look and smell a little more presentable when you meet His Majesty."

Our two early morning visitors turned to face the door. "We'll leave you now; we are both busy men and have other things to do besides taking contemptible robbers like you to speak with to king."

As the two officials left, Sir John gave a signal to the stocky guard behind him. The guard locked the door, leaving the two of us in a sense of wonderment.

"You see, Tom," I could not help gloating. "Something *has* happened. The king wants to talk to us."

"Aye, maybe to see who he's going to hang first, you or me."

"I'm not so sure, Tom," I said, trying to smile. "You heard the Lieutenant say that this is most unusual. Perhaps he won't hang us, after all."

It was clear that Tom was not convinced, but at least now he was talking to me. A few minutes later, our guards brought in two trays. One contained some more-or-less fresh chunks of bread, some pieces of beef which were far less stringy than last time and some apples and pears. The ale was also better this time and I told Tom that this improvement in our food boded well. The second tray held two bowls of scented water and some dry rags to be used as towels. Apart from a few rust coloured stains, they were quite clean.

"I hope you're right," Tom said, as he took a thin piece of rag from the second tray, dipped it into one of the bowls of water and wiped his face. I did the same and for the first time since we had been thrown into the cell I felt clean and hopeful.

We spent the next hour speculating what His Majesty would say and do with us. We also tried to guess why the king was treating us like this. Our discussion was stopped only when we heard the now familiar sound of a heavy key being inserted into the lock of the door of our cell. The door opened and we found ourselves facing Sir John and our two guards. Both guards were carrying long lengths of thick chain, and padlocks. The Lieutenant saw me looking at the chains.

"You didn't think that I was going to allow you two villains out of here without being chained up, did you?" he said. "It would be the end of me if you escaped or attacked the king. You," he pointed to the stockier guard. "Bind the captain up first, and do it well. We don't want him escaping. Just leave his legs free so he can walk."

"Yes, sir," the guard said, and began to bind the rough chains around my wrists and arms and behind my back. He finished his work by locking the end of the chain with a large iron padlock. Once he had finished, he tested the tightness of the chains and then handed the key over to Sir John before turning back and grinning at us.

"I thought you two would like t' know tha'

your friend, Robert Perro', is 'ere now in the Tower. We caugh' him a few days ago. 'e's in a cell jus' like yours."

"Will we be able to see him?" I asked.

The guard shrugged. "Dunno. It's no' up t' me, is it? Ask Sir John."

Sir John's immediate answer was to shake his head. "No, at least, not for the time being. Perhaps in the future. That will depend on any future instructions I receive. Now you," he said, turning to the younger, skinnier guard. "Bind the son up in the same way. And make it just as tight. Being younger, he might be more inclined to risk trying to escape."

A few minutes later, Tom and I clanked our way out of our cell. We were escorted by four guards, carrying muskets and bayonets and marched upstairs. It was good to feel the fresh air and light wind once again on my face and I saw that Tom felt the same. There in the Tower courtyard, a large black horse-drawn carriage was waiting by the White Tower. As we noisily walked over to the carriage, I could not help thinking that, just a week or so earlier this was where I had been caught.

We were pushed inside and another length of thick chain was placed across our bodies and attached to the carriage. It was clear that the authorities were taking no chances with us. As we sat there on the hard plank seats, clanking and rattling with every movement that the carriage made, I wondered if all prisoners were treated like this, or whether my reputation as a potential troublemaker had preceded me. I flattered myself that it was because of the latter.

"Why are you smiling, father? What's so funny?" Tom asked.

"I'll tell you later," I whispered.

Pushing the curtain aside with my head, I looked out and saw that our carriage was being escorted by half a dozen mounted musketeers: two in front, two behind, and one on either side. I was just about to say something when the guard sitting next to me grabbed my hair, pulled my head back inside, and pushed the black curtain back across the window.

"What do think you're doing?" he said brusquely. "You're not the king going out for his Sunday afternoon ride, you know!"

The three-mile journey west from the Tower to the king's palace at Westminster took well over an hour. It was the most uncomfortable journey I had ever undertaken. Every time the carriage bumped over a pothole or a ditch, the chains would bite into me through my clothes. As we clattered over a particularly deep hole I saw Tom wince with pain. He was suffering as much as I was.

"Cheer up, son," I said quietly. "We're going to see the king in his palace. It's not every day that happens."

"If you don't shut up," the pockmarked faced guard said. "You won't be seeing him anywhere. No more talking. Understand?"

We continued in silence. The only way I could

tell where we were was by glancing outside whenever the curtain was blown aside by a puff of wind. Soon after leaving the Tower, we passed London Bridge, and the sight of ten or more heads impaled on tall spikes on its far side caused me to shudder. Would my head and my son's soon be joining them? Later, we passed the church towers of Blackfriars and Whitefriars, and shortly after that I caught sight of the newly rebuilt Somerset House.

It was while I was musing about His Majesty, and how he would receive us, that I felt our carriage come to a halt. We had arrived in the courtyard of Westminster Palace and were roughly manhandled out of the carriage.

"Are we going to see the king like this?" Tom asked. "All chained up?"

"How else?" a burly guard smirked. "In your best Sunday clothes for church?"

Prodded by our guards, and feeling not unlike animals being sent to slaughter, Tom and I were escorted, shuffling and clanking, across the courtyard. Several of His Majesty's courtiers and servants, who happened to be present, witnessed this noisy procession.

"Look!" I heard one of them cry out. "That's Colonel Blood! What's he doing here? And in chains, too!"

As we were being taken down a long corridor, towards the room where we had been told the king would meet us, Tom whispered, "Do you think it will be just us in there with the king, or will he have all of his advisors with him?"

I tried to shrug my shoulders, but the weight of my chains would not allow it.

"I don't know, Tom. We'll just have to wait and see."

We did not have to wait long. A few minutes later we were standing in a medium-sized room, facing the king. Dressed in a dark blue jacket and breeches, he was sitting in a large chair on a raised platform. Several other well-dressed and important-looking men and women were sitting or standing on either side. The king pointed to the centre of the room and told our guards to stand aside leaving us standing there alone to face him.

Sir John looked at the king hesitantly. "Your Majesty, are you sure that is wise? These two are notoriously slippery characters."

The king smiled. "I do not believe I am at risk of losing my life to these two, given that they are both heavily wrapped in chains."

"As you wish, You Majesty." Sir John bowed and instructed his men to move over to the back wall of the room.

I looked at the people standing beside the throne. Some I recognised from the past; others I knew from pictures I had seen. Sitting to the right of the king was his wife, Queen Catherine of Braganza. This plain-faced lady was dressed in a pale green gown, and wore several necklaces of shining stones which sparkled in the beams of light that shone through the windows. She did not look as beautiful as His Majesty's two favourite mistresses whom I had once seen at the theatre. Unsurprisingly, neither Lady Castlemaine nor 'pretty witty' Nell Gwynne were in attendance.

The king's brother, James, the Duke of York, was also present, standing behind the king's chair. He looked ready to whisper into his older brother's ear at any moment. The other member of the king's family present was his cousin, the dashing Civil War commander, Prince Rupert of the Rhine. The handsome Duke of Buckingham sat to the right, near the Queen, and behind him sat Sir Henry Bennet, identifiable by the black bandage on his nose. This he had taken to wear to cover an old war wound. I had met him in the Netherlands, and he winked at me in a conspiratorial fashion. I winked back.

There were three other men sitting on the far left, but the only one I recognized was Sir Joseph Williamson, the unofficial spymaster who was often responsible for carrying out some of His Majesty's secret and murky missions.

"Now, Blood," the king began. "What have you to say for yourself? Why did you demand an audience with your sovereign leader? Do you truly think that I have any desire to speak with a self-styled colonel who fought against my father and then tried to steal my Crown Jewels? Answer me."

"Sire," I bowed, or at least tried to, my chains

preventing me from making much movement. "I know you are a fair man and that you will listen to my plea."

"And you think my officers will not?"

I had to think quickly. I needed to flatter the king but not insult any of the nobles who were present.

"Allow me to explain, Your Majesty," I began carefully. "There are some individuals within your court who are not well disposed to me. I feared that they would allow their perception of me to influence their decisions regarding my escapade—"

"*Escapade*!" Sir Joseph Williamson burst out. "*Escapade*, he says! He calls trying to steal the Crown Jewels a mere escapade. He—"

A quick glance from his royal master halted Sir Joseph's tirade.

The king turned to look at me again and nodded. "Please carry on, Captain Blood. What were you about to tell us? Is it true that, in addition to this 'escapade,' as you call it, you and several of your devilish associates were involved in the attack on the Duke of Ormonde some six months ago?"

Now it was my turn to nod. "Yes, Sire."

"And why did you carry out so bold an assault?"

"Sire, the story behind this engagement with the Duke of Ormonde goes back many years. I do not know if you wish to hear all the details."

"Oh, I do, Blood. I do. And, what's more, I have the time to do so. Please continue."

I bowed again as best I could, the jangling of

my chains echoing around the high-ceilinged room.

"Sire, many years ago, the Duke of Ormonde was responsible for confiscating most of my estates in Ireland, and executing several of my friends—"

The king held out his hand. "You are wrong, Blood. It was I who commanded the duke to confiscate your estates. Did you not fight against my father at Marston Moor, Naseby, and elsewhere?"

I nodded.

"Well then, you can see that I had no choice. You had to pay the price for those treasonous acts."

I stood for a moment, silent and unmoving. Then, after a sidelong glance at Tom, I continued. "Yes, Sire, one's deeds must be paid for, but I am sure that such a generous ruler as yourself did not give the order for several of my friends to be executed. I believe that—"

"Enough, enough," the King said, waving his hand dismissively. "What else do you have to say for yourself? Why should I not have you executed, as the law demands, and as you so richly deserve? What are the names of your accomplices; those who were involved in this wretched attempted robbery at the Tower?"

I shook my head. "Sire, I regret to inform you that I cannot reveal the names of my fellows."

"Pray, why?"

"Because," I replied, looking directly at him. "I could never bring myself to betray my friends in order to save my own life. That would be asking too much."

[318]

"Hmm, how noble," the King admitted. "So, tell us instead why you decided to carry out the robbery in the first place? Surely it was not an act of revenge against the Duke of Ormonde?"

"No, Sire. The truth is, I saw it as a way of righting the wrongs, injuries, and losses I had sustained in Ireland. This taking of the Crown Jewels—"

"*Taking*!" exploded Sir Joseph again. "*Taking*! Stealing, Blood. Stealing. You were—"

Again he was silenced by a sharp look from the King.

"I thought that if I could sell the Crown Jewels," I continued, as though I had not heard Sir Joseph's outburst. "I would be able to buy back my lands in Ireland—"

"And how much do you think my Crown Jewels are worth?" His Majesty asked, leaning forward.

"I assume they are worth at least one hundred thousand pounds, Sire."

The king guffawed loudly and I saw huge grins break out on all the faces of the nobles and officials who stood beside his throne.

"Odd's fish, Blood," he laughed. "One hundred thousand pounds! "Blood, do you have any idea how much they are really worth?"

I shook my head.

He looked at me, grinning. They are worth," he said slowly, "a measly six thousand pounds."

I stood there, stock still. Not a sound escaped

from any of my chains. Tom was the same. Frozen. Silent.

"Blood, you have risked your life, and those of your son and your friends, when we catch them, for a mere six thousand pounds." He paused to let his words sink in. "After you had divided up the proceeds from your precious loot with your criminal accomplices, you would not have had enough money to buy a cowshed in Ireland, let alone buy back all your estates. *Ha*! One hundred thousand pounds indeed."

I must admit that, on hearing this, I felt somewhat foolish. I looked over to Tom, who was now staring at the floor. I am sure he was thinking that he too would be executed, having gained nothing from joining his father in his latest 'escapade'.

The king looked around. "Does anyone here have anything to say about this Hibernian robber who knows nothing about the price of the royal baubles?"

"Sire," the King's cousin, Prince Rupert, began. "I have to admit, when this so-called Colonel Blood was fighting on our side, that is, your father's side, at the beginning of the war, I heard that he was a very stout, bold fellow." He paused, looked around, and continued. "It is true, Your Majesty, that before he was persuaded to turn traitor and fight for the other side, this man did carry out several sterling acts of bravery in the West Country, in the name of your father."

"Hmm, so he has done some good, after all," the king mused. "Interesting."

At this point, I knew I had to think quickly. If His Majesty thought that there was an even more positive side to my exploits, I knew that I had to tell him. And now. Otherwise it would definitely be the Tyburn Tree and a noose around our necks.

"Sire," I said, clanking a step forward. "I have more to say…"

"I am sure you have," he smiled. "The thought of being hung, drawn and quartered often has that effect on people. I mean,the threat of such a death is a rather excellent method for improving a man's rhetorical skills. Am I right, gentlemen?"

His lords and officers smiled, and one or two said, "Hear, hear."

"Carry on, Blood. What do you have to say? We are all listening."

"Sire," I began slowly, knowing that my life and that of my son were dependent on my next few sentences. "Several months ago, I cannot remember exactly when, I was walking alongside the River Thames above Battersea, I saw you bathing in the river."

"So?"

"So, Sire, I was walking along with my musket in my hand when the thought occurred to me that I could shoot you from where I was standing, hidden amongst the reeds, and then escape before anyone in your party could catch me."

"But you chose not to."

"Yes, Sire. I realised that my king's life was

too important for me. To kill Your Majesty would have been a most foolish deed."

"You are correct, Blood. It would have been a very foolish deed, indeed." The king leaned forward, looking at me intently. "Before I make my final decision, do you have anything more to say in your defence? Is there any good reason that I should not give an order for the pair of you to be taken to Tyburn and to be dispatched there as you deserve and also as the law allows me?"

I saw Tom shiver at the mention of being executed at Tyburn and then pulled myself up, standing as straight as I could under the weight of my chains. "Your Majesty," I began as carefully as I could. If you will spare me and my son, I guarantee that you will not have two more loyal subjects in the whole of England, Scotland, and Ireland. We will be prepared to do *anything* for you and this country, Sire, even at the risk of our own lives. And not only that, Sire, but many of my friends and others will also be eager to perform eminent service to the Crown, should we be released."

The Queen tapped her husband on the knee and nodded her head, suggesting that she had been impressed by my words.

Noting this, I continued. "Sire, all I can add is this. If you were to execute myself and my son, I fear that these same people would rise up in a state of hostility and that this beloved country would be plunged into another bloody and unnecessary civil war.

[322]

And, if I may say so, Your Majesty, if you do condemn us to death, what will you have gained? Two dead and mutilated bodies, instead of two faithful and patriotic citizens. Two citizens who will owe their king everything, and be eternally grateful for his magnanimous generosity."

I looked at the King and his courtiers, trying to decipher whether they had been impressed by my words.

His Majesty looked me straight in the eye. "Is that so, Blood? Is it indeed?"

I nodded. "Yes, Sire. It is so."

The king sat back in his chair and leaned over to whisper something in his wife's ear. She nodded, and he leaned forward again, raising his hand.

"Blood," the king said, after a short pause. "What if I should give you your life?"

"I should endeavour to deserve it, Your Majesty."

"I shall consider what you have said and think on this matter. In the meantime, guards, take these two men back to the Tower. This meeting is over."

Within minutes, Tom and I were being escorted back across the courtyard to our carriage. When Tom asked me if I thought we would hang, I told him to be quiet, for now. We would talk about it later. I did not want to say anything that our guards could hear and possibly report back to the king and his officials later.

We rode the whole way back to the Tower in a heavy, thoughtful silence. It was only when we had been unchained and marched into our cell and the door was locked that we could begin to talk about this most fateful and unusual meeting at the palace.

Chapter 25
The Aftermath

The first thing we did once our cell door was slammed shut was to shake ourselves like dogs coming out of the water. Being chained up for several hours had not been a comfortable experience and we both felt stiff and abused. Seconds later, Tom asked me what I thought about the day's events.

"Shh, Tom," I whispered, pointing to the door. "Wait a while. Be patient. There may be someone outside trying to hear what we have to say."

He nodded and we both lay down on the straw as our muscles began to relax.

"Father, do you think it's a good sign that they haven't chained us up this time?" Tom asked quietly.

I shrugged. "I don't know, son. It was hard to tell what the king was thinking while he was questioning us. And who knows what his nobles said to him after we left?"

"The queen looked sympathetic, especially when you said that could have shot him by the river but didn't."

"Yes, I thought so too, but that Williamson fellow did not look very impressed, and I fear his opinion carries a lot of weight with the king. More so than his wife's."

"How do you think the Duke of Buckingham felt about what you said?" Tom asked. "He is, or was, your friend, right?"

I shook my head. "It's a little more complex than that, Tom. He's not exactly my friend; he is more like an associate."

"Meaning?"

"Meaning, Tom, that both the Duke of Buckingham and I cannot stand the Duke of Ormonde. In fact, Ormonde's son, the Duke of Ossory, even challenged Buckingham to a duel once."

"And?"

"Buckingham refused to fight him and Ossory was sent to the Tower for a while to cool his heels."

"So, you and Buckingham are on the same side, aren't you?"

I shook my head again. "It's not as simple as that, Tom. As I told you, the king and Buckingham have a great deal of history, not all of it good." I paused as I thought about the noble who had encouraged me to ambush the Duke of Ormonde several months earlier. "On the one hand, the king appreciates Buckingham, because they fought on the same side during the Civil War and that he went into exile with him, but on the other hand, a lot of bad blood has flowed between them since then. So, at the moment, Tom," I concluded. "I don't think we can count on Buckingham's influence on the king, at least, not for us."

Tom lapsed into a thoughtful silence.

A little while later, our two stocky and skinny guards appeared with their trays of the usual fare. I took the opportunity to ask about Perrot and whether we would be allowed to see him. The stockier guard's reply was that he didn't know but that he would ask Sir John.

After the guards left, we ate quietly, waited a few minutes and then began discussing our situation again.

"Father, answer me honestly. Do you think we're going to hang, or not?"

I shrugged. "I don't know, son. I really don't. As I said, it looked like the queen was impressed by what I had to say, but I've heard that she doesn't have much influence on what His Majesty does."

"Yes, I've heard that, too," Tom replied. "People say he listens more to Lady Castlemaine and Nell Gwynne."

"Aye, it's a shame that actress lady wasn't there this morning," I said. "I'm sure she would have believed me."

"What do you mean?"

"That story I told the king about not shooting him while he was bathing and—"

"Wasn't it true?"

"Yes, Tom, that part was true."

"So, which part wasn't true? The story about you having a whole army at your disposal which will rise up and revolt if he hangs us?"

"Aye, you hit the nail on the head. That was the good old Irish gift o' the gab," I grinned. "How could I raise up such an army? It was all bluff, boyo. All bluff."

"Well, let's hope His Majesty doesn't realise the truth, because if he does…" Tom slid his finger across his throat.

I nodded in agreement and lay down on the straw, staring up at the ceiling. I had played the only card I had left. Now it all depended on what the king decided to do with it.

*

We remained in the cell for another three weeks, before the Lieutenant of the Tower, Sir John Robinson, told us one morning to prepare ourselves for an interrogation by Sir William Morton, a judge of the King's Bench.

"Who is he, father? Do you know anything about him?" Tom asked after Sir John had left.

"Yes, son," I replied. "He is well-known for his

loyalty to the king. He also has a terrible reputation for demanding harsh punishments for those he considers criminals and wrongdoers. To him, sending someone to be hanged at Tyburn is nothing at all. I fear that his coming to interrogate us is not a very positive sign. I've heard that this old man, he's well over sixty years old, is like a hungry terrier with a bone. Once he gets started on something, no-one can stop him."

Tom and I spent the next few days in heavy silence. It seemed that any hope of us being released was about to be dashed by the forthcoming interrogation with the king's fierce and vengeful defender. It was therefore with great trepidation that we wearily stood to attention when the door to our cell was opened a few days later, letting in a stream of bright summer sunshine. Sir John and two armed guards entered.

"Captain Blood," Sir John began. "I have been informed that Sir William Morton will not be interrogating you after all. Sir Henry Bennet and Sir Joseph Williamson have decided that this measure is no longer necessary."

"Are you sure, sir?" I asked.

He nodded.

"Sir John," I asked, sensing that the authorities might agree to my next request. "Would it be possible for my wife, Maria, to visit us here in the Tower? I know that she has not been permitted to come and see us before now, but it's been nearly two months since my son and I last saw her."

"I will make the necessary enquiries, but I cannot promise you anything," the Lieutenant replied. "In the meantime, you will remain here. I will have the straw replaced shortly. Good day to you."

An hour later, our regular guards returned and replaced the straw. It was only after the new straw was laid on the floor that we became aware of how foul the old straw had become.

Soon after replacing the straw, the stockier of our two guards returned with a tray bearing a pen, a pot of ink, and some blank sheets of paper.

"The gov'nor says tha' if you wish for your wife t' come and visit you, you mus' write out a formal request."

"Now?"

"Aye, and I'm to take it to 'im when you've finished."

I sat down and started writing. I chose my words carefully, as I knew that 'the gov'ner', and probably several other officials, would read my petition before allowing Maria to visit us. I wrote saying that our close confinement was affecting our health and that, if it were possible, we would be delighted to see her. I also requested that if she were permitted to do so, then she should bring us each a change of clothes and some specific foodstuffs. Finally, I added that Tom and I both fervently prayed that she would be able to make the journey from wherever she was now living in London. I then handed the letter to the guard, hoping our request would be granted, and that this was not some kind of a trick.

To our great surprise, Maria did succeed in visiting us a week later. She came with two large baskets: one filled with foods that she knew we liked, and the other with clean clothes.

As soon as our guard had locked the door, she put her baskets down and the three of us hugged each other tightly for a few minutes. Then after my wife told us that we smelled somewhat, we immediately changed into our new clothes and spent the next two hours discussing and speculating about our fate. Of course, we asked her whether she had heard anything to our advantage, especially after our interview with the king.

"I don't know what to believe," she said. "As I was entering the Tower, I heard two of the guards say that Sir William Morton is not going to interrogate you after all."

"Yes, we heard that as well," I said. "But do you know why?"

"Not really. The guards just said something about Sir Henry wanting to release you," she replied. "I was thinking of using my feminine charms to try and extract more details but I decided against it. Had I failed, it might have made things worse for you."

This was the first time we had heard anything about being released.

"Why would he want to release us?" Tom asked.

Maria shrugged, but I could see that her eyes

were brimming with tears. "I'm not sure. I asked around and was told that Sir Henry had heard that the king would prefer to use you to catch revolutionaries and people like that," she said. "Sir Henry Bennet and Sir Joseph think you are worth more to them alive working for them, than you are dead, especially since we are still at war with the Dutch."

"What does that have to do with anything?" Tom asked.

"The king and his ministers fear that there are some who wish to use this situation to get rid of the king, and so catching revolutionaries and sympathisers before they can execute their plans is of the upmost importance. I just hope what I was told is true," she said sadly, looking at me for a moment before drying her eyes on her sleeve.

"Listen, Maria," I began. "When you leave here…"

But I wasn't allowed to finish my sentence. Our two guards entered and told Maria, in no uncertain terms, that it was time for her to leave.

"But I was just telling my husband…Can't I have a few more minutes with him?" Maria pleaded.

"Sorry, Ma'am," Stocky said, taking hold of her elbow. "You've got t' go now. If I le' you stay 'ere any longer, then it'll be my 'ead what'll be on the block, not no-one else's. So come on, lady, let's go." He guided her roughly outside, slamming the door as he did so.

Naturally, Tom and I spent the rest of the

evening mulling over what my wife had said, hoping that she had not heard yet another baseless rumour concerning our fate.

The next day proved that there was some truth in what Maria had learned. About midday, Sir John came into our cell, this time without an armed escort. He told us that the king had told him that I was to write a letter to the Duke of Ormonde apologising for my attack. Sir John told us that, if I did this, then His Majesty might consider releasing us from the Tower.

"Are you sure this is true?" Tom asked.

"I'm afraid so," Sir John replied. "If it were up to me, I'd have hanged the pair of you weeks ago." He sighed. "But I must follow the king's instructions. Now, are you prepared to write a letter of apology?"

I nodded, and he promptly left.

"Father, do you think this is a trick?" Tom asked. "You know, a means for them to obtain written proof against you?"

I thought for a moment before replying. "I don't think so, Tom. I mean, when the king agreed to speak to us, he did. There was no trick there, was there? And when they said Maria would be allowed to visit us, she did, didn't she? No, son, I don't think this is a trick, but even if it is, I don't really have much choice, do I? It's us in the Tower, not them."

"I suppose you're right," Tom mumbled, though I could see that he was not happy with this condition of our release. "It's just…to apologise would mean surrendering to your lifelong enemy, the man who stole your land and has forever been the bane of your life."

This time, it was my turn to tell him that he was right, but I knew that if we wanted to leave the Tower and not be hanged, I would have to eat this very large slice of humble pie.

Later that afternoon, the younger of our two guards returned with a pen, a pot of ink, and some paper. He waited by the open door while I wrote my apology:

The greatness of my crimes so far exceeds expression that were not my burdened soul encouraged by finding vent to its grief, though by such an acknowledgement as bears little proportion to my guilt...

I continued in the same vein, filling the letter with flowery language and repetitious apologies...

...by the consideration of your renowned excellency, which I, unworthy monster, was so regardless of, has produced this eruption of humble acknowledgement of my most heinous crime...

With a final flourish, I ended my letter to the duke:

...so should I count it in my happiness to have an opportunity in the most demonstrative way to

[334]

manifest it, Your Grace, unworthy to be accounted
though I am.

      Your Grace's most humble servant,

                      Thomas Blood

I showed the letter to Tom, who thought I was being far too servile. But when I reminded that this was our ticket to freedom, and to keeping our heads on our shoulders, he nodded in agreement.

Later, I heard that Sir Henry Bennet had taken my apology to the king, and the following day, Sir John came to our cell, holding a Royal Warrant.

"Captain Blood," he began. "His Majesty has instructed me to release you from your present captivity tomorrow, the thirty-first of August, the year of our Lord 1671. You, together with your accomplice, Captain Robert Perrot, who has been held here in the Tower in a separate cell since he was captured some four months ago, are to receive a full pardon. It seems that Sir Henry Bennet as well as Sir Joseph Williamson believe that you will be of better use to His Majesty alive rather than hanging from a noose."

Later, I learned that Sir Henry Bennet had asked for...

    ...a full pardon to be given to Captain Thomas
Blood, for all treasons, murders, homicides, felonies,
assaults, batteries, and other offences committed since
25 May 1660 by himself alone or together with any
other person or persons.

"And what about my son, Tom?" I asked.

"He will be held here for a while longer," Sir John said.

"How long?" Tom asked.

"That, young man, will depend on your father's behaviour and his commitment to what His Majesty has in store for him," Sir John answered. He then turned on his heel and left immediately without saying another word.

As soon as he had closed the door, Tom turned to me. "What does this mean, father? I could be stuck here for months. Maybe years!"

"Fear not, son," I said, drawing him to me. "I will not let that happen. We have escaped what we thought would be our fate. I am sure you will be released very soon." I hugged him closer. "You can count on me to do my best to ensure that you are let out of here as soon as possible. I'll go and speak to Sir Henry Bennet and that Williamson fellow and see what can be done. Chin up, son. I'm sure you won't be here for very long."

He smiled wanly for a moment, then sat down on the straw, thinking about his future in the Tower without me.

The following morning, the older of our two guards came to escort me up to Sir John's office. I assumed he would tell me in no uncertain terms about the conditions of my release, so I was completely surprised when he simply handed me a small packet.

"'ere, captain," he said gruffly. "This is for you. 'is Majesty gave me instructions t' hand it over afore you leave."

I took it, thanked him, and left. Despite our close proximity over the past few months, neither of us had anything especially personal to say to each other. "Jus' make sure you behave yourself in the future if you don' want t' return 'ere," was part his final warning. "Remember, we're still 'olding your son" were his last words to me.

As I was escorted out of the Tower, through the Wakefield gate, I looked up at the clear blue sky and breathed in the fresh air. I mused that this was the same gate through which I had made my fateful entrance to the Tower, all those long months ago. Only this time, I was not a fugitive, hiding beneath a parson's robes. I was a free man now. I hoped and prayed that Tom would soon join me. Then it occurred to me. I was so happy to be a free man again that I had forgotten to open the packet Sir John had given me.

I walked over to stand behind a tree and ripped the packet open. Inside was the grand sum of five hundred pounds! *Five hundred pounds.* I wondered what the king would ask for in exchange. His Majesty must have really wanted me free. Hopefully he would release Tom soon.

My head in the clouds, I walked over to the nearest stables, paid a deposit, hired a horse and rode off in the direction of my wife's house, north of the city. I was in sore need of some good food, clean clothes and feminine attention. I hoped that, very soon, I would be enjoying all three.

Chapter 26
On His Majesty's Service

It was a wonderful feeling to be free, to see the sky and to feel the wind in my hair as I rode north. In comparison to many unfortunates, I had been incredibly lucky. Not only had I left the Tower with my head still firmly attached to my shoulders, but I had also been there for only four months. Many people I'd heard about had been imprisoned there for years, and by the time they came out – if they came out at all – they were well and truly broken with no future ahead of them.

While I must admit that the conditions in my cell had not been the best, at least my son had been there to keep me company, and neither of us had been tortured or threatened with serious physical harm. It was a relief to see my wife and children again; to hold them in my arms and know that we did not need to hide anymore. We were safe, for now.

Less than a week after my return to society, I used some of the five hundred pounds the king had given me to buy a new house in Westminster, on the corner of Great Peter Street and Tufton Street. Many of my new neighbours were well-known persons, connected with Parliament and the judiciary. Most of them either ignored me or greeted me well, but one or two made it known that they were going to have nothing to do with that 'devilish villain,' as I heard one MP call me. This did not bother me in the slightest, but I knew Maria felt somewhat hurt, especially when one court official deliberately crossed the road when he saw the pair of us walking towards him one afternoon.

However, the following lines by the oft drunken aristocrat, John Wilmot, Earl of Rochester, did upset me:

> *Blood that wears treason in his face,*
> *Villain complete in parson's gown,*
> *How much he is at court in grace*
> *For stealing Ormonde and the crown!*
> *Since loyalty does no man good,*
> *Let's steal the King and outdo Blood!*

To make matters worse, this nasty piece of doggerel had been written by a man who was widely known as a dissolute rake and womaniser. In contrast, the lawyer and courtier, Sir Thomas Henshaw, said that I looked well in my new suit and periwig and that I seemed to be 'very pleasant and jocose'.

Not long after we had moved to our new house, Tom was released and was greeted with a bath, clean clothes and a very festive supper. Although I was relieved that my son was back with us, having received a full pardon, I was not pleased to find out that the writer and diarist, John Evelyn, had written about me in a most disparaging manner. He had noted in a news sheet that he was horrified to hear that I had dared to attend a dinner at the house of the comptroller of the royal household, Sir Thomas Clifford. This event had also been graced by several of His Majesty's nobles as well as a number of French aristocrats.

It was at about this time that I received a message, requesting my presence at the house of Sir Henry Bennet. I must confess, I was a trifle fearful about this, especially since Sir Joseph Williamson and my former gaoler, Sir John Robinson, appeared soon after my arrival. Sir Henry asked us all to be seated, before opening the meeting. Since all of us had already become acquainted, there was no need for a round of introductions.

"Let us get straight to the point of this evening's meeting," he declared, once everyone had received a glass of his finest claret and partaken of a sweetmeat or two. "I have called you here because His Majesty wishes to promote his policy for dealing with the ever-growing numbers of Non-conformists in this country. Especially here in London." At this point, he turned to face me. "This is where you enter the picture captain or, as you prefer to call yourself, Colonel Blood."

"Why? What do I have to do?" I asked. I had never had anything to do with these people before.

Sir Henry Bennet replied. "We want you to act as a spy, and inform us, that is, myself and Sir Joseph here, about the activities of the aforementioned Non-conformists."

"Why? What have they done, or what are they suspected of doing, sir?"

"We believe that they are dealing with exiled radicals in the Low Countries," Sir Henry replied. "And since we are at war with the Netherlands, it is of vital importance that His Majesty and his chosen officials are aware of what these Non-conformists are doing."

"I see. And what am I to do with any information I might discover?"

"You are to pass it straight on to me or to Sir Joseph," Sir Henry replied. "The quicker the better. But let me tell you a few things about these Non-conformists. Firstly, since the passing of the Conventicle Act—"

"Last year?"

"Yes, Blood. Since then, it has been very difficult for the Non-conformists to hold their prayer meetings. They are not permitted to meet in groups of more than five at a time and if they do, they are heavily fined."

"Excuse me, sir," I asked. "But how do you know about these meetings and how many people attend them?"

He tapped the side of his black-bandaged nose. "Spies, Blood, spies. Spies like you, and others. Now, when you catch these fellows, it is going to cost them five shillings for the first time, and double if you catch them again. Their ministers will be fined twenty pounds for the first offence, and forty pounds after that. In addition, any person who allows these Non-conformists to use their premises will also be fined in the same way as the ministers."

"I see. This could be a very profitable exercise for His Majesty."

"Indeed." Sir Joseph said. "And also for you."

"How so, sir?"

"Because you, Blood, will receive one third of these sums for bringing this information to us and His Majesty."

As a result of my new mission, I came into contact with several dubious people. Including an Anglican clergyman, called Dr Nicholas Butler; a Mr Church, who was an official at the Fleet prison, and a Scottish non-conformist and former rector, called Mr. James Innes. The latter asked me to intercede, as he wanted the king to grant more religious freedoms for the Non-conformists. I told him that I could not do so as His Majesty had spared my life and I could not now go against his wishes.

Because I wished to stay in the king's good graces, I began to work more for the Scottish Secretary of State, John Maitland, Earl of Lauderdale, rather than Sir Henry and Sir Joseph. I saw that Maitland had more influence with the king, and I began to become more involved in court politics. Sir Joseph was not very pleased with this and he considered me untrustworthy from that point onwards.

It was during this period that I was able to use my growing influence and connections and help certain past Non-conformists and supporters of Oliver Cromwell. Naturally, the members of the latter group were hated by the king, as he saw them as the murderers of his father, so I had to work carefully and rely on great discretion to keep everyone happy.

One of the people I managed to save was John Lockyer, my old partner who had helped me rescue Captain Mason from being executed in the past. I was also responsible for securing pardons for Major William Low of Dublin, and Captain Humphrey Spurway of Tiverton, Devon.

"What have these fellows been doing, Colonel, that they need a pardon from me?" the king asked during one of my regular visits to report to him at Whitehall Palace.

"Major Low was a radical, who has now seen the light and wishes to serve Your Majesty, Sire."

"And Captain Spurway?"

"He once planned to kill you, Sire."

"What, when I was bathing in the river?"

[344]

"No, no, Your Majesty," I replied, surprised that he had remembered that story. "He was planning to do so while you were on your way to visit your mother at Greenwich. He wanted to kill you and seize your brother, James, together with the Duke of Albermarle and Sir Richard Brown."

"The same Sir Richard who is now the Lord Mayor of London?"

I nodded.

"Well, Blood, what became of that particular plot? Not much I think. As you can see, I am still here, and my brother is in the room next door."

"Nothing became of it, Sire. He fled to the New World, to live on a plantation there."

"So, good riddance to him. In the meantime, I'm going to watch Mistress Gwynne play Angelica Bianca in *The Rover*. She is such a good actress, and she does amuse me so."

But despite his interest in Nell Gwynne, and several other mistresses, His Majesty did find the time to grant a pardon to Sir Humphrey, as well as to several other persons, including eighteen Non-conformists whom I had tried to help.

It was also during this period that I was able to advance the careers of several of my sons. I managed to obtain commissions in the navy for Edmund and William. They received commissions to serve on the *Jersey,* a forty-gun frigate, while Holcroft, another of my sons, became a Clerk of the Peace and a Clerk of the Crown in County Clare, Ireland.

A few months later, William came to see me in London with some very sad news.

"Father, father…have you heard? Tom, he…he's dead, father. He died in America."

"What? But he's only twenty four years old."

"I know, but…"

"How did this happen! Was he killed? Or did he die of some disease out there?"

William shrugged sadly. "I don't know, father. I asked the same question to the sergeant who told me the news and he didn't know, either."

"What about his wife, and the children?"

William shrugged again. "I don't know, father. All I know is that he died somewhere near Albany, north of New York."

This news truly saddened me. Tom and I had been through so much together, and now he was gone, just like that. I would not even be able to give him a proper burial. His death added a weight to my shoulders that I could never shake and for the rest of my days I felt like a piece of me was missing.

Not long after hearing of Tom's untimely demise, I discovered that one of my projects had failed. When my wife's brother, Charles Holcroft, had died, I had attempted to add the ownership of his estate to mine. The authorities had decided otherwise, and his land was awarded to another member of the Holcroft family. Still, despite this disappointment, I was now at the most affluent stage in my life. His Majesty was paying me one hundred pounds per year and I was receiving five times this amount from my improved and expanded Irish estates.

I liked to think that the reason I was so successful was because I made a daily visit to White's coffee house, near the Royal Exchange. There, I would exchange news and useful tit-bits of information with affluent clients, including the king's brother, James, and Thomas Osborne, the Earl of Danby. In turn, they would keep me informed about what was happening regarding finances in the City, how the war was going with the Dutch, and how certain unsavoury characters were behaving in London.

This uncovering of what was simmering below the surface, especially in London, was an important part of my work as an intelligencer for His Majesty. It was thrust upon me to deal with individuals and groups of people whose aim was to either kill the king or cause chaos and confusion in the capital. Some of these people wished to kill the king because they believed in some form of republicanism, while others thought that he was a secret Catholic, who wanted to bring Catholicism back to England.

"After all," I heard such folks say, on several occasions. "He's surrounded by Catholics, isn't he? His wife, Catherine, is Catholic, and so is his mother. They also say that his brother, James, is a secret Papist."

"That's true. And what about his French mistress, Louise de Kéroualle? She's also one of them."

"Aye, and that other trollop, Hortense Mancini. I think she's also a Catholic. I mean, who was her uncle? That French churchman, Cardinal Jules Mazarin."

One of the places where I heard the most rumours about the king's alleged Catholic connections was the King's Head tavern, in Chancery Lane End. There, a group of radicals would meet frequently to drink and talk politics. They called themselves the Green Ribbon Club. They would all wear such a device in their hats as a way of identifying one another as they walked through the streets of London. Some of the best-known members of this club included the king's oldest illegitimate son, the Duke of Monmouth, as well as the Dukes of Bedford and Buckingham, and the Earl of Shaftesbury. Cromwell's grandson, Henry Ireton, was also a member, and so too was the false priest, Titus Oates.

But these men not only discussed politics and denigrated the king. They also had a great influence over the Whigs, the up-and coming anti-Royalist political group. In addition, they organised the lighting of huge bonfires on which effigies of the Pope were burnt.

Of all of these men, the one I had most to do with and detested was Titus Oates. This fat-faced man was about thirty years old when our paths first crossed. Rupert Smythe, an old army friend of mine, warned me about him when I told him that I had heard him speak at the King's Head.

"Tom, I'm telling you," Rupert said, wagging his finger at me as a father would do to his son. "Don't have *anything* to do with him. He is a terrible liar, and he corrupts everyone who comes into contact with him."

"What do you mean? I heard him talk and I thought that he was quite pleasant and most persuasive."

"Aye, that's the problem. That's how he damn well fools everybody. I'm telling you," he continued. "Most of what he says is only half-true or outright lies. He hates Catholics and is a fearsome rabble-rouser."

"What else do you know about him? He sounds like one of the people I should keep my eyes on."

My drinking companion nodded. "Aye, Tom, you should. But don't believe anything he says. Anything. Here, let me tell you something about him. This Oates fellow was born in Rutland, but was schooled at the Merchant Taylor's School here in the city. He then went to Cambridge but never completed his degree. I've heard it on good record that his tutor thought he was a great dunce and that he preferred men to women…"

"You mean he's…?"

"Aye. However, that didn't stop him from saying that he had a degree and with that, he gained a licence from the Bishop of London to preach. Then, about eight years ago," my friend continued, "he was ordained as a Church of England priest and became a vicar somewhere in Kent. That's when his true nature began to show itself. He accused a schoolmaster in Hastings of sodomy so that he, Oates, could obtain the schoolmaster's post instead."

"Did that dirty trick work?"

"No, Tom. It was found to be a false accusation and he was charged with perjury."

"Good," I said. "Sounds like he deserved it."

"He did, but he managed to escape and fled to London. Then, sometime after, he became a chaplain in the navy, but was thrown out a few months later when he was accused of buggery."

"But that's a capital offence. Why wasn't he hanged?"

"Unfortunately for us, Tom, he was lucky. He was spared because he claimed he was a priest, and thus they couldn't hang him. Then he returned to London and went back to Hastings, but this time, to answer the earlier charges of perjury. He was pardoned and returned once again to London. Then he became a Catholic and—"

"But you just told me he hated Catholics!"

"I know, but that didn't stop him from working with them and becoming acquainted with another odious character called Israel Tonge. These two began to produce a series of anti-Catholic pamphlets. Then passing himself off as a fervent Catholic, Oates went to France and Spain to study for the priesthood, that is, the Catholic priesthood. But when they discovered that he didn't know any Latin and that he blasphemed and spoke against the king here, they expelled him…"

"And he returned to London?"

"Right, and then he told his friend, Israel Tonge, that he was really an Anglican, but had only pretended to be a Catholic so that he could learn their secrets. That's when he started fabricating his Popish Plot which claimed that the Catholics were planning to kill the king and take over this country."

"Yes, I know about that," I said. "I heard a rumour when I was last in the palace that Queen Catherine, together with the king's physician were planning to poison the king. His Majesty heard about it, asked me a few questions about what I'd heard, and then interrogated his physician himself. The king ordered Oates to be arrested, but he had to release him soon afterwards because of some legal clause. And not only did he let him go," I added. "But he gave him an apartment in Whitehall and an annual allowance of over one thousand pounds."

"*One thousand pounds!* I didn't know that."

"Aye, my friend. And then Oates requested the College of Arms to design a coat of arms for him. The last thing that I heard was that he is planning to marry the Earl of Shaftesbury's daughter, or some other lass in his family."

"And *this* is the creature you've been told to keep an eye on? They really do give you the worst of them, Tom."

Rupert was right; Oates was not the only unsavoury character I had been asked to deal with. Thomas Osborne, Earl of Danby, now wasting away in the Tower was there because of two serious charges. He had been impeached for corruption and embezzlement from the Treasury, and he had hidden information about Oates' Popish Plot from the authorities. In addition, Osborne had crossed swords with my past supporter, the Duke of Buckingham.

Buckingham's name had now become a byword for depravity after he was charged with sodomising Sarah Harwood, a London gentlewoman. Buckingham had paid for this lady to go to France, hoping that this would prevent his crime from becoming public, but unfortunately for Buckingham, his plan did not succeed. His reputation for violent behaviour went against him, and to complicate matters even further, the duke had to face two other charges. The first was brought against him by a farmer who claimed that the duke's men had trampled his cornfield while he was hunting, but the second charge was more serious. Buckingham had been accused of being a poisoner. Was it a coincidence that William Leving, a government spy and a man I had briefly met whilst rescuing my friend, Captain Mason, had died from poising shortly after speaking out against the Duke?

Buckingham, of course, had strongly denied all of these charges, two of which could have cost him his head. When the Buggery Act of 1553 was brought against him, he claimed:

But for my innocence in this, I can only call God to witness and rely upon the charity of all men.

God knows I have much to answer for in the plain way, but I never was so great a virtuoso in my lusts.

This claim of innocence was refuted by several witnesses, who claimed that the duke had sexually molested them. Buckingham denied this, and claimed that the wife of his enemy, the Earl of Danby, had paid at least one witness three hundred pounds to speak against him in court.

As this sorry tale continued, I was brought in, and was forced to speak out against the duke. I will not describe the tortuous legal proceedings that followed, except to say that the duke's lawyer, Sir William Waller, had me imprisoned for conspiring against his client. I was committed to the Gatehouse prison in Westminster, and together with three others, was charged with blasphemy, confederacy, and subornation.

Later, it was proved that several of Sir William's witnesses had perjured themselves, and eventually, I was released. This nefarious case had two results. The first was that Sir William fled to Holland, having been sacked as a magistrate, and the second was that the duke sued me for defamation of character.

"Father, how much is he suing you for?" my son, Charles, asked.

"Ten thousand pounds in a civil suit for *scandalum magnatum*."

"But you don't have anything like that amount of money."

"I know, and that's why I'm going to send you to speak to the king's brother, James, and ask him to intercede on my behalf."

My son did so, but the Treasury dragged its feet, leaving me to rot in the Gatehouse again. I had no alternative but to write the following to the new Secretary of State, Sir Leoline Jenkins:

I have been left destitute of the usual supply of money from the court and tantalized from day to day and week to week. The Lords of the Treasury have promised me from three days to three days the payment of that six hundred pounds which the King allowed me for my salary to enable me to do this business.

I desire an immediate supply of thirty or forty guineas to bear the charges of my disentanglement, for I am quite destitute, having pawned my silver plate, I would entreat you to encourage some persons to be bail for me.

Sometime later, on the 21st July 1680, I received a writ of *habeas corpus*, and was moved to the debtors' prison in Southwark. There, an anonymous person bailed me out and I became a free man once again. But my homecoming was not a joyous occasion. My house was empty, as Maria had died during my time in prison. My children had long left home to make their careers and my social standing had been battered by what had happened to me over the past few months. Doors which had once opened to me easily, in the palace and other important places, now remained closed. In addition, I still had to find ten thousand pounds with which to pay the Duke of Buckingham.

On top of this, the time I had spent in prison was now having an effect on my physical well-being. It was now that I began to feel every one of the days of my sixty-two years. I was unspeakably weary for much of the time and found it difficult to communicate with my friends, or the Presbyterian minister who came to visit me in my Westminster home. Each tried to talk me out of my state of melancholy but unfortunately they did not succeed. I grew more and more morose, miserably comparing myself to what I had been in the past and what I had achieved.

I recalled fighting alongside my comrades, both as a Royalist and a Roundhead at Babylon Hill, Marston Moor and Naseby; my obsession with regaining my lands in Ireland, and taking revenge on the Duke of Ormonde. I recalled my past planning and carrying out of the robbery of the Crown Jewels in the Tower, and the strange and unexpected way my actions afterwards had ultimately led me to become an important personage, working for the king. My life had been so full, and yet now, here I was, lying in bed in a small not very pleasant room overlooking the Thames.

The last thing I can remember is responding to my friends' pleas to dictate to them my last will and testament. It did not take much effort to preface this document:

...being at the time sensible of the frailty and mortality of man, afflicted by a weariness of body, I bequeath my soul into the hands of almighty God in full assurance of that blessed resurrection held forth in the Holy Scriptures and that my body shall return to the earth from whence it came.

This document was dated Monday the twenty-second day of August, in the year of our Lord, 1680.

Epilogue

'Colonel' Thomas Blood died at three o'clock in the afternoon, on Wednesday the twenty-fourth of August 1680, two days after writing his last will and testament. He left his family and friends very little, having pawned or sold most of his property in order to pay for his final legal proceedings.

He bequeathed some money to his daughters, **Elizabeth** and **Maria,** as well as to his three surviving sons, **Holcroft, Charles** and **William**. He also left a little money to his daughter-in-law, the widow of his son, **Tom**, who had died in America. In addition, he willed twenty shillings to 'my dear old friend, John Fisher'. The rest of his goods and chattels which included some chairs and some wall-hangings, a beer jug, cutlery, candlesticks, a bedstead, rugs, and blankets were assessed to be worth three hundred pounds, fourteen shillings and twopence.

The last scandal that he was involved in actually occurred after his death. Blood was buried in the New Chapel cemetery at Tothill Fields, Westminster near the grave of his wife, Maria. However, his funeral and its aftermath were not the quiet and orderly events that usually take place. Many people suspected that Blood had not really died and that this was just another of his tricks. It was rumoured that he had staged his death in an attempt to evade paying off his debts to the Duke of Buckingham. So much noise was made about this that the authorities were persuaded to open his grave in order to see that he had indeed passed on to meet his Maker.

In order to prove that the week old body was indeed that of the Irish adventurer, the Westminster coroner and jury called on an old army captain who, under oath claimed that he had known Colonel Blood well. Once the body was exposed, the captain looked at the cadaver's left hand and studied the thumb. He noted that, as a result of a past injury, this was enlarged. It was of 'prodigious bigness.' As a result, the body was confirmed to be that of Captain, self-promoted Colonel Thomas Blood and was returned to the grave.

However, Blood was still not allowed to rest quietly. Several satirical broadsheets gleefully exploited the death of the infamous and newsworthy man and published various articles and poems about him.

A Mr. J. Shorter composed a seventy-six line poem entitled: *An Elegy on Colonel Blood, Notorious for Stealing the Crown*. It began:

> Thanks, ye kind fates for your last favour
> shown
> Of stealing BLOOD who lately stole the crown
> We'll not exclaim so much against you since
> As well as BEDLOE* you have fetched him hence,
> He who has been a plague to all mankind
> And never was to anyone a friend...

*A Popish Plot informer and crook who died four days after Blood.

This nasty poem ended in the same vein:

> Here lies the man who boldly ran through
> More villainies than ever England knew
> And ne'er to any friend he had was true
> Here let him then by all unpitied lie
> And let's rejoice his time was come to die.

With regard to the unfortunate Keeper at the Tower, **Master Talbot Edwards,** he recovered from the blows and stabbing he had suffered and was supposed to come into some money as compensation. He was awarded two hundred pounds, while his son, Wyeth, whose timely homecoming from abroad spelt the end of Blood's would-be robbery, was awarded one hundred pounds. However, typical of that time, the Keeper of the Crown Jewels did not receive even a penny of his reward due to the appalling state of King Charles II's treasury. The old man was forced to sell off some of his property to pay for his medical bills and he died three years later in September 1674. The eighty year old keeper was buried by the south wall of the Tower Chapel of St. Peter ad Vincula, sharing this burial site with Anne Boleyn, Catherine Howard, and Lady Jane Grey.

His son, **Wyeth,** inherited the post as Keeper in the Jewel House, serving for two years before being succeeded by **Martin Beckman**, who had been knighted. Beckman, the guard at the Tower who had prevented Blood from escaping with the Crown Jewels, became the Master of the Jewel Office for the next twenty-four years and married Talbot Edwards' daughter, Elizabeth.

As for Blood's seven children, his oldest son, **Tom,** died in 1675, five years before his father. After trying to help his father ambush the Duke of Ormonde, and later steal the Crown Jewels, he had married, possibly had two children, and died as a captain in the

British Army in Albany, New York State. Blood's second son, **William**, served in the navy, and died near the West African coast in 1688. His third son, **Holcroft**, also served in the navy, but after switching to the army, he had a more illustrious career. He rose to the rank of brigadier-general, became estranged from his wife and died in Brussels in 1707. Blood's fourth son, **Edmund,** also travelled abroad and possibly served with the East India Company. He died in 1679, one year before his father. The youngest son, **Charles**, became, like his father, an intelligencer and worked for King Charles II's brother, James, warning him of opposition to his reign. Later, as a lawyer, he successfully defended his brother, Holcroft, against assault charges brought against him by his estranged wife, Elizabeth.

Little is known about Blood's oldest daughter, **Maria**, other than that she married a Master Corbett and received fifty pounds from the will of her brother, Holcroft. Similarly, little is known about her younger sister, **Elizabeth** who also received fifty pounds from the same will and married a Master Edward Everard.

As for Blood's accomplices in the Crown Jewel robbery, **Captain Richard Halliwell** escaped arrest, and it is thought that he wrote a biography about his friend, 'Colonel' Blood. He signed his book '*Remarks on the Life and Death of the Fam'd Mr. Blood*, R.H.' No more is known about **Colonel William Moore** who was also involved in the Dublin Castle attack on the Duke of Ormonde, as well as the ambush on the same duke in London and the unsuccessful attempt to steal the Crown Jewels. **Robert Perrot**, after being released from the Tower, fought as a major on the side of King Charles II's rebellious son, the Duke of Monmouth, at the Battle of Sedgemoor. He was on the losing side, but managed to escape. However, King James II's men later found him, and like hundreds of others, he was executed at Taunton, Somerset. Nothing is known about his fellow Fifth Monarchist, **William (Bill) Smith**, whose job it was to look after the getaway horses during the robbery at the Tower.

Philip Alden, the government spy and lawyer who featured in the opening chapters of this book, was arrested with Blood *et al* after the unsuccessful attack on the Duke of Ormonde at Dublin Castle. In order to protect his cover afterwards, he was later allowed to escape. He continued spying on radical groups for the government in England, and eventually retired to Ireland. He was granted a pardon and a yearly government pension of one hundred pounds, though this was not paid regularly.

Captain Martin Beckman, the Swedish-born officer who was instrumental in catching Blood after the failed Crown Jewels robbery, received one hundred pounds for 'resisting that late villainous attempt to steal the crown'. He married Keeper Talbot Edwards' daughter, Elizabeth, and in 1667 was appointed the chief engineer for His Majesty's castles and forts. He was knighted in 1686, and naturalized five years later. After his wife died, he remarried and died in 1702 at the Tower, as a resident, not as a prisoner.

Sir Henry Bennet, later the **Earl of Arlington,** sold his post as Secretary of State to his assistant, Sir Joseph Williamson, for six thousand pounds and became Lord Chamberlain of the royal household. In the same way that King Charles II had done, Arlington hid his secret Catholic beliefs until the end and called for a Catholic priest only on his deathbed in July 1685.

Sir Joseph Williamson was born the son of a poor clergyman, but through his hard work and diligence, he became King Charles II's chief spymaster. However, he was dismissed after he ordered the residence of the king's wife, Catherine Braganza, in the Strand to be searched without first obtaining the king's permission. Later, Williamson was suspected of being involved in the Titus Oates' Popish plot. Williamson was arrested, but then released by the king. The ex-spymaster later married the king's cousin, the affluent Lady Clifton, and died a rich man in 1701. He left six thousand pounds and his library to Queen's College, Oxford, as well as five thousand pounds to the Sir Joseph Williamson Mathematical School which he founded in Rochester, Kent.

Blood's lifelong adversary, **James Butler, the Duke of Ormonde**, served as the Lord Lieutenant of Ireland from 1662-1669, and again from 1677-1685. From 1645, for thirty-three years, he held the title of Chancellor of Trinity College, Dublin, but he did not live there for much of this period. This was because he was living abroad with the future King Charles II until

1660. After an exile of fifteen years, he returned to take up his post. The Duke died at Kingston Lacy, Dorset, and was buried in Westminster Abbey. He left debts between £100,000 and £150,000.

George Villiers, the Duke of Buckingham, one of Blood's supporters and one of the Duke of Ormonde's main opponents, was a problematic figure who had a troublesome relationship with King Charles II. During the Restoration, he was elected Chancellor of Cambridge and High Steward of the University of Oxford and was also involved in various love-affairs. Buckingham was later attacked in Parliament for his affair with the Countess of Shrewsbury, but he then appeared to reform his ways. However, he was later sent to the Tower for plotting to embarrass the government. He was active in prosecuting those implicated in the Popish Plot and he supported the Whig party in Parliament. He believed in religious toleration, and in 1685 published a pamphlet '*A Short Discourse on the Reasonableness of Man's Having a Religion*'. As a result, King James II sent a priest to try and convert Buckingham to Catholicism, but to no avail. The childless Buckingham died of a chill in April 1687 feeling 'despised by my country and I fear forsaken by God'.

One of the nastiest individuals to feature in this story is the bogus priest, **Titus Oates.** After fabricating the Popish Plot in 1678, which caused at least fifteen innocent men to be executed, Oates suffered a backlash of public opinion after the violent execution of Oliver

Plunkett, the Roman Catholic Archbishop of Armagh, Ireland, in July 1681. Oates was arrested for sedition after he denounced King Charles II and his brother, James, and was imprisoned and fined £100,000 (over £11,000.000 in today's money). He was ordered to be stripped and whipped for several days, whilst tied to the back of a cart going from Aldgate to Newgate. He also had to stand in a pillory at the gates of Westminster Hall, where he was pelted with rotten fruit and worse. He spent three years in prison but was pardoned by the joint-monarchs, William III and Maria II, who awarded him an annual pension of two-hundred-and-sixty pounds This was stopped in 1698, then later restarted and increased by forty pounds. After serving as an Anglican priest before converting to Catholicism, in 1693 Oates became a Baptist. However, he was expelled from the denomination in 1701, and died forgotten four years later, aged fifty-six.

As for **King Charles II**, he continued to reign until his death in 1685, when his unpopular younger brother, James, Duke of York, succeeded him as King James II of England, James VII of Scotland. Charles, known as 'The Merry Monarch,' was famed for his licentious life-style. Despite being married to the faithful Catherine of Braganza, Charles had many mistresses. His most famous one was Nell Gwynne, the Drury Lane actress and self-styled 'Protestant whore.' The king was often short of cash, and on occasion depended on his cousin, King Louis XIV of

France, to help him out. Charles was skilled at negotiating the fine line between political and religious pressures during his reign, and ruled without a Parliament from 1681 until his death four years later. It was on his deathbed that he admitted to being a secret Catholic. It was also on his death-bed that he is alleged to have said about his former mistress, "Let not poor Nelly starve."

King James II, his younger brother, was an open and devout Catholic. After his second wife, Maria of Modena, bore him a son, there was a growing groundswell of public and political opinion which feared that Catholicism would become rooted once again in England. This led to the bloodless Glorious Revolution of 1688 in which the King was deserted by his ministers and the army. In the end, after reigning for only three years, James II had no choice but to flee to France. He died in exile at St. Germain near Paris, in 1701.

Author's Note

Writing an historical novel is a fascinating task that combines the truth with imagination. It is also true to say that in general, the nearer the historical character or period is to the present day, the easier it is to find more contemporary documentary evidence. The self-styled 'Colonel' Thomas Blood did indeed live from 1618 – 1680 and his most (in)famous act, that of trying to steal the Crown Jewels from the Tower of London, happened 350 years ago. This means that there is written evidence about this foolhardy deed as well as proof in other forms, such as the Jewel House Keeper's burial plaque.

In addition, written records exist which refer to other aspects of Blood's life. These include documents which refer to his estates in Ireland; his ongoing feud with the Duke of Ormonde and other escapades such as, attacking Dublin Castle and his rescue of Captain John Mason.

However, to be strictly honest, Blood's two love affairs described here with Annie Whitcombe and Cathy McAfee as well as the horse-riding accident in which he broke his leg are fictional. They have been added in order to show other facets of this swashbuckling Anglo-Irish adventurer's character. So too are the conversations that he had while plotting the rescue of Captain Mason and the stealing of the Crown Jewels. These fictional discussions are a product of my own 'heat-oppressed'* brain as naturally Blood left no written records of these meetings.

I would also like to take this opportunity to thank my two long-time editors, Marion Lupu and Gary Dalkin, for turning yet another of my historical novels into what I hope will be a pleasurable read.

*Shakespeare: *Macbeth*

D. Lawrence-Young,

Jerusalem, Israel.

May 2021

About the Author

D. Lawrence-Young was an English teacher and lecturer in schools and universities for over forty years until he retired in 2013. He is happiest researching Shakespeare, English and military history or quirky aspects of British social history. In addition to rewriting *Communicating in English,* a best-selling textbook, he has written two crime and twenty historical novels which have been published in the UK, USA and Israel.

He has been a frequent contributor to *Forum,* a magazine for English language teachers and also to *Skirmish,* a military history journal. He is a member of the local historical club and from 2008-2014 was the Chairman of the Jerusalem Shakespeare Club. He is also a published (USA) and exhibited photographer (UK & Jerusalem). He loves travelling, plays the clarinet (badly) and is married and has two children.

His entertaining history of British criminals, *Villains of Yore,* has also been published by Cranthorpe Millner.

Bibliography

Abbot, Wilbur Cortez, *Colonel Thomas Blood: Crown-Stealer, 1618-1680*, Bath, Somerset: Cedrick Chivers Ltd., 1970 (1910)

Baker, Anthony, *A Battlefield Atlas of the English Civil War*, London: Bookmart Ltd., 1986

Codd, Daniel J., *Crimes & Criminals of 17th Century Britain*, Barnsley, S. Yorks., Pen & Sword History, 2018

Davies, Stevie, *A Century of Troubles: England 1600-1700*, London: BBC Channel Four Books, 2001

Diehl, Daniel & Donelly, Mark P., *Tales from the Tower of London,* Glos: Sutton Publishing, 2004

Downing, Taylor & Millman, Maggie, *Civil War*, London: BBC Channel Four Book, 1991

Drake, Jane, (ed.), *The Civil War 1642-1651*, Andover, Hants: Pitkin Guides, 1996

Hanrahan, David C., *Colonel Blood: The Man Who Stole the Crown Jewels*, Stroud, Glos: Sutton Publishing, 2003

Haythornwaite, Philip, *The English Civil War 1642-1651*, London: Arms & Armour, Cassell Group, 1994

Hodgman, Charlotte, (ed), *The Story of the Civil War*, Bristol: BBC Publications, 2017

Hutchinson, Robert, *The Audacious Crimes of Colonel Blood*, London: Weidenfeld & Nicolson, 2015

Jordan Don & Walsh Michael, *The King's Revenge: Charles II and the Greatest Manhunt in British History*, London, Little, Brown, 2012

Peacock, Max, *Colonel Blood*, Toronto: Harlequin Publishing, 1954

Whitley, William Thomas, *Colonel Thomas Blood,* Baptist Quarterly, Vol 4. No. 1, January 1928

Wilson, Derek, *The Tower of London,* London: Allison & Busby, 1998

Wittenbury, Kaye, *Romances and Adventures of the Notorious Colonel Blood*, NL:Fredonia Books (1903), 2001

Take some twenty wicked British villains. Add their dastardly crimes. Then include their miserable backgrounds. Mix in some nefarious conversations and combine all this together to produce an exciting collection of stories: VILLAINS OF YORE.